703-836-5198

Y0-CQW-669

# Democracy and Development in East Asia

## Taiwan, South Korea, and the Philippines

Edited by Thomas W. Robinson

The AEI Press

Publisher for the American Enterprise Institute
WASHINGTON, D.C.

*1991*

Distributed by arrangement with

University Press of America
4720 Boston Way                                3 Henrietta Street
Lanham, Md. 20706                              London WC2E 8LU England

**Library of Congress Cataloging-in-Publication Data**

Democracy and development in East Asia : Taiwan, South Korea, and the
   Philippines / Thomas W. Robinson, editor.
      p.   cm.
      ISBN 0-8447-3715-1 (alk. paper).—ISBN 0-8447-3716-X (pbk. :
   alk. paper)
      1. Taiwan—Politics and government—1988- 2. Taiwan—Economic
   conditions—1975- 3. Taiwan—Social conditions—1988- 4. Korea
   (South)—Politics and government—1960- 5. Korea (South)—Economic
   conditions—1960- 6. Korea (South)—Social conditions.
   7. Philippines—Politics and government—1986- 8. Philippines—
   Economic conditions—1986- 9. Philippines—Social conditions.
   I. Robinson, Thomas W.
   JQ1528.D46   1990
   950.4'28—dc20                                                    90-198
                                                                      CIP


1   3   5   7   9   10   8   6   4   2

AEI Studies 504

© 1991 by the American Enterprise Institute for Public Policy Research,
Washington, D.C. All rights reserved. No part of this publication may be
used or reproduced in any manner whatsoever without permission in writing
from the American Enterprise Institute except in the case of brief quotations
embodied in news articles, critical articles, or reviews. The views expressed
in the publications of the American Enterprise Institute are those of the
authors and do not necessarily reflect the views of the staff, advisory panels,
officers, or trustees of AEI.

The AEI Press
Publisher for the American Enterprise Institute
1150 17th Street, N.W., Washington, D.C. 20036

*Printed in the United States of America*

# Contents

TABLES

FIGURE

# Preface

A startling and near-simultaneous turn toward democracy occurred in Taiwan, South Korea, and the Philippines in the late 1980s: was this change the product of greater economic development, the consequence of a complex relationship between democracy and economic modernization, or the result of international influences? This volume analyzes the relationship between political modernization and economic development in all three countries during the 1980s and beyond. Chapters address the economy, the politics, the sociocultural changes, and the international environment for each entity, followed by four general assessments. In the conclusion the editor draws on the existing theoretical and historical literature relating democracy and development in other countries to forecast the evolution of these two important movements in Taiwan, South Korea, and the Philippines during the 1990s.

Some useful conclusions emerge: political culture and therefore historical tradition are as important as other factors to the timing and success of democratization; the international environment strongly influenced the pace of the transition to democracy as well as providing a framework for economic development; no model yet exists relating democracy and development in a simple and generally accepted manner, and if one does emerge, it will surely be complex; the Taiwanese and Korean cases are surprisingly similar, while the Philippine instance is quite different, demonstrating the difficulty of generalization; and in all three democracy is fragile, dependent on influences over which neither the leadership nor the populace has much control. The future thus contains many pitfalls. In particular, further economic development will not by itself guarantee stable democracy.

The chapters that follow detail, for the first time, the relationship in three important East Asian non-Socialist societies, between the two great forces creating non-Western extensions of the modern world: the spread of political democracy and the transformation of the economy through industrialization. It is not yet clear that a one-to-one relationship exists between the two, that is, that beyond a certain point in a society's economic or political development further progress in one sphere must be directly and closely linked to progress in the other. Yet such a tendency does appear to exist, and some of the links between economics and politics in these Asian societies are becoming apparent. Despite the transforming power of democracy and development, however, the weight of history and culture remains enormous, if not decisive. Neither political democracy nor economic development is inevitable, even once a certain stage of governmental institutionalization or per capita national income has been reached. While plateaus or setbacks can occur, nonetheless, the probability of success rises at a given threshold. In Taiwan and South Korea the power of the past is exceedingly strong, forging a long-standing cultural unity. The contrast with the Philippines is stark. The gradient for the Philippines is thus much steeper than for Taiwan and South Korea. The Philippine people and their government must work hard, have a great deal of patience, make investment of all kinds, and earn the support of other countries to achieve a successful outcome.

The authors of this book provide some guideposts to the lessons learned (and still being learned) by the Koreans and the Taiwanese and to the obstacles that may lie ahead for the Filipinos. In the end, we may be able to generalize their collective experience for application to other situations, as well as speak with more confidence about what to expect in these three Asian societies themselves.

This book is the product of an international conference held in May 1988 at the American Enterprise Institute. Many contributed to the success of that meeting and the present work. Special thanks are due, nonetheless, to Leza Coelho and Angela Miles, who assisted with conference organization and took care of all administrative matters; Isabel Davidov, director of seminars and conferences, and her staff; Pamela Shime and Jennifer Arnold, research assistants who also helped write the introduction; Audrey Weg and Kathleen Walsh, who saw to the further and final production of the book; and to Chong-Pin Lin, the  associate director of the China Studies Program. Needless to say, errors and omissions are the sole responsibility of the editor.

# Contributors

THOMAS W. ROBINSON is director of the China Studies Program at the American Enterprise Institute, adjunct professor at Georgetown University, and chairperson of the China course at the Foreign Service Institute. Dr. Robinson, who was educated at Carleton College and at Columbia University, writes on China, Asia, the Soviet Union, international relations, and national security.

AHN BYUNG-JOON is professor of political science at Yonsei University, Seoul. He received his Ph.D. from Columbia University and has taught at Western Illinois University, the University of Michigan, and the University of California at Berkeley. He has been president of the Korea Association of International Relations and is the author of *Chinese Politics and the Cultural Revolution: Dynamics of Policy Processes*.

JOHN T. BENNETT is president of the Korea Economic Institute of America and former counselor for economic and commercial affairs at the U.S. Embassy in Seoul, 1975–1978. Dr. Bennett holds degrees from Harvard and the University of California at Berkeley. In 1978–1979 he was international affairs adviser at the National War College in Washington., D.C.

DAVID S. CHOU received a B.A. from National Chengchi University and an M.A. and Ph.D. from Duke University. He is associate professor in the Department of Diplomacy and deputy director of the Institute of International Relations, National Chengchi University. Dr. Chou is also editor in chief of *Issues and Studies*.

NICHOLAS EBERSTADT is a visiting scholar at the American Enterprise Institute and a visiting fellow at the Harvard University Center for Population Studies. He is editor of *Fertility Decline in the Less Developed Countries* and author of *Poverty in China*. His two most recent books are *The Poverty of Communism* and *Foreign Aid and American Purpose*.

RAYMOND GASTIL originated and directs the Comparative Survey of Freedom at Freedom House, appearing annually as *Freedom in the World: Political Rights and Civil Liberties*. Dr. Gastil is also vice-chairman of the Committee for a Community of Democracies/USA. He is author of *Social Humanities: Toward an Integrative Discipline of Science and Values*.

CAROLINA G. HERNANDEZ is professor of political science and director of the Center for Integrative and Development Studies at the University of the Philippines. During the 1987–1988 academic year she was a Fulbright Asia Scholar-in-Residence at the Southeast Asia Program, Cornell University.

RICHARD HOOLEY is professor of economics and public affairs at the University of Pittsburgh Graduate School of Public and International Affairs. He received his B.A. in economics from New York University and his Ph.D. from Columbia University. His articles have appeared in such journals as *Foreign Affairs* and *Journal of South Asian Studies*.

KIM KYONG-DONG received a Ph.D. from Cornell University, has taught at North Carolina State University, and has served as research fellow at the East-West Center and the Wilson Center. Currently he is professor of sociology and dean of planning and coordination at Seoul National University. He has also been president of the Korean Sociological Association.

MARTIN L. LASATER is president of the Pacific Council and visiting professor at Pennsylvania State University. Formerly, he was senior research fellow at the Naval War College and director of Asian Studies at the Heritage Foundation. He is the author of many books and articles dealing with U.S. relations with Taiwan and China. His most recent book is *Policy in Evolution: The U.S. Role in China's Reunification*.

LU YA-LI is professor of political science at National Taiwan University. He has a B.A. from the National Taiwan University and an M.A. and Ph.D. from Indiana University-Bloomington. He has published many books, articles, and reviews on Asian politics.

DARYL M. PLUNK is vice president of the Richard V. Allen Company, an international business consulting firm in Washington, D.C. He is also senior fellow at the Asian Studies Center of the Heritage Foundation, where he was a staff member from 1984 to 1987. From 1978 to 1980, Mr. Plunk served as a Peace Corps Volunteer in Korea's South

Kyungsang Province. He received a B.A. in political science from Millsaps College in Jackson, Mississippi.

JAN S. PRYBYLA is professor of economics at Pennsylvania State University and a fellow at the Pennsylvania State University Center for East Asian Studies. His books include *The Political Economy of Communist China, The Chinese Economy: Problems and Policies, Issues in Socialist Economic Modernization,* and *Market and Plan under Socialism: The Bird in the Cage.*

SEGUNDO ROMERO teaches political science at the University of the Philippines, where he served as assistant dean for student affairs. He has been course director at the Philippine Foreign Service Institute, supervising fellow for the Countryside Development and Public Opinion Projects at the Development Academy of the Philippines, and a member of the executive board of the Philippine Social Science Council.

DAVID ROSENBERG is professor of political science at Middlebury College. He spent a year as a Fulbright Research Professor at the University of the Philippines, studying dictatorship and democracy in the Philippines. He is a contributor to the World Bank's *1988 Report on the Philippines,* the *Encyclopedia of Asian History,* and the *Yearbook on International Communist Affairs.*

W. SCOTT THOMPSON, formerly a resident associate at the Carnegie Endowment for International Peace, is associate professor of international politics at the Fletcher School of Law and Diplomacy at Tufts University. A Rhodes Scholar and a graduate of Stanford and Oxford Universities, he has been a White House Fellow, an assistant to the Secretary of Defense, and an associate director of the United States Information Agency. He is the author or editor of numerous books and articles on foreign policy.

TING TIN-YU is associate professor of sociology at the National Taiwan University. He has been a visiting associate professor at Kansas State University and at the National Chengchi University. He received his B.A. in sociology from the National Taiwan University and his M.A. and Ph.D. from the University of Michigan. He is author of *Industrial Pollution and Regional Variations of Life Expectancy at Birth in Taiwan.*

# 1
# Introduction

*Thomas W. Robinson*
*with Jennifer A. Arnold*
*and Pamela J. Shime*

A startling and near-simultaneous turn toward democracy occurred in Taiwan, South Korea, and the Philippines in the late 1980s. Was this movement the product of higher levels of economic development, the result of a complex relationship between democracy and development, or the consequence of international influences? This volume analyzes these relations between political modernization and economic development in the three countries during the 1980s and beyond.

Chapters on economics, politics, sociocultural changes, and the international environment for each country precede assessments by four generalists. The final chapter suggests a synthesis by relating the data on these countries to existing theoretical and historical literature on democracy and development in other countries and by forecasting the evolution of these two important movements during the 1990s.

Some interesting conclusions emerge:

- Political culture and historical tradition are as important as other elements in determining when democratization appears and whether it succeeds.
- The international environment strongly influences the timing of the transition to democracy as well as providing for a framework in which economic development can take place.
- No "model" yet exists relating democracy and development in a simple and generally accepted manner, and if one does emerge, it will surely be complex.
- The Taiwanese and Korean cases are startlingly similar while the Philippine instance is quite different, demonstrating the difficulty of generalization.

- In all three cases democracy is fragile, dependent on a series of influences over which neither the leadership nor the populace has much control.

The future thus contains many pitfalls. In particular, further economic development will not by itself guarantee stable democracy.

## Taiwan

**Political and Economic History.** The October 1986 announcement of a democratic reform package signified a change in the political climate in Taiwan. In his chapter, Lu Ya-li reviews the political and economic history leading up to the announcement, assesses the prospect for democratic development, and analyzes the case of Taiwan in the context of a general framework of democratic transition in developing countries.

Through the 1950s and 1960s, land reform and economic growth satisfied the agricultural class and the growing urban middle class. In the 1970s, however, when the authoritarian political system confronted often insurmountable challenges, the middle class, as well as the more radical elements of society, began to demand liberalization and democratization.

In the 1980s, President Chiang Ching-kuo led the way to reform. The six-part reform package he initiated modifies the most fundamental aspects of Taiwan's authoritarianism, most of which date back to the late 1940s. The most salient elements of this package are the reforms that lift martial law, end the ban on parties other than the Kuomintang (KMT), alter the composition of the national legislature, and change the method of choosing local government.

None of these reforms is easily implemented. Controversies over the need for a national security law to replace martial law, over the legitimacy of an opposition party, and about when and how to retire senior members of the legislature and restructure the local political apparatus all have delayed and complicated the transition to a democratic system. Yet resolutions to these problems are emerging, and reform is taking effect.

Both external and internal changes have influenced the leadership to initiate democratic reform. External factors such as peace and prosperity in the Asian-Pacific region and a deteriorating international diplomatic status for Taiwan have resulted in such changes as an increasingly politicized and powerful middle class, an unofficial opposition with rising political and popular power, and a populist leader with Western-educated advisers. The outcome has been peaceful supersession of authoritarianism in Taiwan.

Nevertheless, obstacles render further democratization difficult. Relations between the two parties, the KMT and the Democratic Progressive party (DPP), are hostile. On the one hand, the DPP remains intransigent on the composition of the national legislature and local government reform, the legality of the Temporary Provisions of 1948, and the legitimacy of the KMT. On the other hand, the KMT refuses to establish warmer relations until the DPP defines more clearly its use of the term "self-determination." Further complicating these obstacles is the lack of democratic norms, evidenced by the plethora of violations of law and order that sometimes are neither peaceful nor justifiable.

As a result, the transition stage of democratization in Taiwan will be far from easy. Yet Taiwan has some advantages over other developing countries. Already a modern industrial society, Taiwan has a large, well-educated middle class with democratic values. Moreover, in many respects the people have been prepared for a democratic system by local elections establishing a precedent of democratic participation, an education policy that successfully combated illiteracy, an income redistribution policy creating a highly equitable society, and a foreign policy pointing to the democratic West as a role model for the younger generation. By evaluating Taiwan in the general framework of democratization, Lu provides a realistic forecast of short- and long-term expectations and comes to optimistic conclusions regarding democratic development in Taiwan.

**Economic Record.** Jan Prybyla summarizes the economic record of Taiwan since 1952, provides explanations for its amazing success, looks at contemporary economic problems and Taipei's response to them, and links latter-day economic modernization to political developments on the island.

The record is clear. Between 1952 and 1987, gross national product (GNP) and GNP per capita have increased by more than six times. Each Taiwanese resident had an income of about $7,000 by the end of 1989. Taiwan is therefore a "modern" country, if $5,000 GNP per capita is an accepted criterion. Moreover, population control has been accomplished: annual growth has declined from 3.7 percent to 1.1 percent, without a state-imposed population policy. By using the price mechanism to allocate economic goods, the government has avoided misallocations of resources, and the economy has been geared to user needs. Growth has been smooth, without disruptive fluctuations in output, employment, and inflation. Structural balance has come about through coordinated advances and strategic restraint,

3

without the "storming" characteristic of centrally planned economies. While major sectoral shifts have occurred within the economy, balance has been maintained among agriculture, industry, transportation, and communications. There has been a conscious effort to move up market: to intensive growth, high value-added products; toward manufacturing and services and out of agriculture; and away from government domination of the economy. Distributional equity has been maintained and even enhanced.

Most of the reasons for this success are internal to Taiwan. Most important, the economy is a market system, based on private property rights under state protection. Initiative, incentive, and ingenuity have thereby been released so that production is for consumption and costs are constantly reduced. The state does intervene in the economy but only for necessary purposes (defense, education, money supply regulation, taxation, welfare, income redistribution, and encouragement of growth), and the rule of thumb has been that such intervention should be short-lived, subsidiary, indirect, general, and persuasive as opposed to coercive. Market spontaneity has thereby been balanced with government action. Price stability, balanced budgets, savings invested in new capital, tariff reductions, land reform, income equity, full employment, and encouragement of foreign investment have resulted.

Other reasons also exist for this success, the most obvious of which is the informed rejection of conventional wisdom. Taiwan early on rejected the import substitution model of economic development and avoided the pitfall of stimulating investment through low interest rates amid high inflation. Instead, Taiwan was the first economy to emphasize export-led growth. As a result, labor moved from low marginal-output agriculture to low-wage export industry, where it held a comparative advantage. Hence, the marginal productivity of labor *and* wages rose, and the combination of high unemployment and low productivity, characteristic of other developing economies, was avoided. In addition, Taiwan has emphasized education. Literacy rates have been very high (92 percent), most students graduate from high school and attend college, costs have been kept low and quality high, and education has been esteemed in the culture. That helped set the stage for the recent movement to high-technology production and moving up market. Further, Taiwan has enjoyed social stability, the joint product of the Confucian cultural influence (thrift, industriousness, family loyalty, respect for learning, orderliness, and discipline) and modern attitudes imported from the West (willingness to take risks, competitiveness, personal responsibility, timeliness, and innovativeness). A stable government follows, as does, at least until recently, absence of labor unrest.

4

Two external factors buttress these internal reasons for Taiwan's economic success: the American and the Japanese connections. The United States supplied economic assistance (to 1960), advice (for example, with regard to land reform), guaranteed Taiwan's security, and opened its own market to Taiwanese products. These helped Taiwan to grow and to export, fast. Japan saw to the early modernization of Taiwan during the fifty-year colonial period ending in 1945 and invested heavily in Taiwan after 1952.

Taiwan has encountered two economic problems in recent years, mostly the product of its success. One is the changing nature of its relations with the United States. Essentially, Taiwan sold too much to America and imported too little, thereby amassing a very large trade surplus for itself and contributing substantially (about 9 percent) to the American foreign trade deficit. Washington has made its discomfort known, charging Taiwan with government subsidization of exports, wide-scale pirating, erection of nontariff barriers, supporting financial restrictions, permitting discriminatory trade practices, and deliberately posing difficulties to American firms attempting to enter the Taiwan market. Taipei, however, has taken these criticisms seriously and has begun to change its economy and also to engage in "buy America" campaigns. The problem remains that American bids, goods, and prices are not competitive.

The other problem is how to restructure the economy in response to rising competition from lower-wage countries and the trade surplus with the United States as well as to two growing internal difficulties: the labor question and environmental degradation. Faster movement toward high-technology, high value-added, and skill-intensive production, an emphasis on the service industry, and relocation of labor-intensive industries off shore would help, depending on the political acceptability of such changes. Required as well are a sound tax system, transition from family firms to large publicly held corporations, less dependence on the American market, and more trade with Western Europe. Moreover, the labor situation is problematic: workers' attitudes are changing, the work force is aging, and population growth has slowed greatly. These developments have been accompanied by slackening labor quality, less willingness of young people to work, politicization of the work force, and the continuation of the government (which owns six of the eight largest companies) to act as an economic player as well as a referee. The government needs to divest itself of these companies, address growing income disparities, encourage greater consumer demand and domestic consumption, invest heavily in social programs and the

5

environment, provide a more favorable investment climate, and solve labor disputes.

Already Taiwan is proceeding to address these shortcomings. Tariffs have been reduced, the currency has greatly appreciated, private capital investments in other countries are now permitted, foreign firms are no longer so limited in conduct of business in Taiwan, and a crackdown has taken place on theft of intellectual property. The currency is being allowed to float upward, inflow of hot money is being curbed, and the trade surplus with the United States is being decreased at $1 billion per year. Industrial restructuring is also proceeding through investment in low-labor-cost Southeast Asian nations (especially Thailand, Malaysia, and the Philippines) at about $4 billion a year, buying into technologically advanced Western industries, getting into service industries, and attempting to rejoin international economic organizations. The effort to join the international organizations is important, since if successful it may enable Taiwan to break out of its political isolation as well. Thus Taiwan sent a delegation to the Asian Development Bank meeting in Beijing, is attempting to rejoin the General Agreement on Tariffs and Trade and the Organization for Economic Cooperation and Development, and has a new $1.1 billion foreign aid fund. These measures, plus the modernization of the financial and banking structures, should enable Taiwan to become an international center of finance, insurance, and shipping. Opening up Taiwan's stock market to foreigners, allowing the Taiwanese to invest in other stock markets, and opening trade ties with the Soviet Union and Eastern Europe complete the list of restructuring measures.

As for the relation between economic development and political modernization in Taiwan, some generalizations are possible. First, a market system is a necessary but not sufficient condition of political freedom. A market system can coexist with authoritarianism but not with totalitarianism. Moreover, in the end, authoritarianism is not well suited to the market, since it strains toward political freedom and the institutionalization of that freedom in democracy. Equilibrium between economic and political freedom does not, however, come naturally; it requires a conscious act of political will. That is what is occurring on Taiwan.

**Taiwanese Society.** Writing on Taiwanese society, Ting Tin-yu hypothesizes that the degree of socioeconomic development can be predicted by the level of KMT-DPP competition. He regards political competition as a measure of democracy and stable democracy, in turn, as closely linked to socioeconomic development. Consequently, to assess the process of democratization in Taiwan, he first reviews its socioeconomic development since 1949 and then traces the growth of the opposition movement and the DPP. Finally, he analyzes competition in the townships to test his hypothesis.

Socioeconomic development in Taiwan between 1950 and 1986 occurred in three stages. In the 1950s the government initiated land reform and rebuilt the agricultural sector, thereby transforming the rural social and economic structure. The establishment of labor-intensive light industry in the 1960s followed naturally as the next stage of a program of economic development. By the 1970s and 1980s the final stage of development manifested itself in the general improvement in society, evident not only in the economy but also in health, transportation, communication, education, and other areas.

These changes have strongly influenced the emergence of democracy in Taiwan. In the wake of the transition from an underdeveloped to a newly industrialized country, many now demand political change commensurate with economic progress, believing that Taiwan is ready for democracy. In addition, a new, well-educated generation with democratic values has been making its presence felt. At the same time an independent elite of entrepreneurs and intellectuals has differentiated itself from the governmental sector. Further, environmental concerns and worker exploitation have raised the general consciousness concerning the need for political change. Finally, the oversimplified propaganda regarding the conflict between the KMT and the Chinese Communist party has inspired the new generation to question rather than blindly accept the KMT party line.

In this atmosphere, an opposition movement developed. For a long time localized elections, media control, and restrictions on popular assembly kept the opposition fragmented. Only after the rapid socioeconomic changes and the growth of political elites in the early 1970s did an urban-oriented grass-roots opposition succeed in creating the DPP. Its victories in the 1986 Supplementary Legislative Yuan and the 1989 Legislative Yuan elections legitimized the DPP as the most competitive opposition in Taiwan.

After reviewing these socioeconomic developments and the consequent emergence of a political opposition, Ting constructs a township model to test the hypothesis that socioeconomic development significantly intensifies political competition. He examines the connections between socioeconomic development (which he measures by urbanization and education) and both the growth of opposition power and the intensity of party competition.

The author finds three reasons for these connections. First, greater urbanization fosters access to more information, especially

7

regarding democracy. Second, those with a higher education value democracy more than others. Third, nonagricultural employment often leads to more diverse occupations among workers, enhancing party competition. Ting concludes that his findings support the hypothesis that socioeconomic well-being is linked to the advent of democracy in Taiwan.

**International Pressures.** Martin Lasater explores the relationship between the international environment and Taiwan's move toward greater democracy. The international environment affects Taiwan's security, economy, and politics, including political reform. Taiwan's domestic environment often accounts for its attitude toward international pressures promoting democracy.

Taiwan's security is uncertain. The major security threat, the People's Republic of China (PRC), is omnipresent, and although that danger has eased somewhat for the short term, it will not disappear completely. In the political arena Taiwan is in a similar position. Recognized by only twenty-six governments, Taiwan has a deteriorating diplomatic status. China's improved relations with Taiwan's top diplomatic partners, the Republic of Korea (ROK) and Saudi Arabia, cause concern in Taipei. In response, Taiwan is demonstrating increasing flexibility and pragmatism regarding participation in international organizations, accepting membership even when Beijing is the only officially recognized representative of China in that body.

Taiwan's economic standing, however, is more certain, usually friendly, and strongly competitive. Direct and indirect trade rank Taiwan the world's twelfth largest trading nation. The future holds major challenges, however, including protectionism of major partners and pressure to provide access for foreigners to Taipei's stock and financial markets. In the long term, Taiwan must restructure its industrial sector to remain competitive in the world market. Lasater stresses the importance of U.S. support in all areas of international influence, given the threat of the PRC to Taiwan's security and political status.

Taiwan's domestic politics affect its receptivity to international pressures for reform, with four factors influencing its willingness to change. First, Sun Yat-Sen, founder of the KMT, early on identified constitutional democracy as the last stage of development in the Republic of China (ROC). Second, the ROC has always allied itself with democracies against Communist countries. Third, many students from Taiwan, educated in the United States and Western Europe, believe in democracy and human rights. Finally, with an eye trained on economic success, Taipei cannot ignore the link between economic success and democratic politics in other Asian countries. Rather than "if," the question concerning democracy in Taiwan has always been "when."

Having determined that Taiwan is affected by the international situation and that the domestic environment is receptive to democracy, Lasater analyzes the international influences on political reform. First, uppermost in the minds of the leaders of Taiwan are its relations with the United States and the PRC. The effects of democratization on both relationships will benefit Taiwan. The more democratic Taiwan becomes, the stronger the support from the United States will be. South Korea and the Philippines are constant reminders of the effect of democratization on relations with Washington. In addition, pressure from the American administration, Congress, and the media regarding human rights will ease as democracy takes root. At the same time, democratization will strengthen Taipei's hand when confronting the issue of reunification with the PRC, both by presenting Beijing with the united front of Washington and Taipei and by improving Taiwan's international image. As Taiwan becomes politically and economically more open, it can stand as a model for the PRC, altering the relationship of the two countries.

Second, economic as well as political influences have also affected the attitude toward democracy in Taiwan. The international economic environment helped create a strong, educated middle class, demanding a more open society, political checks and balances, and government accountability. Moreover, Taiwan's experience in overcoming obstacles in the international sphere contributes to its self-confidence in instituting a potentially destabilizing program of domestic reform.

Third, another impetus for reform is international opinion. Overwhelming support for the political competition between the KMT and the DPP encouraged progress and strengthened the position of the reformers in the KMT leadership. Finally, the international environment provided models of representative government. Democratization in Taiwan is planned and implemented by design, based on lessons from other developing and developed countries.

Most significantly, the international environment provides democratic models, exerts pressure to democratize, and challenges Taiwan to make good on its claim that it is less authoritarian than the PRC. The attitudes and activities of the PRC and the United States are the key elements of the international influence. Yet, domestic pressures will be the most influential factors contributing to the success of democracy. International support and influences serve only to pace and support the domestic dynamic in the ROC.

9

## South Korea

**Democratic Reforms.** Daryl Plunk reviews the path to reform in Korea, looks closely at the Sixth Republic, and assesses the outlook for democracy. In evaluating the potential for successful democratization, he examines party diversification and voting trends. Plunk distills the essence of the changes in the ROK, building up to, explaining, and examining what ensued after critical changes in the political history of the ROK. Plunk traces the advent of democracy in Korea from the 1985 National Assembly elections, when the New Korea Democratic party emerged, through Chun Doo Hwan's April 1986 statement of support for limited democracy. He follows Chun's retrenchment a year later down to the appointment of his successor Roh Tae Woo, whose June Declaration advocating constitutional reform and open direct presidential elections initiated a new era of changes. Determined largely by a split between Kim Young Sam and Kim Dae Jung, the "race for the Blue House" divided progressives into Reunification Democratic party (RDP) and Peace and Democracy party (PDP) supporters. Because the two Kims split the vote, Roh gained a majority and won, with Kim Jong Pil emerging as a new opposition force. Using demographic surveys of voters, Plunk concludes that regionalism, rather than issues, was still a driving motivation for voters in the elections.

Beginning the Sixth Republic with promises of democracy, economic reform, national reconciliation, and an end to authoritarianism, Roh purged Chun's associates, appointed a committee to address the explosive 1980 Kwangju issue, investigated corruption, and formed a new cabinet.

When the April 1988 elections upset the ruling party's control of the legislature for the first time in thirty years, the PDP became the key opposition. Plunk again analyzes voting trends and among other conclusions recognizes regional loyalty as a major factor in voter decision making. Following the election of Roh's minority government, significant changes in the constitution affected the decision-making process and social and political life. New legal rights and rights for employees accompanied greater freedom of the press. Most noteworthy, however, was the new balance of power between the National Assembly and the president, who could now be impeached.

Both affected by reform and affecting the degree and pace of that reform are media, labor, business, and politics. Obstacles remain, such as the tradition of using aggressive tactics by the opposition, the legacy of corruption under Chun, and the necessity for a full accounting by Chun. In addition, the prominence of regional loyalty as the driving force in voters' decisions and the lack of information about foreign policy, security, and international issues impede evolution to a more open, democratic system.

The orderly transfer of power in 1986 imbued the reform program with stability. Two years later, the Olympic Games brought a changed Korea into the international limelight. If Korea can develop a democratic culture so that consensus can coexist with differing views, success in domestic and international spheres will continue.

**Economic Dangers.** In the next chapter, John Bennett assesses seven potential dangers for the Korean economy. In his exploration of the relationship between economic and political development, he discusses Korean values and the ways that culture affects the interaction between economics and politics.

Technology is the first potentially unstable area in Korea's economy. Food management and a contract manufacturing system that renders technology cheap have been the prime reasons for the technological success Korea has experienced. At the same time as the transfer of technology to Korea has been successful, however, the small size of the sector leaves Korea with few options for the development of its own leading technology. Koreans need to learn from Japan so that they too can use basic science to create innovative products. Korea is now addressing this problem of too much production and too little innovation by developing technology abroad.

Markets for export could also cause trouble for the Korean economy. Although exports are strong, they rely too heavily (40 percent) on the American market, now increasingly complicated by the trade deficit. Overcoming these difficulties will be difficult as protectionism and a declining U.S. dollar threaten further participation in the U.S. market. To preempt a crash, Korea must increase investment in domestic (both North and South Korean) and in third-country markets. Yet this solution creates new problems, as payment from these customers is less sure than payment from Washington. Nevertheless, despite this potential obstacle, Bennett asserts that Korea should play a significant role developing third-party trade and will not suffer as long as it explores new markets.

World depression, often identified as potentially dangerous for the Korean economy, would certainly cause protectionism to rise. This danger would be overcome more easily for Korea than for others, however, because foreign companies would still need Korean manufacturers. Hence Korea would be able to adapt to a depressed world economy more quickly and successfully than most.

While global automation could make Korean manufactures less important in the international market, say some economists, Bennett argues that, on the contrary, this possibility would not endanger the Korean economy as long as trade is advantageous to both countries and Korean outputs are cheaper than those of Korea's competitors. Since automation is still much more expensive than manual labor, Bennett does not regard this threat as a real danger for Seoul.

Many believe that changes in Korea's employment structure could harm the job market. A declining proportion of the labor force depends on agriculture, and a growing proportion is attending university. Both groups face potentially insufficient job markets. Yet these problems are deceptive since possible solutions exist, including downward wage-demand adjustment, emigration, immigration, automation, and increased leisure.

A breakdown in labor-management relations attributable to increasing freedom for unions also threatens the economy. As labor becomes accustomed to independence, however, explosive situations will become less frequent. Certainly, Bennett argues, labor problems will not cause economic failure.

The increasing complexity of the economy and the decreasing capacity of government to control it may become a crisis in both the political and the economic spheres. The uneasy transition from government to business control must be handled with care by officials and businessmen alike, if it is not to imperil economic success.

Bennett does not see insurmountable dangers for the economy; rather, he acknowledges problems and offers solutions. After analyzing the economy, he discusses models of interaction between economics and politics. He explains both economic success and future obstacles by pointing to Korean values and philosophies manifested in the economic and political systems. Finally, he concludes that as democracy becomes entrenched, external pressures on the economy will diminish. The connections between political and economic liberalization will then serve only to cement the stability of the Korean economy.

**Culture and Politics.** In his chapter on sociocultural aspects of political democracy in Korea, Kim Kyong-dong introduces the yin and the yang of political leaders and methods of reform, of culture and politics. He discusses both the current state of democracy and the future challenges to reform in Korea. Kim seeks answers to why, what, and when events occurred by superimposing theories of cultural and political change on a history of pivotal events; underlying those events are cultural causes and effects. The yin and the yang now permeating events and culture are change and resistance to change: that is, those forces attempting to change the existing balance of power and influence and the forces attempting to retain power and control over decision making. Moreover, international influence and domestic adaptive change present another interplay of yin and yang. The yin of a positive influence, such as that of the political and bureaucratic elite, counters the yang of a negative influence, such as that of intellectuals and the working class.

Since World War II a dialectic has operated between militaristic, bureaucratic, authoritarian political culture and resentment of political suppression linked to democratic ideals bequeathed by the U.S. occupation.

Student protesters toppled the Rhee regime in April 1960, altering the dialectic. Yet conflict between international ideals and Korean culture and a lack of democratic norms threatened the stability of democracy. Strong beliefs in egalitarianism countered a widespread desire for upward mobility, resulting in an approach that Kim calls "popularized elitism." A lag between the end of authoritarianism and the creation of a democratic system created a tension of rising expectations and aspirations growing out of rapid economic progress.

In June 1987 the government finally yielded to demands that had exploded that spring. Kim reviews the history of the republics leading up to the June declarations—the technocracy after Rhee fell, the tradition of student protesters under the increasingly authoritarian, questionably legitimate Chun Republic, and, finally, the disappointment after the coup of 1980 and the Kwangju incident when democracy did not materialize.

The bureaucracy's resistance to change is a central obstacle to democracy; yet the lack of democratic process within the opposition does not bode well for future democracy. Intellectuals, entrepreneurs, labor activists, farmers, and women could all form active— even disruptive—groups in society. At the same time, it is the economic sector and labor that advocate change, the latter often explosively, while bureaucracy and universities are slow to adapt. Kim notes that a trend toward greater autonomy for institutions coincides with a lingering bureaucratic resistance to change.

Rapid changes render liberalization unstable. The many labor disputes since the June Declaration have sometimes been violent. Minority support in the National Assembly handicaps the executive, as does the perception of the Sixth Republic as a continuation of the corrupt Fifth Republic. Regional divisions constantly emerge, undermining reforms and affecting the outcome of elections. Kim concludes that hope lies in compromise as a solution and the gradual fading of the collective in cultural memory.

**International Influences.** Ahn Byung-joon views the international environment as a less powerful influence on reform in Korea than domestic dynamics. Economically, however, the country has been subject to a new global interdependence and a strengthening of relations between Western and Asian nations. Ahn reviews the momentous changes in Korea over the past two years and analyzes the political evolution and economic transition now occurring. He explains why and how the international environment affects Korea and asks how changes today influence the ROK's transitional political economy. Finally, Ahn outlines the challenges and prospects for post-Olympics Korea.

The changes in Korea have carried the country from an era of "crisis politics" to one of "interest politics." Korea no longer suffers from a crisis of security, authority, and legitimacy; rather, society-led pluralism is resulting in a reconciliation of conflicting interests. Access to Western ideas, as well as American influence, helps sustain the ideals of competitive politics, freedom of the press, and an independent judiciary. These changes may be a pivotal point in Korea's history of alternating civil and military regimes.

Korea's economic growth has been extraordinary. Economic development has benefited from the state's role in reform, that is, its system of incentives based on tax benefits and subsidies. Society's demands for welfare, business desires for autonomy, and American pressures to open Korea's market to outside investors all push the government to relinquish control over the economy. Both external and internal forces constrain Korea to initiate internationalization of the economy and a general devolution of power. State-led developmental capitalism has given way to market-led welfare capitalism, with increasing power wielded by agricultural interests and small and medium-sized industries. The challenges that now confront the economy are the conflict between the domestic need for economic autonomy and the international pressure for an open market.

Since 1948, under Rhee, Park, and Chun, South Korea has aligned with the United States against North Korea, using security risks and economic development as excuses to delay democratization. As the superpowers turn inward and address domestic problems, however, Korea loses the excuse to delay reform. In this environment Seoul has made great strides in security, economics, and politics, becoming a middle-power economy in the international arena and a democracy at home.

Further, since the United States ended its troop withdrawal in 1981, security relations with the United States have improved. The choice of Seoul as the location for the summer 1988 Olympics affirmed the increasingly positive tone of relations between the West and South Korea.

While trade friction with the United States and Japan strains economic relations, it indicates that South Korea now has leverage in the global economy. The end of American hegemony has led to an American attempt to impose defense burden sharing on Seoul. That is one reason for the anti-American sentiment expressed most visibly by protesters over the past few years. This sentiment in turn discourages the very burden sharing Washington seeks to impose on Seoul.

These problems with South Korea's strongest ally and trading partner are occurring against a backdrop of a newly confident and assertive policy by Seoul toward Pyongyang. American policy, Soviet and Chinese involvement in the Olympics, expanded trade with Moscow and Beijing, and American and Japanese attempts to communicate and trade with Pyongyang all encourage negotiations between the governments on the peninsula. The lessening of tensions between the global powers forces the issue, leaving no ally for Pyongyang should the South reject negotiations.

Korea is in a good position as the international economic center shifts to Asia; in addition, the PRC, Eastern Europe, and the USSR are expanding trade with certain Asian nations, including Korea. As a "trading state," Korea can only increase its influence. The establishment of an Overseas Development Fund indicates that Korea is already seeking new horizons.

Thus, the international environment has evolved as a strong foundation for the development of an advanced economy and political democracy in Korea. After the Olympics, trade volume indicates that Korea will become one of the ten leading industrial powers.

In the economic sphere the government must negotiate with labor, liberalize trade, and sustain the economic growth that has occurred so rapidly over the past few years. While the future looks bright for Korea, Seoul needs to meet the requirements of redistribution and reinvestment. As a result of its strong economy, in its foreign policy South Korea has greater confidence in dealing with the United States and a solid advantage in relations with North Korea. The Olympics helped Korea move from the margins of the international community toward the center. If in the future Seoul confronts the challenges inherent in change, it will become a leader in security and development in the region.

## The Philippines

**From Dictatorship to Democracy.** Carolina G. Hernandez addresses key political developments in the Philippines, specifically, the decline of Philippine politics under Marcos from democracy to dictatorship, redemocratization in the context of the Marcos legacy, and the factors that will determine democracy's future in the Philippines.

The change from democracy to dictatorship during the Marcos regime supplies a critical element for analyzing present trends and future prospects for democracy. The declaration of martial law in September 1972 not only marked the collapse of democracy but also encouraged the growth of an insurgency dedicated to forcibly over-throwing the established order and American-style democratic insti-tutions. With martial law also came the arrest of opposition politi-cians, a ban on all political parties and political activities, the closing of many newspapers and radio stations, presidential decrees sus-pending and curtailing civil and political liberties, and a tearing apart of the Philippine Congress.

Marcos then went on to centralize power in his own hands and to expand the role of the military. By improving the training and equipment of the army and integrating all constabularies into the national police, Marcos effectively gave the military a free hand for the next fourteen years. Moreover, to ensure dictatorial control over society, the 1973 Constitution was amended to allow presidential power of legislation even under martial rule and after election of a regular legislature. This measure gave him absolute control over the entire electoral and political process.

The regime's assassination of opposition politician Senator Be-nigno "Ninoy" Aquino, Jr., on August 21, 1983, rebounded against Marcos to seal the fate of his dictatorship. Massive public protests and demonstrations signaled a revolt against a regime afflicted by cronyism, corruption, and rapid economic decline. These pressures ultimately combined to force Marcos to hold presidential elections. He attempted, nonetheless, through electoral engineering, to jimmy the results to allow him to remain in office. Unfortunately for Marcos, opposition groups not only delivered an impressive majority vote to Corazon Aquino but also caught him in the act of electoral manipu-lation. A tumultuous turnabout then ensued in which the military, faced with the prospect of civil war, switched its support to Aquino. When the United States also abandoned Marcos, his fate was sealed, and Aquino was installed as president. In the face of blatant election fraud, Aquino led the way back to democracy for the Philippines. What would she do with it?

To ensure long-term survival of democracy, democratic political institutions obliterated during the Marcos dictatorship would have to be rebuilt. Among institutions targeted for restoration were the press, the judiciary, the election of local officials, and a genuine bureaucratic reorganization. A new democratic constitution was also ratified in February 1987, legitimizing Aquino's assumption of office and providing mechanisms for separation of power, checks and balances, and legislative recall; guaranteeing human rights; and restricting the powers of the presidency. The new Constitution thus made a dictatorship legally impossible. Although legislative elections proved Aquino's tremendous popularity, problems in carrying out policy formulation soon surfaced. The early Aquino administration was a collection of disparate, conflicting politicians lacking a common ideological base. This failure of cohesion caused a split in proadministration votes and the election of opposition candidates, thus making it difficult to form policy. These trends continued in the early 1990s.

Two difficult tasks confronting the Aquino administration were establishment of civilian control over the military and neutralizing the Moro front and the Communist insurgency. The emergency powers of the presidency were strictly limited by the new constitution, reducing the probability of another government-military partnership similar to the past regime. Could the administration continue to overcome military opposition, and intermittent coup attempts, to reform along constitutional lines? It was not easy to reduce powers deeply ingrained in such a dominant sector, and to be successful, Aquino would have to undertake a major military retraining program to turn a demoralized army into an effective antiinsurgent force. The Aquino government would also have to root out traditional military corruption, assert dominance over a politicized army, and continue efforts to rectify Philippine socioeconomic problems at the grass roots. If the government were unsuccessful, the threat of insurgency and persistent military coup attempts would continue to impede the future of a country desperate for political stability.

Fourteen years of suppressed political competition held the Philippines "in a state of suspended animation" by the Marcos regime. The 1988 elections, however, saw the return of these politics and politicians and indicated that traditional political elites had indeed survived Marcos's domination of politics. Unfortunately, and much to the distress of Filipinos expectant of a legitimate government, private gain at the expense of public benefit also survived.

The future of democracy in the Philippines will depend on reviving a shattered economy, undertaking a comprehensive land reform program, stepping up foreign investment, revamping the military, curbing endemic corruption, and thwarting Communist insurgency. Likewise, if the Aquino government maintains the confidence and support of the people, military attempts to overthrow the government can be avoided.

For lack of a better alternative to the present government, Corazon Aquino and her administration continue to be popular, if on a declining curve, and the Philippine economy is finally on the upswing. Moreover, the harsh memory of dictatorship is still fresh on the minds of Filipinos, serving as a powerful incentive toward democratization. With the continued persistence of the Aquino government to check the political ambitions of local politicians, with military support, and with international assistance, one can be cautiously optimistic regarding prospects for democracy—otherwise, not.

**Economics and Political Unrest.** Richard Hooley analyzes the economic factors underlying sociopolitical stability and dissension in the Philippines. He concludes that economic growth generally leads to democratic development in the absence of such economic shocks as rapid changes in income distribution. Acknowledging the difficulty of measuring income distribution for developing countries, Hooley proposes real wages as an indicator. Because it excludes windfall profits reaped by the upper strata, this index provides a closer approximation to the real economic position of most working-class consumers than such indicators as real per capita income.

Hooley undertakes to determine the relationship, if any, between changes in real wages and the manifestations of discontent with the political system. Calculating real wages for skilled and unskilled workers from various statistical sources and quantifying discontent as "the number of persons involved in movements of armed protest," he divides twentieth-century Philippine history into five distinct periods to illustrate the correlation between the two. In each of these cases, rising or high real wages have been accompanied by sociopolitical tranquillity, while periods of falling or low wages have witnessed clear instances of discontent. Furthermore, the more severe the decline in wages, the more militant the dissent is likely to be.

Thus from 1897 to 1902, the depreciation of the peso combined with minimal increases in money wages to produce extremely low real wages. The marked decline during the 1890s was followed, after a short lag, by rebellion against Spain and then against the United States between 1898 and 1902. Between 1903 and 1927, by contrast, both real per capita income and real wages grew steadily and quickly, and the country experienced neither armed uprising nor any other serious political dissent.

During the years 1928–1946 Philippine workers received unprecedentedly low real wages and expressed persistent discontent. Until the outbreak of World War II, real per capita income held constant, but real wages declined slowly and steadily. At the same time, the Philippine populace showed the first signs of dissatisfaction with the American administration: the appearance of the Kalipunang Pambansa ng mga Magsasaka sa Pilipinas (KPMP) in the late 1930s capped nearly a decade of rising discontent, and the Sakdalan movement expressed the frustration of tenant farmers in central Luzon with their deteriorating economic situation.

The outbreak of war in 1941 took a more serious toll on the Philippine economy, and by 1946 the real wage rate had plummeted to its level at the beginning of the century. In the 1940s both the most dramatic and prolonged decline in real wages during the American period and the most striking case of sociopolitical discontent, the armed and widespread Hukbalahap (Huk) rebellion, occurred.

The end of the war ushered in an era of rising real wages and strengthened democratic institutions, as wage increases outpaced the growth of per capita income and Ramon Magsaysay succeeded in ending the Huk rebellion. The real wage rate peaked in 1960, however, and grew only slowly in the next decade as real per capita income increased steadily. This discrepancy signifies the beginning of a less equitable distribution of income; and indeed, while democratic institutions remained functional throughout the 1960s, such signs of rising unrest as the establishment of the New People's Army (NPA) became visible.

During the 1970s, real wages declined decisively while real per capita income continued to rise. As a result, relative to real per capita income, real wages are now at their lowest point in the twentieth century. At the same time, democratic institutions were trampled, and the NPA grew exponentially in size, organization, and strength. Despite important gains since the fall of Marcos, Philippine democracy remains at a precarious point.

Hooley concludes that the relationship between real wages and sociopolitical discontent is inverse, while the correlation between discontent and real per capita income appears tenuous at best. Furthermore, the ratio between real wages and real per capita income indicates with remarkable accuracy both the timing and the magnitude of outbreaks of discontent. The interval between a change in the direction of the wage curve and the onset of popular uprising appears to be approximately three to four years.

Examining the present, Hooley notes that real wages continue to fall while real per capita income continues to rise, signifying a further

19

decline in the living standards of working-class households. A sharp transformation of the domestic labor market explains this disturbing trend. The rate at which agriculture and industry provide new jobs is insufficient to clear the labor market, which has swelled considerably as the population has grown at record rates. Demand for agricultural labor has shrunk as output per unit of land has increased, and a switch from lower- to higher-value crops has occurred, changes that have entailed increased use of nonlabor inputs in agricultural production. In addition, the industrial sector remains highly inefficient, and the price system is badly in need of restructuring; until these conditions are alleviated, industry cannot create enough new jobs to relieve the pressures on the labor market.

The effectiveness and flexibility of the Aquino government in devising a long-term economic strategy to counter this most serious threat to Philippine democracy are limited by the decreased effectiveness of the bloated bureaucracy and the burdensome national budget deficit. Political and administrative steps to ensure economic reform must complement economic measures, but cleavages among the nation's political elite complicate that agenda. The stakes are high, for democratic institutions in the Philippines are at a critical point. To ensure the increase in real wages and distributive equity necessary to mute sociopolitical discontent and keep democracy functioning, the Aquino government must deal effectively with such difficult but fundamental issues as land distribution, agricultural productivity, wages and income distribution, industrial restructuring, and the national deficit. Recent land reform legislation represents a useful first step, but much remains to be done to retain popular confidence in the economy and the government necessary for Philippine democracy.

**Social and Cultural Factors.** David Rosenberg examines the complex influence of social and cultural factors on political change in the Philippines. Beginning with a brief look at political and economic factors, Rosenberg lays a foundation for understanding social and cultural determinants of development and democracy.

Ferdinand Marcos, who proclaimed martial law in 1972, ruled under presidential emergency powers until the ascension of the Aquino leadership in 1986. Marcos's rule was further bolstered by his firm grip on the military as his major power base, but his promise of a new society fell far short of ending feudalism and political instability. The "people power" movement and Cory Aquino, in contrast, renewed the hope and opportunity of transcending the corrupt

dictatorship, revitalizing the economy, and reforming the civilian and military bureaucracies.

The most pressing responsibilities that first faced the Aquino leadership were to devise a strategy for land reform, to alleviate poverty, to generate more productive employment, and to promote equity and social justice. However necessary and attractive these ideas are to democratization, even in the Aquino administration they have been compromised by poor administration and corruption. Inefficiencies and inadequacies in the government have become steadily more manifest, and politics seems to be reverting to the rule of landed oligarchs. Further, the gap between potential and achievement remains wide. Socioeconomic progress also depends on the growth rate and hence, among other factors, on foreign investment. Near-term prospects are not good, however, given the volatility in global markets and relatively poor prospects for traditional Philippine exports.

Social and cultural factors have also played instrumental roles in determining the latter-day structure of Philippine society. Some of these have reinforced traditional values while others have led to their deterioration.

Agriculture, the foundation of the Philippine economy, employs a disproportionate part of the labor force. That means widespread poverty is concentrated in rural areas. The high rural population growth accounts for the great rise in the labor force, which, without strong economic expansion, merely aggravates the historical Philippine cycle of poor economic health, unemployment, and rural poverty. The consequence is a burgeoning underclass of landless poor that is growing faster than available jobs. The Aquino government, therefore, needs to place the massive creation of new jobs high on the list of priorities. To do this, the government must implement a large-scale redistribution of capital, particularly investment funds, to populous rural areas where wealth is lowest.

The present configuration of the Philippine economy is not natural, however, and did not happen on its own initiative. Specific Marcos-era government policies have intensified high population growth, unequal distribution of wealth, and stratification of social classes. Although the Aquino government has adopted many constructive policies to address these problems, so far its policies are foundering in a litigious maze of bureaucratic incompetence, lack of money, and opposition of vested interests. Is not the Aquino government running out of steam?

The government answer to rural poverty is land reform for the entire country, but how does one persuade those who have land to

transfer it to those who do not? The Philippine elite is hardly likely to surrender its privileges voluntarily. Aquino hopes that a comprehensive agrarian reform program will facilitate a breakup of private estates and achieve a just distribution of agricultural lands.

Such cultural factors as the tradition of political dynasties and the merely symbolic value of elections reinforce class stratification. Usually, family name, not policy, is the key to success. The familial aspect of politics was a distinct feature of the Marcos leadership. Most friends and relatives placed in key positions of authority were indebted to Marcos even after he was forced out. Aquino, in contrast, came into power with no significant debts to old political families; neither does she have the benefit of such personal alliances and reciprocal obligations. Traditional, family-based political dynasties are thus being revived, making it difficult for policies favoring economic and social reforms.

Of equal importance to electoral success are the power of symbols and the ceremonies of authority. In the Philippines, where elections have become a synonym for democracy, the use of mass psychology has in the past proven tremendously successful in gaining public political participation. Marcos used the traditional persona of *machismo*, while Aquino employs the persona of a traditional housewife, honest and unpretentious.

The short-term legitimacy of such a demonstrably popular president cannot be challenged; yet the prospect for continuing divisiveness within her administration also seems strong. Although the Aquino government has achieved some political reforms, uncertainty still hangs over deep-rooted problems such as the inequality of wealth, income, and opportunity. Eventually, the popularity of the Aquino government may wane in the face of these potentially explosive issues.

Finally, the continuing issue of American bases in the Philippines complicates prospects. The Philippine dilemma over its own identity is acute; yet much of the dispute over the bases symbolizes Philippine independence from the United States. The United States should reassess this issue, consider bearing a larger share of the cost of maintaining the facilities, or perhaps relocate or phase out some of its military missions on the islands. The United States must remember the inevitability of change in its promotion of development in the Philippines. Above all, political change is necessary if there is to be any further social or economic progress.

**International Influences.** W. Scott Thompson focuses on the international environment and its implications for democracy and development in the Philippines. He describes two new factors affecting the

Philippines' international position—the anti-Marcos revolution, which led to the installation of the Aquino government, and increasing international recognition of the effectiveness of the Association of South East Asian Nations (ASEAN). Given the assumption that states will always attempt to maximize their sovereignty, these changes in international status would seem to prescribe a Philippine foreign policy markedly independent from the United States. Thompson argues, however, that the excesses of the Marcos reign drained the nation's resources, precluding any immediate assertion of autonomy in Philippine foreign policy. Manila's foreign relations are therefore essentially reduced to relations with Washington and with the other ASEAN capitals.

The major factor complicating U.S.-Philippine relations is the debate over the American military installations at Clark Field and Subic Bay. While many in the United States deem these bases vital to American security interests, their presence is another embarrassing reminder of imperialism for Filipino nationalists. Thompson recognizes this conflict but concludes that public opinion in Philippine provinces enjoying the economic benefits from the U.S. bases, the support of other Asian nations such as Thailand and China for a continued American presence in the region, and the growing threat of the New People's Army (NPA) make likely an extension of the agreement allowing the U.S. bases.

Having described these two constraints on Philippine foreign relations, Thompson turns to a discussion of economic development and reform in the Philippines. Defining revolution as an event introducing significant social and economic change, he charges that the post-Marcos events qualify more as a restoration than a revolution. Citing recent abuses of power by landlords and government figures, he describes the present situation as a return to the system of rule by the pre-Marcos elite.

Indeed, the current debate over economic development strategy is essentially the same argument heard in preceding decades. The fundamental question is whether aid worsens or alleviates economic problems. Thompson finds this argument indicative of a desire to maintain protected Philippine markets for inefficiently produced goods.

The Multilateral Aid Initiative/Philippines Aid Program magnifies the intensity of this debate. This program, advocated by the Reagan administration, found international support in three areas: encouraging further economic reforms, improving the economy's absorptive capacity, and organizing further economic aid. At an aid donors' summit held in July 1989 in Tokyo, it appeared that the plan would provide the Philippines with $10 billion over a five-year period.

Just as the U.S. bases are an essential criterion in assessing the possibilities for Philippine foreign policy, they also figure prominently in economic considerations. The connection between American aid and continued military presence became clear when difficulties arose over renewal of the bases agreement. During the period of disagreement, progress on the Philippine Aid Program came to a halt at U.S. insistence. Once the base negotiations were settled, aid discussions were resumed.

Finally, Thompson assesses the future for democracy and development in the Philippines. He prefaces this by noting that the Philippine definition of democracy is quite different from its understanding in the West. This difference stems from two factors: sociopolitical psychology and Philippine history as a Spanish colony. Culturally, the Philippines are best compared to Malaysia, where respect for and acceptance of authority are strong and where conflict and dissent are discouraged. The legacy of Spanish colonialism is a Filipino population with little or no understanding of the notion of individual rights. These underpinnings of Philippine politics may not be a solid basis for a democratic system.

As the NPA grows stronger and the debate over appropriate response to the insurgency continues, the United States will confront difficult decisions concerning its Philippine policy. Indeed, a U.S. armed intervention is neither impossible nor unthinkable. Protection of American military bases, a sense of responsibility for the colony, and the strong connections between Philippine and American elites could all precipitate a U.S. decision to intervene.

Assuming this scenario is possible, Thompson examines how the United States could avoid it. He believes the answer lies in the relationship between American security interests and Philippine economic development. Essentially, the protection of U.S. bases and other security interests in the Philippines is contingent on the stability of democracy. From this perspective, a shift in emphasis in U.S. policy from protecting military access to promoting economic development and reform may prove more beneficial in the long run. Thompson's projections for the future are based on three factors: the political will of the military, the increasing strength of the New People's Army, and the dedication of a sector of the Philippine polity to a democratic future.

### Political and Economic Assessments

**A Global Context.** Acknowledging the difficulty of generalizing about political and economic development in the third world, Raymond

Gastil examines the cases of South Korea, Taiwan, and the Philippines in the context of democracy and development throughout the world over the past two centuries. He first traces the rise of the modern democratic polity and industrial economy from their origins in eighteenth-century Great Britain through their diffusion and entrenchment in Europe and beyond during the nineteenth and twentieth centuries. From this, Gastil concludes that the relationship between development and democracy is not strictly causal. While economic woes have been the downfall of many democratic regimes, it does not follow that economic growth and development are sufficient bases on which to sustain a democratic system. Something more seems to be required, perhaps historical experience with democracy or a political culture broadly sympathetic to democratic processes.

He next applies these lessons to South Korea, Taiwan, and the Philippines. The prognosis is mixed. The Philippines, beset by social cleavages and economic difficulties, nonetheless possess a hardy, if tumultuous, democratic tradition that has spanned decades. Even if socioeconomic crises temporarily overwhelm it, the democratic tradition in the Philippines is deep-rooted and has acquired a legitimacy that may allow it to sprout again.

In South Korea and Taiwan, economic conditions seem much more amenable to democracy. No democratic political culture, however, has been built up in the past. South Korea not only has a long tradition of military rule but also is vulnerable to nationalist appeals for Korean unification. Taiwan's historical experience encompasses traditional Chinese authoritarianism, decades of Japanese occupation, and forty years of rule by the Leninist-style Kuomintang. As a result, recent trends toward democratization in both societies are still experimental. One is left with the hope, but not the certainty, that these departures will be enduring and successful enough to take hold as legitimate traditions in their own right.

**Recent Events in the ROC.** David Chou begins his assessment of the prospects for democracy in the Republic of China on Taiwan with an overview of the changes that have transformed the political life of that society since 1986. Even before the forty-year-old martial law decree suspending citizens' constitutional rights was lifted in July 1987, progress toward democracy was under way. The opposition Democratic Progressive party (DPP) was founded in September 1986 and, though technically illegal, won some 29 percent of the vote in the November 1986 supplementary elections for the Legislative Yuan and National Assembly. The establishment of additional new parties soon followed. Lifting martial law also heralded a significant expansion of press freedom: the number of newspapers published has more than tripled since 1987, and once-taboo subjects are reported and discussed much more freely.

The peaceful transition of power following the death of President and KMT Chairman Chiang Ching-kuo in January 1988 marked a further step away from authoritarianism. Vice President Lee Teng-hui assumed the presidency as mandated by the Constitution and was subsequently elected KMT chairman at the Thirteenth Party Congress. Under his leadership, the KMT continued along the reformist path initiated by the late president. Because the KMT is so firmly institutionalized and opposition strength is offset by weak organization and serious factional disputes, the KMT is likely to dominate ROC politics even in a multiparty system. This strong presence may help to ensure political stability in an increasingly democratic society.

While prospects for democracy thus appear quite favorable, recurrent calls for Taiwan's independence and a profusion of demonstrations and strikes threaten to undermine political reform. Anathema to the KMT (as well as to Beijing), the independence issue impinges directly on the relationship between the Mainland and Taiwan and remains highly sensitive. While the DPP has not incorporated independence in its party platform, some radicals have urged its inclusion, and the party has detailed conditions under which it would reverse its position.

Strikes and demonstrations have proliferated as a result of the rising expectations induced by democratization. The government must therefore endeavor to institutionalize recent democratic advances to meet popular demands. Institutional inability to keep pace with the societal transformation under way may lead to political instability.

Chou next examines the relationship between democratization and such variables as socioeconomic development, political culture, and international environment. He finds both socioeconomic development and political culture supportive of a democratic system in the ROC, citing as evidence a high degree of distributive equity, a large middle class, traditional Confucian values of moderation and consensus, and Sun Yat-sen's Three Principles of the People—nationalism, democracy, and people's welfare—which provide the framework for political thought in the ROC. The international environment, too, has influenced Taiwan's progress toward democracy. Close relations with the United States, political change in neighboring Asian countries, and competition with Beijing for Chinese and international support have all played a role in the retreat from authoritarianism.

The international environment remains less important, however, than domestic factors in explaining political change in the ROC.

Finally, Chou compares the political development of the ROC with that of South Korea and the Philippines. He notes the similarities first: all three societies are engaged in a transition from authoritarian to more democratic political systems. Furthermore, the United States has been instrumental in pressuring the governments of each to democratize, although the American role has been most pronounced in the Philippines.

He then outlines these differences: the governments of the ROC, South Korea, and the Philippines enjoy varying degrees of domestic political support. Taiwan's ruling Kuomintang has generally garnered some 70 percent of the popular vote (60 percent in the December 1989 elections), while the Korean government pulled less than 40 percent of the vote in the 1987 parliamentary elections. In the Philippines, the new constitution promulgated by the Aquino government received 77 percent of the vote, but that government represents a coalition rather than a single party with a coherent ideology. Moreover, popular enthusiasm for the government may wane if it is unable to alleviate the nation's severe economic problems.

**The Future of Democracy.** Nicholas Eberstadt views the marked economic and political changes that have swept South Korea, Taiwan, and the Philippines in recent years more as discrete phenomena than as evidence of a general trend. He highlights those factors that may particularly affect progress toward democracy and economic development in each case but remains doubtful about the future of liberal democracy in East Asia as a whole.

Surveying Taiwan's political and economic development, Eberstadt notes that the ruling Kuomintang has been heavily influenced by the Leninist tradition. This influence was both intellectual and material, as evidenced by visits of Comintern advisers from Moscow to help the young party build its organization in China. The KMT (the only Leninist-style party in existence that does not subscribe to Marxism) has, however, taken economic and political strides rarely associated with the Leninist tradition. For instance, significant gains in total factor productivity have played a key role in Taiwan's economic transformation. Moreover, the KMT appears to be the first Leninist party to undertake a voluntary diminution of its power. Finally, moves toward political liberalization represent not tactical exigencies but a desire to reorient the relationship between party, state, and society.

In the Philippine case, Eberstadt points out that despite serious economic difficulties, the economy has been progressing, if slowly. Statistics demonstrate favorable changes in such indicators as infant mortality, life expectancy at birth, and death rates for very young children. The incidence of extreme material hardship seems therefore to have declined in the Philippines over the past generation.

Widespread knowledge of English may also affect development and democracy in the Philippines. From an economic perspective, fluency in the primary language of international business should facilitate greater integration in the world economy. Such aptitude also avails the population of the literature of the Anglo-American political tradition in a way that selective translation cannot.

Surveying economic and political changes in South Korea, Eberstadt notes that the nation's economic success is generally attributed to government policies conducive to growth. Official policies on credit allocation, agriculture, public health, and other matters, however, would seem instead to impede development. The adoption of an export-oriented economic strategy seems to explain South Korea's outstanding economic progress. (Indeed, while South Korea's economic performance may not have been optimal in theory, in real terms the results have been significant.)

Politically, it is premature to speak of liberal democracy in South Korea. While notable strides toward political liberalization have occurred since 1987, Korean society is still governed by a system other than the rule of liberal law. Government administration remains highly personalistic and frequently arbitrary. No political community of the sort required for liberal democracy yet exists, and its establishment is impeded by the Korean tendency toward racialism in the guise of nationalism. The 1988 political reforms have set the forces of racialism and liberalism at odds, and the ensuing tension is manifest in the rise of anti-American and pro-unification sentiment. The Korean people, however, have traditionally been receptive to foreign ideas and influences, as their widespread embrace of Christianity has demonstrated, and the values of liberal democracy are no more alien to the Korean cultural tradition than are those of the Christian faith.

Eberstadt concludes his assessment with a less sanguine outlook for East Asia as a whole. A survey of the political landscape of the region over the past two decades reveals that the achievements of South Korea, Taiwan, and the Philippines are more the exceptions than the norm. In addition, the decline of American power in East Asia is unlikely to hasten the process of democratization, as some observers have predicted. Indeed, liberal democracy has to date taken root only in those Asian societies with a distinct historical legacy of Anglo-American influence. The vacuum left by a diminished American presence in the region is not likely to be filled by a profusion of newly democratic states.

**Threats to the Future of the Philippines.** Segundo Romero reiterates the consensus that while the Aquino administration has achieved considerable success in revitalizing the democratic institutions and processes that languished during the Marcos years, socioeconomic problems constitute the gravest threat to a democratic future for the Philippines. After surveying a spectrum of opinion on the roots of the crisis and the prognosis for resolution, he draws his own conclusions on the nation's prospects for democracy and economic development.

Romero emphasizes the importance of certain intangible factors mitigating the socioeconomic threat to democracy. He points out that Filipinos from the Left and from the Right now defend the "democratic space" carved out by Corazon Aquino after her victory in 1986. Particularly in the aftermath of the Marcos dictatorship, Filipinos are unlikely to acquiesce in a political system that disregards personal liberties. Indeed, by allowing the progressive movement to take its grievances to the streets freely and legally, the Aquino administration has channeled some of its opposition away from the armed insurgency and into mainstream political life.

The charisma of Aquino herself serves as an additional intangible factor favoring democracy. With the exception of Ramon Magsaysay, no leader of the postwar Philippines has commanded such respect from the population. Indeed, the democratic institutions Aquino has established would be difficult to dismantle largely because she stands staunchly behind them. It is nonetheless true that the strength of such intangibles has dissipated since the euphoric days of the 1986 election. The exaggerated hopes that abounded after Aquino's victory have given way to sober realism and some disappointment: although real change has occurred, much remains the same.

Certainly, the most important task of the Aquino administration will be to hasten development and reduce distributive inequity. The challenges Aquino faces, however, are not solely economic. While her government has clearly passed the test of legitimacy, it has yet to tackle the problem of political participation, a crisis that threatens to undermine the stability of the very democratic institutions and processes Aquino has worked to entrench. National electoral politics notwithstanding, Philippine society is not broadly democratic. Political participation at the local level is scanty, and overcentralized administration has been a persistent problem since 1946.

Romero suggests, too, that Aquino may have erred in failing to institutionalize the "people power" behind her success at the polls. Her administration early embarked on a generally successful and politically astute effort to dissociate itself from the tactics of the Marcos regime. In so doing, however, Aquino has been reluctant to establish a political party or mass movement, rebuild popular organizations at the village level, or undertake a nationwide political education and public information campaign to disseminate and promote her political program. Such steps may be necessary to eradicate the remnants of pro-Marcos sentiment and consolidate support for the ideals that underlay her 1986 victory.

Finally, Romero concludes that while both the economic and the political challenges facing the Aquino administration are formidable, the prospects for an enduring democratic system are favorable. It is far less likely, however, that the government will prove competent to bring about widespread economic development and implement an equitable distribution of wealth.

## Conclusion

The chapters that follow detail, for the first time, the relationship between the two great forces that are creating non-Western extensions of the modern world in three important East Asian societies: the spread of political democracy and the transformation of the economy through industrialization. It is not yet clear that a one-to-one relationship exists between the two: that is, that beyond a certain point in a society's economic or political development further progress in one sphere must be directly and closely linked to progress in the other. Yet such a tendency does appear to exist as some of the links between economics and politics in these Asian societies emerge more distinctly. Despite the transforming power of democracy and economic development, however, the weight of the historical and cultural past remains enormous, if not decisive. Neither political democracy nor economic development is inevitable, because even once a certain stage of governmental institutionalization or per capita national income has been reached, plateaus or setbacks may occur. Nonetheless, the probability of success rises once a threshold has been attained. Such success seems the case in Taiwan and South Korea but not in the Philippines. In Taiwan and South Korea, cultural unity and a long history intensify the power of the past. The contrast in the Philippines is stark on both counts; the gradient is thus much steeper than for Taiwan and South Korea. It will therefore take a great deal of hard work by the Philippine people and their government (and a great deal of patience), investment of all kinds, and fortitude on the part of others to see the matter through to a successful outcome.

The chapters in this volume may provide guideposts to some of the lessons learned (and still being learned) by the Koreans and the Taiwanese and to pitfalls that may lie ahead for the Filipinos. In the end, we may be able to generalize their collective experience for possible application to other situations, as well as to be more confident about what to expect in these three Asian societies themselves.

# PART ONE
# Taiwan

# 2
# Political Developments
# in the Republic of China

*Lu Ya-li*

In 1986, the leadership of the Republic of China (ROC) on Taiwan decided to launch political reforms aimed at transforming the island's authoritarian system into a constitutional democracy. Two items in the reform package have already been realized, while the others are still to be implemented. Although Taiwan has not yet attained its final goal, observers generally agree that it is on its way toward becoming a democracy and the process seems irreversible. Since only a few developing countries have democratic systems or have succeeded in transforming their authoritarian political structures into viable democracies, the case of Taiwan merits our attention, the more so as in this case the process of transition has been to a considerable extent initiated by the leaders themselves.[1]

This chapter attempts to explain why the leadership in Taiwan made the decision to reform the political system in the 1980s, to assess the prospect for democratic development in Taiwan, and to place the case of Taiwan in a general framework of democratic transition in developing countries. The chapter has four sections: first, a brief account of the past political development in Taiwan, with the emphasis on recent reforms; second, an analysis of the internal and external factors contributing to the reforms; third, an analysis of the problems hindering Taiwan's democratization and future political development together with an assessment of the prospects for democracy in Taiwan; and fourth, an effort to put the case of Taiwan in a broader context of democratic evolution in developing societies.

## The Past

The political system in Taiwan just prior to recent reforms has been variously characterized as "soft authoritarianism" or "authoritarianism with developmental features."[2] To handle the problem of national security, the government of the ROC imposed martial law on May 20, 1949, which in effect suspended the operation of key constitutional provisions guaranteeing people's rights to form political parties and to engage in mass activities such as labor strikes, street demonstrations, and the like. Until 1969, national parliamentary elections had not been held.[3] Local elections, held regularly since 1950, provided the major vehicle for people's political participation and gave politicians of Taiwan origin some preparation for assuming national office. At the central level, the Kuomintang (KMT) virtually monopolized power, while at the local level, non-KMT politicians sometimes won important offices by defeating KMT candidates in elections. Of the twenty-one county magistrates and city mayors in Taiwan Province, for example, four were not KMT members.

In the 1950s, the government carried out land reform and earned support in much of the countryside. Although recent troubles in agriculture have eroded the government's popularity among farmers somewhat, by and large the KMT still wields considerable influence in the rural areas as a result of the successful land reform. In the urban areas the KMT did not enjoy the same degree of undivided support, though it would be an oversimplification to say that the remarkable political stability in Taiwan throughout the 1950s and 1960s was simply the result either of the government's effective system of control or of political apathy. While these factors naturally played their part, more important was that rapid economic development in Taiwan has made Communist propaganda entirely irrelevant, and people's attitudes toward the system fell within the range of active support to passive tolerance. Those who were intensely hostile toward it were very few. At the first stage of KMT rule, roughly from the early 1950s to the early 1970s, the government was largely an administration of technocrats committed to rapid economic growth. With a strategy that emphasized balance between state intervention and private entrepreneurship, Taiwan achieved remarkable economic growth, averaging a 9 percent annual increase in GNP from 1952 to 1972.[4] The urban middle class, whose number increased by leaps and bounds during this period,[5] was the main beneficiary of the ever-enlarging economic pie. At this stage, the general attitude of this pivotal class was nonpolitical.

Throughout the 1970s and the early 1980s, developments within Taiwan and abroad put the system to new and tough tests. The leadership was aware that the old system needed major changes. Liberalization and democratization became not only the fervent desire of many people but an urgent necessity for the country to meet new challenges.

In March 1986, the KMT convened the third plenum of the Central Committee of its Twelfth Party Congress amid high expectations of the public, who demanded fundamental reforms. The result of the plenum was a disappointment. With the benefit of hindsight, it is certain the decision to launch reforms was made by late President Chiang Ching-kuo, then the KMT chairman, prior to the plenum, but for tactical reasons he chose not to reveal it even during the party meeting. In May and June of that year, the press reported that a twelve-member blue ribbon panel was appointed by the president to study a six-item reform package. The formal announcement of the reforms was made by the late president when interviewed by a *Washington Post* delegation in October. A brief account of the reforms follows.

**Lifting of Martial Law.** For the past fifteen or so years, lifting martial law was a popular demand. Non-KMT political activists wanted it repealed so that they might have more room for political activities while intellectuals voiced the same demand to promote academic freedom. Even some firm supporters of the old system urged the government to lift martial law, since they were also aware that by the early 1970s martial law no longer served a useful purpose and its continued imposition was too costly. The conservatives, however, were opposed. So for a long time, the government was indecisive on this matter.

Once the decision to lift martial law was made, its dismantling became a matter of controversy. Some people demanded that a national security law should be enacted prior to the end of martial law while others staunchly opposed such an enactment. After a period of heated dispute and hard bargaining between the KMT and the Democratic Progressive party (DPP) members in the Legislative Yuan, a much diluted national security law was passed, and martial law was duly lifted on July 15, 1987.

**End of Ban on Parties.** The ban on new parties had been imposed together with martial law in 1949. In 1960, some intellectuals and local politicians led by Lei Chen, the editor of *Free China* magazine, tried to form a new China Democratic party, an effort that produced no result as Mr. Lei was jailed and his magazine closed. From then until the early 1970s, no one made another attempt to defy the party ban. In the early 1970s, politicians in the opposition running for seats in the national legislature formed various campaign organizations, which were eventually amalgamated into a quasi-party called the *dangwai* (outside the Kuomintang) group. Since the group consistently received approximately 25 percent of the votes in a series of elections, after several futile attempts to dissolve it, the government believed it politically wise to tolerate its existence. On September 28, 1986, 112 *dangwai* leaders met in a hotel room and announced the founding of the Democratic Progressive party, the first genuine opposition party in Taiwan. As the new party was established before the lifting of martial law, technically it was illegal, but the government chose to ignore this fact and throughout has treated it as an opposition party. The new party won twelve seats out of 288 in the Legislative Yuan in the election held in November 1986. (Of these, 193 are senior members whose seats were not contested.) In November 1987, another new party, the Labor party, was founded. The Labor party, despite its small membership, has been very active in the labor movement.

**Reform of the National Legislature.** The national legislature (actually three bodies, the Legislative Yuan, the Control Yuan, and the National Assembly) is composed of two categories of members: those elected in 1947 on Mainland China, and those elected in Taiwan and chosen from overseas Chinese communities. The first category forms the majority; but not having stood for election since 1947 and consequently being elderly, the legislature is thus regarded by many in Taiwan as insufficiently representative of the people. To remedy this defect, two proposals have been offered. The opposition and some intellectuals demand the immediate retirement of the senior legislators and the holding of a general election to form a new legislature of reduced size. The KMT and some other intellectuals prefer a more moderate approach. According to the KMT plan, which forms the basis of the government policy, senior legislators are encouraged to retire of their own volition; and those who fail to attend any functions for two successive legislative sessions are regarded as having retired voluntarily. Those who choose to retire are entitled to a generous pension. The policy was implemented in January 1989 with results less satisfactory than popularly expected.

**Reform of the Local Government System.** This controversy pertains to the way by which the governor of Taiwan Province and the mayors of the two major cities, Taipei and Kaohsiong, are chosen. According to current practices, these officeholders are appointed by the central government. Some people demand that they be popularly elected. So far, the government has decided that although the provincial governor will be appointed by central authorities, the provincial assembly will be consulted prior to the appointment. The local press has reported that the government has decided that the two mayors will be popularly elected, but an official announcement was not yet made by late 1989.

## Factors Affecting Democratization in Taiwan

In the mid-1980s, several east Asian countries began to march toward democracy almost simultaneously. Some explain this phenomenon as a domino effect, while others attribute it to the influence of the United States. Some believe it is the natural outcome of economic development and the rise of the middle class in those countries, while others consider exposure to Western ideas on the part of young intellectuals the principal reason for democratization. Although these single factor explanations all have some merit, they fail to yield a really satisfactory theory.

An explanation of Taiwan's democratization requires both external and internal factors to be taken into account. The major external factors are two: the general political and economic situation in the Asian-Pacific region in the mid-1980s and Taiwan's international position.

**The Asian-Pacific Region in the Mid-1980s.** In the mid-1980s, the East Asian–Pacific region enjoyed peace and prosperity. With the termination of the war in Vietnam in 1975 and the U.S.-PRC normalization (1972–1979), the United States and the PRC discovered parallel interests in the region. These two countries, together with Japan, appeared to have reached a tacit agreement to maintain the status quo in the region, at least for the foreseeable future.[6] Moreover, by the mid-1980s, most countries in the region had had three decades of rapid economic growth and were enjoying the highest prosperity in their recorded history. The ROC on Taiwan, confident that military conflict in the Taiwan Strait was a remote possibility and that its past economic performance and present prosperity ensured moderation in domestic political matters, believed that the situation was propitious for launching political reforms. In a crisis, the conservatives could always use national security as a reason to resist democratic reforms. But the situation in the Asian-Pacific region in the mid-1980s deprived the conservatives of an important excuse to resist democratization.

**Taiwan's International Position.** While peace and prosperity in the East Asian–Pacific region give Taiwan's political leadership a tactical advantage in launching political reforms, the deteriorating international position of the ROC since the late 1970s makes such reforms a political imperative.

After the ouster of the ROC from the United Nations in 1971 and the American recognition of the PRC in 1979, more and more people in Taiwan became concerned with the diplomatic isolation of the country and its political future. Many were convinced that only by becoming fully democratic could the ROC win the good will of the democratic West and the moral support of the non-Communist countries. With such sympathetic support, the ROC would eventually improve its international position. The pressure from the United States and political events in neighboring countries, such as the ascendancy of Corazon Aquino in the Philippines and the unrest in South Korea caused by student demonstrations in the early 1980s, also played their parts.

In pursuance of the Taiwan Relations Act, the U.S. Congress since 1980 has assumed the role of monitor of the human rights record of the ROC. The Committee on Foreign Affairs of the U.S. House of Representatives has held open hearings on such issues as martial law and Taiwanization. The activities of the Congress and certain individual congressmen such as Stephen Solarz have also exerted pressure upon the government to speed up reforms.

Important as these external factors are, however, they do not play a role as determinative as domestic factors in influencing the decision of the ROC leadership, such as the attitudes of the middle class and the activities of the opposition.

**Role of the Middle Class.** It is widely assumed that the main obstacle to democratization in most developing countries is the absence of a large middle class to make strong demands for democratic reforms and to give sustained support to such reforms, once they are made. This assumption is probably correct. Nevertheless, the presence of a large middle class may not guarantee the adoption of democratic reforms unless that class has a firm commitment to democratization and is willing to use its economic and social influence to bring about the necessary political changes.

In less than thirty years, Taiwan has moved from an agrarian society to an industrial and urban one. The middle class, composed mainly of professionals, salaried employees of public and private institutions, and business people, has been increasing rapidly, and by the mid-1980s about 35 percent of the gainfully employed could be classified as members of the middle class. Until quite recently, the middle class in Taiwan had not been particularly political, their main preoccupation being the improvement of their economic condition and the social status and welfare of their own families. In recent years, however, some of them have become intensely interested in politics, inspired by their concern for Taiwan's political future, their own ambition to achieve important positions, or their desire to use political influence to promote their economic interests or to advance certain personal ideals, such as environmental protection.

The middle-class political activists, mostly young, well-educated, and of Taiwanese origin, identify themselves either with the liberal wing of the KMT or with the opposition. These people are the main supporters of political reforms. Their demand for reforms cannot be ignored for two reasons: they provide financial support to political parties and they are society's most skilled and talented elements.

**Role of the Opposition.** The opposition served as the main catalyst of democratization. In the early 1970s, various opposition candidates running for seats in the national legislature in the so-called supplementary elections pooled their resources and formed a campaign organization for mutual help. This campaign organization, together with the *Formosan Magazine (Melitao)* became the core of a movement for founding an opposition party. The opposition, once having acquired an organizational basis, was able to play an active role in pressuring the government to reform the system. The confrontational tactics of the opposition were sometimes counterproductive; yet the leadership's decision to launch reforms was undoubtedly motivated partly by a desire to accommodate the opposition, since failure to do so would in the long run probably destablize the political system, as by the early 1980s the opposition had already become a significant political force.[7]

**Role of President Chiang Ching-kuo.** Despite these external and internal factors, democratic reforms would not have been carried out without the personal initiative of the late President Chiang Ching-kuo. Chiang was a populist who frequently met with ordinary people to discuss various issues with them. Through such contacts he acquired an accurate understanding of the wishes of the people. Moreover, through these contacts, he found groundless the fear of some conservatives that democratization might give those who advocated Taiwan's independence more room to maneuver and consequently not be in the best interest of the state. He believed that "because the times have changed and the circumstances have changed, the government and the party also have to change." His personal power and prestige reduced the conservative resistance to an exercise in futility. In formulating his strategy for reform, Chiang relied on a group of personal assistants, who were usually young, Western educated, and pragmatic in their approach to problems. Among them, notable examples include James Soong and Ying-chiu Ma. Soong, then deputy secretary general now secretary general of the KMT Central Committee, received his doctorate from Georgetown University. Ma has a J.D. from Harvard and was another deputy secretary general of the committee until July 1988. Both were chosen by Chiang as his assistants and interpreters. These political technocrats seem to have played a role more important than that played by the twelve-member panel, which served only as the front for the president. The president was therefore the single driving force to push for reform.

### Obstacles to Democratic Development

The relationship between the ruling KMT and the main opposition, the DPP, remains the key to Taiwan's future democratic development. The animosities have been caused by a variety of factors: past history, differences in personality, background, values of the two sets of leaders, and the like, but, above all, by the diametrically opposed positions of the two parties on four issues:

1. With regard to the reform of the national legislature and that of the local government system, their positions are almost irreconcilable. On the legislative issue, the DPP has declared that unless its proposal of total replacement of senior members is accepted, it will not cease its struggle. To force the government to change its position, the DPP resorts to drastic tactics, including mass street demonstrations and disruption of sessions of the national legislature. But the KMT and the government have with equal determination refused to change their position. As for the reform of the local government system, the DPP demands the government honor the people's "constitutional" right of electing the governor of Taiwan Province; but the KMT and the government, arguing that at a time of national emergency the popular election of the governor of Taiwan Province is not a constitutional right of the people, have refused to do so. This problem will become a very divisive issue.

2. The issue of the alleged illegality of the Temporary Provisions is another difference. In 1948, the Legislative Yuan passed the Temporary Provisions during the Period of National Mobilization and Rebellion Suppression. These provisions had the effect of changing the government system of the ROC from a quasi-cabinet system into a quasi-presidential system, thus reducing the role of members of the

Legislative Yuan. Recently, the opposition has repeatedly challenged the legality of these provisions, but the government insists that their legality is unquestionable.

3. The role of the KMT is another issue that has become quite divisive. The KMT, as the ruling party for four decades, enjoys high prestige and has accumulated much power. With 2.4 million members, it maintains party branches in all social institutions. The DPP demands that the role of the KMT should be curtailed and that the ruling party's branches in public institutions should be dissolved. But the KMT maintains that although no political party should be granted special privileges, there is no reason for the KMT to reduce its role in society, particularly if by so doing the right of an individual citizen to join the party of his choice is infringed upon.

4. The DPP's adoption of a "self-determination" position is a very divisive issue. The DPP platform states: "The future of Taiwan should be jointly determined by all inhabitants on the island in a free, uncoerced, universal, fair, and equal way. No government or coalition of governments has the right to determine the future political affiliation of Taiwan." This idea of "self-determination" is susceptible to a variety of interpretations. Some believe it is the code word for "Taiwan independence." Some others think that by advocating "self-determination" the DPP wants only to show outsiders that the people in Taiwan refuse to accept Communist rule. Still others regard the whole matter as the opposition's means to force the political authorities in Taiwan to speed up democratic reforms and to carry out the policy of "Taiwanization" in a more thorough way. No matter what the correct meaning is, the idea of self-determination has made the difficult relations between the two groups even more difficult.

On several occasions, the KMT asked the DPP to clarify its position concerning Taiwan independence, but the DPP refused to do so on the ground that the ruling party's request implied condescension. The conservatives in the KMT have viewed the DPP's refusal as its tacit admission of being a party for Taiwan independence.

Although most DPP leaders are probably not for Taiwan independence, one faction, labeled as "New Wave" (Hsinchaoliu), is now working to promote it. The activities of this small yet active and articulate faction not only have put the DPP leadership's ability to maintain party unity and discipline to a hard test but also have caused a severe strain on the relationship of the two parties.

In addition to lacking a normal pattern of interaction between the government and the opposition, Taiwan also lacks a healthy civic culture or proper sense of democratic norms. Since the lifting of martial law, street demonstrations or open-air rallies have become daily events in Taiwan.[8] On many of these occasions, demonstrators, police, and bystanders hurl insults, come to blows, and the like. Minor violence is present in some. Law and public order are often violated. Although some of these demonstrations and rallies represent the legitimate exercise of the people's right to petition the government to redress their grievances, some are not justifiable. Many, however, mistakenly believe that with the lifting of martial law, people are free to do almost anything. The lesson drawn from this state of affairs is that mere institutions and a legal framework do not guarantee the proper functioning of a democratic system. In the absence of a healthy civic culture or proper democratic norms, the line between democracy and anarchy can sometimes become tenuous. Taiwan is in urgent need of developing proper norms of citizen conduct.

The prospects for democratic development in Taiwan are thus by no means brilliant. Taiwan will have to undertake an uphill fight to achieve the final goal of democratization. On the one hand, the two obstacles just mentioned are not easy to overcome or eliminate. On the other, as the experiences of many other countries that have made the transition from authoritarian systems to democracies show, to make the transition is often easier than to consolidate the democratic system.[9] Taiwan is now still in the transition stage, but it may take much longer for the new system to consolidate itself.

This, however, does not mean the democratization process in Taiwan will fail. In the short run, Taiwan will certainly encounter many difficulties, but eventually it will probably establish a viable democratic system. There are several reasons to support an optimistic assessment.

First, Taiwan has already become a modern, industrial society with a sizable, well-educated middle class who possess progressive and enlightened values. Even though the political maturation of the middle class still leaves something to be desired, it can be relied upon to provide firm support to democratic reforms. The middle class is now becoming increasingly influential, and as economic development proceeds, its support will become indispensable for any government to rule effectively. The presence of this class has made democratic reform inevitable and guarantees the irreversibility of the democratization process.

Second, unlike many other developing countries, Taiwan has a number of advantages as far as democratization is concerned. The government has done many things, which either inadvertently or intentionally have paved the way for democratic development: regular local elections have given people some training in democratic participation; education policy has eliminated illiteracy and has enabled those under the age of forty to have at least nine years of compulsory education; the redistribution policy has made Taiwan one of the most equitable societies in income distribution; and the policy to stand by the democratic West through thick and thin has inevitably made the democratic system the model to emulate in the minds of the young generation.

Third, under the leadership of the late President Chiang Ching-kuo the Kuomintang underwent significant changes. The conservative old guard are gradually retiring from active political life, and a new generation more sympathetic to democratic values has emerged and has already begun to assume leadership positions. Moreover, with the ascendancy of President Lee Teng-hui, leaders of Taiwanese origin are replacing many senior leaders from the Mainland. The result of this new phase of Taiwanization is shown in the composition of the KMT Central Standing Committee—the inner core of the ruling power—following the thirteenth Party Congress, July 7–9, 1988. For the first time, the majority of the thirty-one-member committee are natives of Taiwan who now hold sixteen seats, up from fourteen in the previous lineup.

Fourth, it is not impossible that the KMT and the DPP will improve their relationship. The ruling party, with the retirement of the ideological conservatives, will become more pragmatic and more tolerant of the diversity in views and values of its membership. The KMT will be forced by circumstances to cease calling itself a "revolutionary-democratic" party and will have to regard itself as a mere "democratic" party. The DPP will likely also have to moderate its actions and attitudes. The improvement in relations will not come at all too soon, as two preconditions must exist beforehand. First, the issue of representation in the national legislature must either be solved or fade away in time. A satisfactory solution to the problem is not possible now, given the firm commitment of the ruling party to its own policy. The other outcome is more likely. Since the average age of the senior members is over eighty, the problem though troublesome now, will fade away in less than ten years. The other precondition is that the issue of Taiwan independence mut be properly settled. Since this issue has become quite emotional, it appears very difficult to find a solution mutually acceptable to both parties. But in reality it should not be such a difficult problem. If public opinion polls are reliable indicators of the general attitudes of the people, it is evident that only a very small number of people are

45

interested in Taiwan's independence according to a survey reported by the *United Daily News* on March 12, 1988; 65 percent of those questioned disapproved of it. Opinion leaders of various shades almost all agree that the idea of an independent Taiwan will not win widespread popularity or public support, though it will probably retain its firm grip upon some adherents as long as Taiwan's international position remains unchanged. In the future, the DPP will remain under pressure to find a way to duck the issue of Taiwan independence. The KMT, on the other hand, would be well advised to cease pressuring the DPP to clarify its position on "self-determination" as it is a futile and counterproductive strategy. Once both parties become aware that the most productive course to pursue is to concentrate on social and economic problems of genuine concern to the electorate, they will develop a normal relationship.

## Conclusion

The establishment of a viable democratic system, the ultimate political goal in a developing country, consists of two phases: the transition from an authoritarian system into one with some democratic and liberal features, though not yet a full democracy, and the consolidation of the new system and its evolution into a full democracy. The transition is facilitated by a variety of factors: a healthy economy, a sizable middle class, political elites who value commitment to a democratic system, and counterelites who put consistent pressure upon the elites to initiate the transition. The existence of a strong leader in favor of changing the system facilitates the transition, while the presence of such a leader against change is a serious obstacle to democratization.

In the consolidation process it is more difficult to achieve tangible results, since in the transition phase the dismantling of the old structure is the main objective, while in the consolidation phase institutionalization of the new system is the main goal. But during this phase the dispute between the elites and the counterelites is intensified, since the former are usually unwilling to dismantle the old structure completely, particularly in an elite-initiated transition. (Moreover, to retain part of the old structure is often part of the original purpose of initiating the transition.) The counterelites often accuse the elites of bad faith, cosmetic democratization to deceive the people, and the like. In addition, the transition often unleashes new social forces, who often ally with the counterelites to engage in a variety of conflicts with the elites. The disputes between elites and counterelites make institutionalization a difficult and prolonged process. The underdevelopment of proper norms and civic culture increases the social costs of the consolidation. Whether the consolidation process will result in the establishment of a democratic order, the restoration of the old system, or an anarchic state of affairs depends upon a number of variables, including the international environment, the pattern of government-opposition interaction, and the basic attitudes of such strategically placed groups as the middle class and the military.

The above represents the author's summary of the views of some scholars.[10] The case of Taiwan may fit some of these ideas, but it may not fit all. Taiwan has begun the transition: the lifting of martial law and the formation of opposition parties are watersheds in its democratic development. The transition, however, is far from complete. But the process is irreversible and will eventually lead to the second phase of democratization. The consolidation is much harder, but since Taiwan is endowed with many advantages to meet the challenge, the author is optimistic about the long-term prospects for democracy in Taiwan. He does not, however, believe that Taiwan will have a stable, well-functioning democratic system shortly.

# 3
# Economic Developments in the Republic of China

*Jan S. Prybyla*

This chapter concentrates on four themes:

- the economic record of the Republic of China (ROC) on Taiwan since the 1950s
- the endogenous and exogenous reasons for that record
- the problems facing the ROC economy and responses to those problems
- the relationship between economic and political modernization and the lessons that others can draw from the ROC's experience

## Economic Record

The economic record of the ROC on Taiwan has been remarkable under the major indicators of performance, which include the following:

- growth
- user satisfaction
- stability
- structural balance
- structural shift
- equity

**Growth.** The growth of real gross domestic product (GDP, in 1981 prices), gross national product (GNP, in 1981 prices), real per capita GNP (in 1981 prices), and real per capita national income (in 1981 prices) is shown in table 3–1.

Such growth rates are phenomenal. They mean that from 1952 through 1987, real GNP and national income per capita increased more than six times. Per capita GNP (in current prices) in 1988 was U.S.$6,053 and was expected to reach nearly U.S.$7,000 by the end of

49

TABLE 3–1
AVERAGE ANNUAL GROWTH OF REAL GDP, GNP, GNP PER CAPITA,
AND REAL PER CAPITA INCOME, REPUBLIC OF CHINA, 1952–1987
(percent)

| Period | GDP | GNP | GNP per Capita | Income per Capita |
|---|---|---|---|---|
| 1952–1987 | 8.7 | 8.8 | 6.3 | 6.2 |
| 1953–1962 | 7.3 | 7.3 | 3.8 | 3.6 |
| 1963–1972 | 10.9 | 10.9 | 8.3 | 8.5 |
| 1973–1987 | 7.8 | 8.0 | 6.2 | 6.1 |

SOURCE: Council for Economic Planning and Development, ROC, *Taiwan Statistical Data Book 1988.*

1989.[1] Because of the "creative accounting" practiced by many of Taiwan's businesses, these figures understate the actual situation. The Ministry of Finance estimates that tax evasion in 1986 amounted to the equivalent of U.S.$600 million.[2] In other words, there is much lively underground economic activity that eludes official statistics. It would not be unreasonable to conjecture that such activity, if properly accounted for, would add perhaps as much as U.S.$2,000 to the official per capita GNP, giving a GNP per head of a little more than U.S.$8,000 in 1988. Whichever figure is taken, the ROC economy is clearly well on the way to modernity if U.S.$5,000 per capita is accepted as one of several criteria of economic modernization.[3]

The ROC, it should be noted, has undergone a modernizing evolution with respect to population growth. Without resort to the kind of Draconian population control methods applied on the mainland since the mid-1970s (before which mainland population policy was subject to wide ideologically induced swings), the rate of natural population increase fell gradually from 3.7 percent in 1952 to 1.1 percent in 1987 (the crude birth rate declined from 4.7 percent in 1952 to 1.6 percent in 1987; the death rate from 1 percent to 0.5 percent).[4]

**User Satisfaction.** Rapid product growth is not meaningful to material welfare if the product produced is useless in the judgment of potential users, that is, if what the economy produces is not what people want or it is not available at prices they are able and willing to pay. This unfortunate situation may arise if the product (or some of it) is at odds with user needs and preferences (for example, when its volume and assortment are imposed on the users by planners in response to the planners' own preference schedules), if the quality of the product is defective, if input-output coefficients are uncoordi-

50

nated, if the product is available in improper locations, and for a variety of other reasons that are regularly encountered under conditions of central administrative command planning.

By and large this situation has been absent from the growth experience of the ROC (whereas it has been much in evidence in the growth experience of the People's Republic of China, PRC, on the mainland). The price mechanism of the ROC's economy has been sufficiently flexible most of the time to eliminate quickly occasional resource misallocations (demand-supply mismatches) and avoid the massive shortages of wanted goods side by side with surpluses of unwanted ones that are a chronic feature of the centrally planned system. The ROC economy has done what any sane economic system is supposed to do: supply increasing quantities and qualities of goods and services that people want at a price they are willing and able to pay. As we shall see, the rapid growth of useful products was combined with a pattern of distribution that ensured ability to pay. The economy, in other words, is geared to user needs. In simple language, it serves the people. In this important respect, the ROC economy conforms to another criterion of modernity. Private consumption, which in 1952 came to 12.7 billion New Taiwan dollars (N.T.$), had by 1987 risen to N.T.$1.4 trillion (current price basis).[5]

**Stability.** Despite the fact that the ROC economy has been heavily dependent on foreign trade (especially since the 1960s) and consequently highly sensitive to economic cycles beyond its shores (especially in the United States), growth has been relatively smooth, devoid of disruptive fluctuations in output, employment, price level, and the balance of trade experienced by many developing and newly industrialized economies. Although mostly disguised (for example, in the form of fluctuating underemployment and suppressed inflation), such instability has been much in evidence in the growth record of the PRC, which includes the great depression that followed the contrived short-lived boom known as the Great Leap Forward of 1958–1959. The comparative stability of the ROC price level and employment can be seen from table 3–2.

From 1985 through 1988 wholesale prices declined at an average annual rate of 2.7 percent, and retail prices rose at an average annual rate of 0.6 percent. The average annual unemployment rate during those years was 2.3 percent.[6] Thus economic growth in the ROC took place in a setting of comparative price stability and practically full employment.

**Structural Balance.** Economic modernization requires movement to-

51

TABLE 3–2
STABILITY OF PRICES AND UNEMPLOYMENT, REPUBLIC OF CHINA,
1953–1987

| Period | Price Increases | | Unemployment Rate[a] (annual average rate, percent) |
| --- | --- | --- | --- |
| | Wholesale (index, annual average) | Retail | |
| 1953–1962 | 7.6 | 8.7 | 1.8 |
| 1963–1972 | 1.8 | 2.9 | 1.4 |
| 1973–1987 | 6.0 | 7.9 | 1.1 |

a. Percentage of labor force.
SOURCE: *Taiwan Statistical Data Book 1988,* pp. 14, 181.

ward industrialization. The movement, moreover, should be such as to minimize (but not avoid) structural disruption. This, in turn, means coordinated advance on all fronts and avoidance of "breakthrough" (or "Stalinist") strategies of industrialization that sacrifice (in fact, exploit) one or more sectors of the economy for the benefit of a leading sector. By the same token, it means strategic restraint, that is, deliberate rather than rushed advance; the avoidance of leaps and "storming" that have characterized Soviet, East European, and mainland Chinese industrialization. Although it does not exclude shifting sectoral emphasis over time to adapt to changing constellations of cost, demand, technology, and comparative advantage, it merely requires the absence of excess in this regard. At all times industrialization should not lose sight of its fundamental rationale, which is to enhance the material welfare of consumers.

In this respect, the industrialization process on Taiwan has been modern. It has been balanced, with agriculture, industry, transport, communications, commerce, and other service trades working in harmony. Unlike what happened on the mainland, serious inter- and intrasectoral imbalances have been absent. Contrary to the Stalinist-type argument, strategic restraint has resulted in rapid industrialization. Most important, industrialization has benefited the consumer.

**Structural Shift.** Economic modernization requires not only across-the-board industrialization but a transformation of the structure of the economy. Such restructuring (or "going up-market") comprises three elements: (1) increasing reliance on improvements of factor productivity as the engine of growth (that is, transition from "extensive" growth relying on simple addition of factors embodying known technology to "intensive" growth based on better performance of factors through improved skills, techniques, and incentives); (2) movement toward higher value-added, higher skill production (from rice to robotics); and (3) change in the composition of output and employment, away from primary industry (mainly agriculture), toward manufactures (light industry, heavy industry, in that sequence, plus transport and communications infrastructures), and increasingly specialized and sophisticated services. Whereas in 1952, 56 percent of the Taiwanese labor force was employed in agriculture, 12 percent in manufacturing, and 13 percent in services (mainly retail commerce), in 1987 the proportions were 15 percent in agriculture, 35 percent in manufacturing, and 42 percent in services, including a rising share of banking, finance, engineering, education, and communications. Whereas in 1952, agriculture contributed 36 percent of net domestic product (NDP), industry (including public utilities) 18 percent, transport and communications 4 percent, commerce 19 percent, and other services 23 percent, in 1987 the shares were agriculture 6 percent, industry 47 percent, transportation and communications 6 percent, commerce 16 percent, and other services 25 percent.[7] The structural shift in exports can be seen from table 3–3. Clearly, the restructuring of the ROC economy has been of a modernizing kind.

Another kind of restructuring that has often gone unnoticed by economists is the shift in the economy's ownership structure. The land reform carried out between 1949 (rent reduction) and 1953 (Land-to-the-Tiller Act) replaced the former landlord-tenant system with independent farmer-owners. Many of the former landowners—compensated for the land they had to sell with commodity bonds

TABLE 3–3
STRUCTURE OF EXPORTS, REPUBLIC OF CHINA, 1951–1987
(percentage shares)

| Year | Agricultural Products | Industrial Products |
|---|---|---|
| 1951 | 91.9 | 8.1 |
| 1955 | 89.6 | 10.4 |
| 1960 | 57.6 | 32.3 |
| 1965 | 54.0 | 46.0 |
| 1970 | 21.4 | 78.6 |
| 1975 | 16.4 | 83.6 |
| 1980 | 9.2 | 90.8 |
| 1987 | 6.1 | 93.9 |

SOURCE: Taiwan Statistical Data Book 1988, p. 213.

and stock in government enterprises—became the nucleus of Taiwan's dynamic industrial-commercial entrepreneurial class. While in the early years the government originated much industrial activity, its share of industrial ownership declined dramatically over the years. In 1952 public ownership of industry, on the basis of the value of industrial production, was 57 percent. By 1962 it had fallen to 46 percent. In 1972 it was 19 percent. In 1982 the government's share was 18 percent and in 1987 14 percent.[8] Although 100 percent of the electricity, gas, and water supply output originates in the state sector, none of the building construction business and only 10 percent of manufacturing output do. I think privatization of property rights is an important component of the economic modernization process because it enlarges the area of creative individual decision making, encourages entrepreneurship and innovation, improves work and investment incentives, and contributes significantly to the proper conservation of assets. Legally recognizing the individual's right to the use, transfer, and income from goods and services and the personal responsibility that goes with private property is an expression of trust in the fullness and maturity of the human person. It is more than a technicality, for it goes to the very core of the notion of modernity.

**Equity.** The market system does not guarantee even a rough equality of outcomes. Indeed, given the inherently unequal marginal contributions to output of different individuals and factors, distributional equality is contrary to the market's operating as a mechanism of efficient resource allocation. Equity, however, is not synonymous with equality, and equity of distribution exercises an important moral influence on productivity. Disparities in income and wealth that are perceived by some participants in the market process as unjust—that is, offensive to their ethical value system—will have adverse effects on incentives and perhaps, in the longer run, lead to political unrest.

The benefits of growth on Taiwan appear to have been equitably shared, increasingly so as the product grew larger (table 3–4). It serves little purpose to quantify with illusory precision the Gini coefficient that is sufficiently equitable to be deemed "modern." It is certainly true that the trend of income distribution in the ROC since the early 1950s qualifies under this heading.

The Gini coefficient, which was 0.558 in 1953, declined to 0.322 by 1986 (the lower the coefficient, the lower the inequality of income distribution). For the same years the ratio of income share of the richest 20 percent of households to that of the poorest 20 percent declined from 20.5 (1953) to 4.6 (1986).[9] The bright picture of income

## TABLE 3–4
### DISTRIBUTION OF PERSONAL INCOME BY INCOME QUINTILE, REPUBLIC OF CHINA, 1964–1986
(percent)

| Household Income Level | 1964 | 1966 | 1968 | 1970 | 1972 | 1974 | 1976 | 1978 | 1979 | 1980 | 1981 | 1982 | 1983 | 1984 | 1985 | 1986 |
|---|---|---|---|---|---|---|---|---|---|---|---|---|---|---|---|---|
| Lowest fifth | 7.7 | 7.9 | 7.8 | 8.4 | 8.6 | 8.8 | 8.9 | 8.9 | 8.6 | 8.8 | 8.8 | 8.7 | 8.6 | 8.5 | 8.4 | 8.3 |
| Second fifth | 12.6 | 12.5 | 12.2 | 13.3 | 13.3 | 13.5 | 13.6 | 13.7 | 13.7 | 13.9 | 13.8 | 13.8 | 13.6 | 13.7 | 13.6 | 13.5 |
| Third fifth | 16.6 | 16.2 | 16.3 | 17.1 | 17.1 | 17.0 | 17.5 | 17.5 | 17.5 | 17.7 | 17.6 | 17.6 | 17.5 | 17.6 | 17.5 | 17.4 |
| Fourth fifth | 22.0 | 22.0 | 22.3 | 22.5 | 22.5 | 22.1 | 22.7 | 22.7 | 22.7 | 22.8 | 22.8 | 22.7 | 22.7 | 22.8 | 22.9 | 22.7 |
| Highest fifth | 41.1 | 41.5 | 41.4 | 38.7 | 38.6 | 38.6 | 37.3 | 37.2 | 37.5 | 36.8 | 37.0 | 37.1 | 37.6 | 37.4 | 37.6 | 38.2 |
| Ratio of highest fifth's income to lowest fifth's | 5.3 | 5.3 | 5.3 | 4.6 | 4.5 | 4.4 | 4.2 | 4.2 | 4.3 | 4.2 | 4.2 | 4.3 | 4.4 | 4.4 | 4.5 | 4.6 |

NOTE: Figures may not add up to 100 because of rounding.
SOURCE: *Taiwan Statistical Data Book 1988*, pp. 61–62.

distribution in the ROC conveyed by the official statistics has, however, been questioned. We shall return to this matter later in the section "Problems and Responses."

Various periodization schemes have been used to explain the developmental process of the ROC economy on Taiwan. A serviceable scheme divides the Taiwanese experience into three phases. The first, roughly the 1950s, was dominated by policies of import substitution and characterized by high tariffs, quantitative restrictions on imports of "nonessentials," financial regulations (especially currency controls), and overvalued exchange rates. The objective was to reduce Taiwan's hard currency expenditures by substituting as many domestically produced goods as possible for those imported from hard currency areas (principally the United States). Considerations of national security encouraged, no doubt, this early drive for a greater degree of self-reliance. While for many other developing countries, import substitution with its protectionist and autarkic overtones became an irresistible temptation and a permanent way of life, this was not the long-term strategy chosen by the ROC. In the 1960s a second phase emphasizing export promotion was inaugurated and continued through the 1970s. The main component of this approach was a substantial reduction in the overvalued N.T.$ exchange rate and the fashioning of a pattern of output geared to the American market. In the 1960s and 1970s Taiwan became a vast processing zone for goods designed principally for export to the United States. Export promotion, however, did not mean the elimination of import substitution. Indeed, until quite recently the two policies were pursued concurrently with, however, a progressive but unhurried withering away of protection. The third phase began—with considerable prodding from the United States—in the mid-1980s. It consists of accelerated import and payments liberalization through the reduction of tariffs and quotas, the easing of financial restrictions, removal of some obstacles to the entry of foreign firms into the ROC's growing home market for services, encouragement of domestic consumption, export diversification, easier travel, more flexible market-determined exchange rates, and enforcement of laws against piracy by local firms of foreign patents, trademarks, copyrights, and other intellectual property. The new strategy is not merely a reaction to American pressure and the fear of losing a lucrative market. It is also a logical outcome of the ROC economy's higher income level and the country's increased ability to compete with the industrial democracies on the world market and the desire to rejoin various worldwide and regional economic organizations such as the General Agreement on Tariffs and Trade (GATT). The results of these policies may be seen from table 3–5.

### Reasons for the ROC's Success

**System of Economic Organization.** The main reason for the positive performance of the ROC economy has been the adoption of the right system of economic organization. The ROC is a model of the market system with private property as the dominant form of ownership and state intervention in behalf of the market and private property. The system permits the release of individual enterprise, initiative, and ingenuity. It is flexible and dynamic. Most important, it is committed to the principle that "consumption is the sole end and purpose of all production; and the interest of the producer ought to be attended to only so far as it may be necessary for promoting that of the consumer."[10] The system is capable, both in theory and in practice, of satisfying consumer wants efficiently, that is, with the least possible real resource cost at a point in time (statically) and over time (dynamically). Of course, like any human creation, the market system is subject to occasional breakdowns and suffers from failures (for example, informational uncertainty and incompleteness, externalities, and public goods problems).[11] Also, as suggested earlier in connection with equity, the market does not address all human economic concerns. It is not a panacea.

That is where government steps in. The notion of laissez faire does not exclude government from participating in the market process. It has never been a question of whether government should intervene in the economy, but how and how much.

The answer to how is, in support of the market and private property, not against them (which has been the principal purpose of

TABLE 3–5

EXTERNAL TRADE, REPUBLIC OF CHINA, SELECTED YEARS, 1952–1987
(1952 = 100)

| Year | Total Trade | Exports | Imports |
|---|---|---|---|
| 1952 | 100.0 | 100.0 | 100.0 |
| 1960 | 419.0 | 406.4 | 426.3 |
| 1970 | 3,008.4 | 4,036.6 | 2,412.6 |
| 1980 | 35,581.8 | 48,514.6 | 28,086.6 |
| 1987 | 70,049.1 | 116,019.6 | 43,406.8 |

SOURCE: *Taiwan Statistical Data Book*, p. 210.

intervention by Socialist governments). This means that public intervention should be primarily general, indirect, and persuasive rather than direct, specific, and mandatory. It should induce behavioral changes in buyers and sellers through alteration of price signals achieved by "legitimate" means, not through administrative command (price freezing, for instance). This may not always be possible, but it should be the rule.

As for how much government intervention, support of the market and private property covers a variety of functions, including (1) the provision of a legal order (protection of contracts and property rights); (2) external defense (critical in the case of Taiwan); (3) money supply and the use of monetary instruments of macroeconomic management; (4) taxation; (5) provision of public goods; (6) action against those who act in restraint of trade (insider traders, monopolists); (7) dealing with externalities (through the market mechanism whenever possible); (8) taking care of those who cannot take care of themselves; (9) initiation and encouragement of the process of economic growth and development through, for example, land reform that encourages more widespread private ownership of land, and research and development expenditures designed to promote an up-market restructuring of the economy that accords with international market trends; (10) support for education (provision of equal opportunities for all at the start); (11) correction of highly skewed, politically explosive, and morally repulsive income and wealth disparities where these are due to market imperfections; and even (12) temporary (but they must be temporary) policies of "sheltered growth" for infant industries and export promotion. Clearly, the list of legitimate governmental interventions in the market process will be longer or shorter depending on one's normative perspective, and the answer to "how much" eludes precise quantification. A useful rule of thumb is that intervention should be limited, that is, that it should be subsidiary, not all-intrusive. As James Buchanan puts it: "Even in success, the state necessarily closes off (or narrowly restricts) the exit options of its members. . . . Man is, and must remain, a slave to the state. But it is critically and vitally important to recognize that ten percent slavery is different from fifty percent."[12]

Having a good vehicle is one thing; using it to good purpose is another. Despite occasional mistakes, the ROC on Taiwan has used the market system well and has succeeded in striking the right balance between market spontaneity and government action. The government has consistently adhered to the principle of supporting and encouraging the market and private property. Given this principle, the government's economic policies have been well informed and pragmatic. Price stability has been promoted through strict control of the money supply and of government expenditures. Almost every year since 1964 government revenue has exceeded expenditure, the savings being used for fixed capital formation. A special agency has been set up to monitor and take action against oligopolistic price fixing. Tariff reductions and the gradual removal of nontariff barriers have been pursued for some years not only as a matter of principle (market liberalization) but as a means of containing inflationary pressures, which in Taiwan are closely related to import prices. As already noted, growth and equity were helped along by the nonviolent land reform of 1949–1953. Growth and equity of income distribution were also promoted by government restraint (or tacit encouragement) with respect to the spontaneous development of small and medium business enterprises. In 1982 these businesses represented 95 percent of all firms, provided 70 percent of employment, 65 percent of total business revenue, and 65 percent of export earnings. They were in large measure responsible for the condition of almost full employment through their high rates of job creation, contributed to the economy's extraordinary flexibility (Taiwan's famous rapid adaptation and response to changing international market conditions), and provided avenues of social mobility for local talent. Public enterprises performed economic, fiscal, and social functions within the market system. The economic function consisted in the provision of raw materials and energy (at "reasonable" prices) and of managerial and engineering personnel to the private sector and, before 1980, the maintenance of employment stability (as a rule state firms did not lay off workers even during recessions). In other words, over stretches of time, the public sector subsidized the development of private enterprise in important areas. During the early years of development, public enterprises were an important source of income for the government, providing more than one-fifth of total government revenue before 1972. They also supplied various social security and social welfare services to their employees (for instance, subsidized housing and transportation, and medical insurance) in a situation where such services were not being adequately provided by the market.[13] Development and expansion of the market economy dominated by private property rights were facilitated by state measures taken to encourage foreign private investment (particularly in recent years in high-technology areas) and by government expenditures on research and development (R&D). Total R&D expenditures as a percentage of GNP remain relatively modest in comparison with industrialized market economies: 1 percent in 1986 compared with 2.8 percent for West Germany, 2.7 percent for the United States, 2.5 percent for Japan, 2.3

percent for France, and 2.2 percent for Britain (the figures for these countries refer to 1985, except Britain, which are for 1983). The relative contributions of private (domestic and foreign) and governmental expenditures on R&D can be seen in table 3–6. In 1986 basic research absorbed 11 percent of the total (6 percent in 1979), applied research 38 percent (28 percent in 1979), and development 51 percent (67 percent in 1979).[14]

**Informed Rejection of Conventional Wisdom.** ROC policy makers were the first to jettison two fashionable post–World War II economic theories: (1) import substitution as the most effective method of development; and (2) the stimulation of industrial investment through maintenance of a low interest rate even in the face of significant inflation. It is difficult today to appreciate the theoretical boldness and vision involved in this double rejection of the conventional wisdom of the time. The ROC abandoned the low-interest-rate policy in an inflationary setting, devalued its currency to a level at which the lowering of tariffs and nontariff restrictions became possible, and shifted to a strategy of export-led industrialization. Although, as we have noted, import substitution was not totally abandoned, it was considerably diluted. The relative liberalization of trade, with emphasis on export promotion, resulted in a large transfer of labor from land-intensive (low marginal productivity) agriculture to labor-intensive, export-oriented industries in which Taiwan had a comparative advantage. This modernizing shift of labor resources resulted in a large net increase of the marginal productivity of labor and of the real wage rate. The abandonment of the low-interest-rate policy (early 1950s) saved the ROC from selecting—like many other developing countries at that time—a capital-intensive, labor-saving (politically prestigious) variant of industrialization dictated by artificially cheap investment capital. It thus made it possible for the ROC

TABLE 3–6
R&D EXPENDITURES OF THE REPUBLIC OF CHINA, 1979 AND 1986
(percent shares)

| Year | Government | Private | |
|------|------------|---------|---------|
| | | Domestic | Foreign |
| 1979 | 64.8 | 31.7 | 3.5 |
| 1986 | 60.1 | 39.4 | 0.5 |

SOURCE: *Taiwan Statistical Data Book 1988*, p. 113.

to avoid the unemployment and widespread low-productivity employment experienced by economies that have elected the illusory "prestige" industrialization path.[15]

**Education.** The emphasis put on education has been an important contributor to the ROC's modern economic growth. The literacy rate is 92 percent. In 1987–1988 practically all school-aged children were enrolled in primary and junior high schools. (The period of compulsory education is nine years, and no tuition fees are charged.) Of the 1987–1988 junior high school graduates, 77 percent were enrolled in senior high schools, and 86 percent of senior high school graduates went on to colleges and universities. In 1987, 6,600 university students were studying abroad, most of them in the United States. Almost one-third of them studied engineering, and another quarter, business administration and social or behavioral sciences. The return rate of such students has risen since the early 1980s.[16] Not only is education widespread, financially accessible, nondiscriminatory, and of good quality, but it is held in high esteem within the culture, not just because of its usefulness in promoting social and economic advancement, but on its intrinsic merits. Top administrative and managerial levels are staffed by graduates of higher educational institutions, both domestic and foreign. (The incidence of U.S.-trained Ph.D.s in the top echelons of the government is probably the highest in the world.) The quality of the blue-collar labor force has been dramatically upgraded. Workers readily master new technologies and adapt without much difficulty to increasingly sophisticated production methods. In these circumstances, and barring labor unrest, prospects are good that the ROC will successfully move—as it intends to—toward high-technology production and stay several steps ahead of the competition from developing countries whose labor costs are lower and natural resource endowments more generous. Lacking minerals, energy sources, and land, the ROC devoted its attention to an extraordinary upgrading of its labor skills.

**Social Stability.** There has been much speculation about the role that Chinese cultural tradition has played in the successful performance of the ROC economy. Cultural influences can surely shed light on comparative economic development. From the time of Max Weber and R. H. Tawney, considerable attention, albeit at the margin of economics, has been given to this subject. It has been remarked that wherever the Chinese settle, they succeed economically (often better than the native populations), except within the system of central planning on the mainland. In a market setting, it is argued, the

Confucian virtues of thrift, industriousness, family loyalty, and respect for learning are given the opportunity to express themselves in an economically constructive, expansionary way. Even the notion of hierarchical authority, which appears to conflict with the iconoclastic rules of the marketplace, contributes a sense of orderliness and discipline, without which the market cannot function and private property cannot be preserved from depredations. Added to these traditional virtues are modern attitudes advocated by Sun Yat-sen and reinforced by sustained contact with the West: readiness to assume business risk, competitiveness, personal responsibility, respect for time frames, and innovation, among them.

Social stability has yet another dimension that is equally difficult to quantify and define with precision. It has to do with stable government. There can be little doubt that Taiwan's ability to compete on world markets has been aided by the absence of significant labor unrest at home. Although the reasons for it are not exclusively political, it is not unconnected with the authoritarian political structure that until recent years prevailed on the island.

**The U.S. Connection.** The Taiwan economic "miracle" owes much to the ROC's American connection. The relationship between the United States and the Republic of China is in many ways special: forged during World War II, later sustained by common strategic concerns, and reinforced by a shared economic system. It has manifested itself most recently in the Taiwan Relations Act indicative of the unwillingness of the U.S. Congress to cut ties with the ROC following President Carter's diplomatic derecognition of Taipei and in the explosive growth of commercial exchanges between the United States and Taiwan since 1979. The ROC's American connection has had two major components since 1949. The first, which came to an end in the mid-1960s, took the form of U.S. economic aid that made it possible for the ROC to weather the many storms it faced in its early years on Taiwan, particularly the acute shortages of raw materials, capital, and foreign exchange. American advice was instrumental in the decision to launch Taiwan's land reform, and the strategy of import substitution was adopted and later transformed into export promotion with U.S. concurrence. American power provided the military protection needed by Taiwan to initiate the process of economic development, and arms sales by the United States continue to be a crucial constituent of the ROC's defense capability.

The second component of the ROC-U.S. connection is even more relevant to the materialization of Taiwan's economic miracle: the accommodating stance taken by the United States toward Taiwan's access to the U.S. domestic market. Despite accusations of protectionism, the United States, more than any other Western economic power or Japan, actually practices what it preaches in matters of international trade liberalization. Not only are U.S. tariffs and other restrictions (both formal and informal) on the entry of foreign goods and services less burdensome than those of most other industrialized market democracies, but also in the specific case of Taiwan, various measures had been implemented over the years to make such entry even easier. This included the application to Taiwan of most favored nation treatment and, until recently, of the general system of preferences (GSP) under which imports from Taiwan were treated more leniently than those from industrialized countries. In 1987 exports represented 55 percent of the ROC's gross national product. Exports to the United States accounted for 44 percent of total ROC exports. The export concentration on the U.S. market can be seen from table 3–7. Over the years Taiwan has benefited from foreign technology transfers. In this process the United States played a leading role through its direct investment in Taiwan.[17]

**The Japanese Connection.** Taiwan's Japanese connection also has two components: the first more controversial than the second. An argument may be made that despite much that was exploitative and abusive in Japan's fifty-year occupation of Taiwan, the painful experience was—from a developmental standpoint—not altogether negative.[18] On balance, so goes the argument, the Japanese presence improved the island's infrastructural facilities and modernized its managerial attitudes. Whatever the merits of that argument, it is certain that the post–World War II economic ties between the ROC and Japan have significantly benefited Taiwan's developmental effort.

TABLE 3–7
EXPORTS TO THE UNITED STATES FROM THE REPUBLIC OF CHINA,
1952–1986
(percentage of total exports)

| Years | Share |
|---|---|
| 1952–1960 | 5.9 |
| 1961–1970 | 26.2 |
| 1971–1980 | 37.6 |
| 1981–1986 | 44.2 |

SOURCE: *Taiwan Statistical Data Book 1988*, p. 222.

From 1952 through 1987 Japan was the main source of government-approved direct foreign investment in Taiwan in number of projects (28 percent, or 1,195 projects, compared with the U.S. share of 15 percent, or 635 projects). In value, approved Japanese direct investments during that time were second (24 percent) to the United States (31 percent). Except for the period 1952–1960, Japan has been the main source of ROC imports (roughly one-third, compared with imports from the United States of about one quarter). Japan's share of ROC exports during the 1961–1987 period (16 percent) was second only to the United States (42 percent).[19] Geographical proximity, quality, excellent after-sale service, and a certain cultural affinity have been cited to explain the apparent ROC preference for Japanese imports.

## Problems and Responses

**Problems.** Two major problems face the ROC economy as it moves toward the twenty-first century: economic relations with the United States and domestic restructuring.

At the center of commercial tensions between the United States and the ROC is the deficit that the United States has experienced continuously since 1968 on its Taiwan trade. The deficit itself would not be much of an issue, were it not for the large increase in its size after 1975, particularly since 1980, and the reasons—as Americans see them—for the large and, until recently, growing imbalance. (See table 3–8.)

Using a somewhat different statistical methodology from the Taiwanese, U.S. sources arrive at a 1987 Taiwan trade surplus of roughly $18 billion. In 1988 the surplus was reduced to $10.4 billion (Taiwan count). About $4 billion of the reduction was due to ROC gold imports from the United States. Although a respectable theoretical argument can be made that inclusion of gold imports in commodity trade is legitimate, such imports do not have much impact on employment in the exporting country, and that is what is partly at issue.

Theoretically, the alleged dangers of a trade deficit are debatable. The erroneous mercantilistic viewpoint of equating trade surpluses with good and deficits with bad has been fashionable of late in protectionist circles in the United States and Taiwan. No matter what the theoretical argument, however, the large and persistent U.S. trade deficit has become a political issue in the United States. Given the number of powerful interests hurt by the influx of foreign imports, strong pressure is brought to bear on Congress and the executive branch to do something about it. The Trade Act of 1988 reflects this

TABLE 3–8

ROC Exports to, Imports from, and Trade Surplus with the
United States, Selected Years, 1968–1987

(U.S. dollars)

| Year | Exports | Imports | Balance |
|------|---------|---------|---------|
| 1968 | 278,194 | 239,494 | 38,700 |
| 1975 | 1,822,737 | 170,608 | 170,608 |
| 1976 | 3,038,699 | 1,797,540 | 1,241,159 |
| 1980 | 6,760,300 | 4,673,486 | 2,086,814 |
| 1981 | 8,158,392 | 4,765,671 | 3,392,721 |
| 1982 | 8,757,795 | 4,563,255 | 4,194,540 |
| 1983 | 11,333,712 | 4,646,443 | 6,687,269 |
| 1984 | 14,867,709 | 5,041,643 | 9,826,066 |
| 1985 | 14,772,990 | 4,746,274 | 10,026,716 |
| 1986 | 18,994,694 | 5,415,788 | 13,578,906 |
| 1987 | 23,637,083 | 7,628,346 | 16,008,737 |

Source: *Taiwan Statistical Data Book 1988*, p. 215.

pressure, although something much worse was narrowly avoided. In 1987, Taiwan's contribution to the overall U.S. trade deficit of some $170 billion was just over 9 percent. Even though that is not a large share, Taiwan seems to be on the receiving end of American anger over an apparent inability of the United States to deal with its huge trade imbalance with Japan. Since the Japanese appear impervious to U.S. threats, Americans seem to be taking out their frustrations on the "little guy."

Table 3–8 shows that the first reason for the deficit is that Taiwan's exports to the United States since 1980 have grown much more rapidly than Taiwan's imports from the United States. While Taiwan's exports grew by leaps and bounds, imports stagnated until 1986 and then, in response to threatening noises from Washington, jumped a bit. From 1980 through 1986, ROC exports to the United States increased nearly 3.5 times, while ROC imports from the United States rose a little more than one and a half times. From the American standpoint, the situation was the result of the already mentioned combination of export promotion and import substitution policies pursued by Taipei. While exports to the United States were buoyed not just by comparative advantage and (for a while) a strong dollar, but by open and hidden government subsidies and piratical practices with regard to patents, copyrights, and the like, imports from the United States were obstructed by tariffs, nontariff barriers, financial restrictions, and discriminatory practices on the expanding domestic services front. The American view was summed up by an article in the *Wall Street Journal:*

> For almost four decades Taiwan has hampered domestic consumption through high tariffs and financial regulations such as currency controls, leaving only the dollar-earning export sector free to function on a level with the rest of the world economy. That free market export sector has been the driving force behind Taiwan's impressive growth rates. . . . Today, Taiwan's mercantilism is hurting domestic invest-ment, damaging its ties to the West, threatening its export growth, and ultimately endangering its security.[20]

The U.S. argument has concentrated on the difficulties experi-enced by U.S. exporters in penetrating the services market in Taiwan, particularly banking and financial services, insurance, advertising, retail marketing, and transportation, especially shipping. Despite hints from Taiwan that the United States is not competitive enough with the Japanese and the West Europeans and that it does not treat exports to Taiwan as seriously as others do, the U.S. argument is that in many sophisticated services the United States clearly has a com-parative advantage and that its inability to make a sale is due to the ROC's "unfairness." The charges and countercharges are many and well known by now.[21] To the ROC's credit, it has not restricted itself to answering the U.S. accusations of protectionism in kind but has admitted the vestigial influence of the import substitution philosophy on its import policies and has taken steps to alleviate U.S. concerns on this subject (see the section "Responses"). Although Frederick Chien, chairman of the ROC Council for Economic Planning and Development, has gone on record as approving of outside pressure on Taiwan for removal of its remnant protection, too much pressure from the United States is likely to be psychologically counterproduc-tive, especially when it comes to imports of U.S. agricultural goods and the marketing of American cigarettes.[22]

The ROC points to its annual "Buy American" missions to the United States as evidence of its good will. In fact, argues Taipei, the European Economic Community accuses the ROC of favoring U.S. imports, a charge that cannot be taken lightly in view of the enor-mous market potential of an economically united Europe. The United States answers that what the "Buy American" missions purchase would have been bought anyway and that when it comes to big-ticket items for Taiwan's currently developing mass transportation and telecommunications systems, airline maintenance facilities, and heavy industrial equipment, the United States loses out most of the time—to France, Japan, West Germany, or Sweden. The ROC answer is that other bids are more competitive.

The domestic economy requires restructuring to meet emerging external and internal challenges. The external challenge takes two forms: increasingly sharp competition on the world market for manufactures of exports from lower labor cost, industrializing economies, particularly in east and Southeast Asia (for example, Thailand, the Philippines, Malaysia, Indonesia, and mainland China), and the need to lower the trade surplus with the United States. The internal challenge also takes two forms: an increasingly problematical labor situation and advanced environmental degradation. Fortunately, the external and internal challenges call for broadly similar responses.

Competition from third world comparatively low-cost producers strengthens an already powerful (and well-recognized) case for continuing to restructure the economy in a high-technology, high value-added, skill-intensive services direction. This involves the relocation of some labor-intensive export industries offshore, which is already happening, and the transformation of others. Such restructuring is always painful and accompanied by resistance from the affected interests. In the more democratic setting of contemporary Taiwan, those being economically restructured out of existence might be expected to find political channels for the expression of their grievances. This constituency includes not only businessmen whose profit margins are squeezed and who object to the continuing (if less than before) restrictions on financially and physically moving elsewhere (to Shenzhen and Fujian or Guangdong Province, for example), but also workers in declining industries like textiles, garments, and footwear. Importation of cheap labor from abroad (including the mainland) has been considered and informally practiced as a short-term expedient but officially rejected as a longer-term remedy. In 1987 exports of technology-intensive goods from Taiwan grew by 26 percent, while labor-intensive exports increased hardly at all (0.7 percent).[23] Restructuring also requires the modernization of financial information and organizational infrastructures. This involves the creation of conditions favorable to the generation and dissemination of reliable financial and accounting information on which a sound taxation system can be built and to the transition from family-based firms to modern corporations, whose stock is held by the public at large.

An effort must be made to diversify export markets both to stake out a share of the large West European unified market scheduled to materialize in 1992 and to lessen dependence on the U.S. buyer. Based on past experience, this will not be easy, especially when export diversification is extended to include Japan; but it has to be tried.

The labor situation on Taiwan is potentially volatile. It is not just a question of labor shortage in certain areas, such as construction, but also of changing attitudes, aging, and a declining rate of natural population increase (expected to reach zero by the year 2020). There is concern that some of the shortage is caused by the growing unwillingness of Taiwan residents to do certain types of manual and blue-collar work and a new reluctance on the part of potential young recruits to enter the labor force or to study. Reportedly 180,000 single people between the ages of fifteen and twenty-four have chosen neither to pursue their studies nor to join the labor force—and this at a time when the labor supply accommodates only two-thirds of the private sector's demand for labor.[24] There are complaints about slackening quality of labor in the midst of full employment, the politicization of workers, and rising labor unrest: "Haggling over . . . bonuses, salaries, and other fringe benefits, including vacation days has become commonplace in Taiwan and worrisome to those who fear that the island's traditional stability is coming unglued."[25]

Li Pei Wu, chairman, president, and chief executive officer of the General Bank of Los Angeles, places some of the blame for the labor disputes on the ROC government's role in the labor market and on what he perceives to be unsatisfactory distribution of income and wealth. Six out of the eight largest companies on Taiwan are government owned. The government, he argues, should act as referee in labor disputes. In the ROC, however, the government tries to be at once referee and player. Wu contends that since government-owned enterprises are usually less efficient than those of the private sector, the government should continue to divest itself of its direct involvement in production and use the proceeds to improve the economic environment. The government's data on income distribution are flawed because they fail to take into account unreported income, a consequence of an unsatisfactory tax system. This makes actual differences in income much more skewed than they appear in official statistics. Large income disparities hurt labor relations, and poor labor relations hurt investment.[26]

The domestic challenge of restructuring includes the need to increase domestic consumer demand and investment in the physical environment, and in social programs (public health, public welfare, and old-age insurance). Expansion of domestic consumption, coordinated with distributional equity, will tend to reduce labor-management frictions, contribute to social stability, provide a favorable investment climate, and lessen Taiwan's currently heavy dependence on exports. (Exports contribute about one-fifth of the Japanese GNP compared with between two-fifths and one-half in the ROC.)

**Responses.** Much progress had been made in the past in addressing the problems that beset the mutually beneficial economic relationship of the United States and the ROC. The ROC has been responsive to the concerns expressed earlier, although some ambiguities and a suspicion of incomplete enforcement of liberal measures, evasion, and a tendency toward postponement in some areas still exist. The ROC has reduced tariffs and quantitative restrictions on imports (the effective tariff rate, for instance, has been cut to 5.3 percent with a projected reduction to 3.5 percent by 1992); significant (more than 40 percent since 1985) appreciation of the N.T.$ against the U.S. currency, a sore point with the ROC, has occurred; ROC government restrictions on private outward capital flows have been relaxed; limitations that had formerly been placed on the operation of American firms (including banks, brokerage firms, and insurance companies) within Taiwan have been reduced; and some well-publicized crackdowns have occurred on what used to be widespread theft of U.S. intellectual property, including infringement of copyright with respect to videos, sound recordings, computer software, books, and translation rights. The ROC has resisted U.S. pressure to let the exchange rate of the N.T.$ be determined by market forces, arguing that such a step would result in a violent restructuring (bankruptcy) of many of Taiwan's export firms with all the imaginable social and political consequences. The ROC has, however, agreed (as of April 1989) to eliminate the daily limit of 2.25 percent on the N.T.$'s fluctuations and the weighted central exchange rate between the N.T.$ and the U.S.$ as determined by the Central Bank and to permit the currency's value to be worked out by daily meetings of nine banks (five government run and four Taiwan and foreign private ones) on foreign exchange transactions.[27] At the same time, to curb the inflow of hot money (speculative capital), ceilings have been placed on the inflow of U.S. dollars. The reform was intended to reduce the likelihood of Taiwan's being blacklisted by the United States under the Omnibus Trade Act as a country that manipulates its exchange rate. The ROC has made known a schedule for the reduction of its trade surplus with the United States, which involves an annual decrease of about $1 billion over the next several years.

Because of its resolve to move up-market to higher-skill, high-technology production, partly to escape the competition from low-cost exporters (in the two years 1987 and 1988 labor costs in Taiwan rose 20 percent), partly as a deliberate act of modernization, Taiwan has been restructuring its industries over the past several years by investing heavily in a number of Southeast Asian countries where labor costs are comparatively low and beginning to invest in advanced industries of the industrial market democracies. According to official ROC data, approved Taiwan foreign investment in 1988 came to $218 million, including $123 million for forty-two projects in the United States. These figures vastly understate the actual size of Taiwanese investments abroad that year, and the same has been true for years past. In 1988, Thailand alone acknowledged that it had approved $2.1 billion of Taiwanese investments, that is, about ten times the official ROC figure. Actual Taiwanese investments in Malaysia and the Philippines that year are believed to have been at least $500 million each. In fact, in 1988, Taiwanese investments represented one quarter of all foreign investment in the Philippines, and the Philippine parliament, risking Beijing's ire, contemplated the passage of a Philippine-Taiwan Beneficial Relations Act, a Philippine version of the U.S. Taiwan Relations Act. Taiwanese businessmen are also investing in Singapore, Hong Kong, mainland China, the United States, and Canada. The actual size of Taiwan's foreign investment is a matter of speculation since most of it is illegal under ROC laws (but even the official ROC press discusses it openly).[28] In Southeast Asia alone it must currently run at around $4 billion a year. It is the second fastest-growing foreign investment flow in Asia, second only to Japan. Buying into technologically advanced industries in the West is understood to be a rational way to acquire state-of-the-art technology, which—given the ROC's educational base—can be transplanted to Taiwan and put the huge foreign exchange reserves (about $75 billion, mostly in depreciating U.S. securities) to productive use. This is well understood by the second generation of well-educated, cosmopolitan entrepreneurs who are energizing the passage of the ROC economy into the industrial and postindustrial era. In 1988 the number of workers hired in manufacturing decreased by 2 percent, the decline being largest in labor-intensive industries such as textiles, apparel, and footwear. It is projected that over the next ten years, more than 80 percent of the incoming labor force will be absorbed by increasingly sophisticated service industries.

From political considerations (to break its political isolation from the international community) but also because it is now a regional economic power with the world's second largest foreign exchange reserves, the ROC seeks to rejoin international (mainly regional) organizations from which it had been ousted in the 1970s. This drive is part of a new diplomatic flexibility adopted by the ROC government and is vigorously pursued despite its risks. It includes willingness to send the minister of finance to a meeting of the Asian Development Bank in Beijing (1989) despite the bank's insistence on designating the ROC delegation as China-Taipei. Rejoining the GATT and entering the Organization for Economic Cooperation and Development (OECD) are on the agenda. The ROC has established a $1.1 billion fund for overseas economic cooperation and development financed out of state budget appropriations. By early 1989, ten countries had applied for loans from the fund. Liberalization and modernization of the ROC's hitherto regulation-ridden and relatively antiquated financial and banking structure are rightly considered essential if Taiwan is to become an international center of finance, insurance, and shipping and successfully compete with others (Japan and Singapore) for succession to the role played by Hong Kong once Hong Kong reverts to the Socialist motherland.[29] Import and financial liberalization—including investment in foreign stock markets by Taiwanese investors, permitting foreign brokerage houses to establish markets in Taiwan to help local investors, the purchase of foreign banks by Taiwanese banks, and the listing of state-owned enterprises on the stock market—is seen by many Taiwanese economists as not only progressive restructuring measures but as a way to curb emergent inflationary pressures.

These days the drive for market diversification includes the pursuit of direct trade with most East European countries and of indirect (via Hong Kong) trade with the mainland (much direct trade takes place informally)[30] and the Soviet Union. Preferential reciprocal import tariffs have been extended to East Germany, Hungary, and Yugoslavia. As Taiwan becomes increasingly high tech, the United States begins to worry about exports from Taiwan of advanced dual-use technology to Socialist countries, especially since Taiwanese businessmen are adept at exporting and importing such things sub rosa, an activity to which the ROC government often turns a blind eye. To allay these apprehensions, the ROC proposes to enact legislation that would establish machinery (on the lines of the Paris-based COCOM) to monitor technology transfers to Socialist buyers. Indirect trade with the mainland rose 80 percent in 1988, from $1.51 billion in 1987 to $2.72 billion, but probably substantially more had everything been counted properly.

## Economic and Political Modernization

The relationship between a workably competitive market system (economic freedom) and political freedom and democracy is a subject that has increasingly come to the attention of social scientists as the failure of the centrally planned Soviet-type of system to provide people efficiently with high-quality goods that they want became manifest even to many devotees of Socialist administrative command. The subject, surrounded by controversy, is being explored on the theoretical plane. It is not possible to do justice to it here beyond stating some general positions.[31] I think that the market system is a necessary condition of political freedom but not a sufficient condition and that political freedom is a necessary but not a sufficient condition of democracy (for example, pre-1997 Hong Kong). A market system can coexist with authoritarianisms of various sorts (but not with totalitarianism of any sort), but the coexistence is uneasy: it is a state of ideological, institutional, psychological, and moral disequilibrium, which sooner or later has to be righted. The presence of a market system (economic freedom) exerts a strong influence in favor of political freedom, but it does not guarantee the outcome. Similarly, the presence of political freedom exerts a powerful influence in favor of the institutionalization of that freedom in democratic rule, but it does not guarantee such an outcome. To establish full economic and political equilibrium (free economy with political freedom and democracy) requires a conscious act of political will.

Taiwan is witness to this process of political democratization with the help of a free economy and by an act of political will. It is not only one of the most successful economies in the contemporary world in its ability to cater efficiently to rising consumer wants but also a model of the way in which economic development can be translated into a pluralistic and democratic society and polity.

## Bibliography

Galenson, Walter, ed. *Economic Growth and Structural Change in Taiwan.* Ithaca, N.Y.: Cornell University Press, 1979.

Gregor, A. James, with Maria Hsia Chang and Andrew B. Zimmerman. *Ideology and Development: Sun Yat-sen and the Economic History of Taiwan.* Berkeley, Calif.: University of California, Institute of East Asian Studies, Center for Chinese Studies, 1981.

Hsiung, James C. and others, eds. *Contemporary Republic of China: The Taiwan Experience.* New York: American Association for Chinese Studies, 1981, chap. 3.

Kuo, Shirley W. Y. *The Taiwan Economy in Transition.* Boulder, Colo.: Westview Press, 1983.

Kuo, Shirley W. Y., Gustav Ranis, and John C. H. Fei. *The Taiwan Success Story: Rapid Growth with Improved Distribution in the Republic of China, 1952–1979.* Boulder, Colo.: Westview Press, 1981.

Lau, Lawrence J. *Models of Development: A Comparative Study of Economic Growth in South Korea and Taiwan*. San Francisco: Institute for Contemporary Studies, 1986.

Li, Kwoh-ting and Tzong-shian Yu. *Experiences and Lessons of Economic Development in Taiwan*. Taipei: Academia Sinica, 1982.

Rabushka, Alvin. *The New China: Comparative Economic Development in Mainland China, Taiwan, and Hong Kong*. Boulder, Colo.: Westview Press, 1987.

Simon, Denis Fred. *Taiwan: Technology Transfer and Transnationalism*. Boulder, Colo.: Westview Press, 1985.

Wheeler, Jimmy W., and Perry L. Wood. *Beyond Recrimination: Perspectives on U.S.-Taiwan Trade Tensions*. Indianapolis, Ind.: Hudson Institute, 1987.

Woronoff, Jon. *Asia's 'Miracle' Economies*. Armonk, N.Y.: M. E. Sharpe, 1986.

Wu, Yuan-li, *Becoming an Industrialized Nation: ROC's Development on Taiwan*. New York: Praeger, 1985.

Wu, Yuan-li, and Kung-chia Yeh, eds. *Growth, Distribution, and Social Change: Essays on the Economy of the Republic of China*. Baltimore, Md.: School of Law, University of Maryland, Occasional Papers/Reprints Series in Contemporary Asian Studies, no. 3, 1978 (15).

Yang, Martin M. C. *Socio-Economic Results of Land Reform in Taiwan*. Honolulu: East West Center Press, 1970.

# 4

# Sociocultural Developments in the Republic of China

*Ting Tin-yu*

The rise of opposition political power in Taiwan has become one of the most important factors contributing to the democratization of the island. Despite martial law, the earlier efforts by Taiwanese opposition politicians to organize quasi-party coalitions, such as the *Formosa* (*Melitao*) *Magazine*, the Tangwai (that is, non-Kuomintang) Central Supporting Association for the 1983 Supplementary Legislative Yuan Election, and the Tangwai Public Policy Association, stimulated the establishment of the Democratic Progressive party (DPP) on September 28, 1986. Two months later the DPP, the first national opposition party organized in Taiwan since 1949, participated in the supplementary Legislative Yuan election and won a surprise victory.

In the year after the 1986 Legislative Yuan election Taiwan experienced a series of reforms that led to the beginning of full-fledged democracy.[1] Martial law and restrictions on newspapers were lifted by the ruling Kuomintang (KMT); life-long members of the Legislative Yuan, the National Assembly, and the Control Yuan were encouraged to retire by an official proposal presented to the public for review; and the opposition DPP was allowed to operate as a de facto political party even without legal permission. These developments demonstrate that the KMT had decided to promote democracy. The KMT's decisions for change, however, were made under strong pressure from street demonstrations organized by opposition camps, especially the DPP.

The acceleration of democratization in Taiwan in 1987 was closely associated with the 1986 election. During the campaign most opposition politicians were unified under the DPP. The KMT candidates faced the first organized challenge from an opposition party. The process was intense, and the result was unforeseen. Twelve of the DPP-nominated candidates won posts in the Legislative Yuan, and

75

one DPP candidate was elected among the quota for union representatives to the legislature. The unexpected success of the DPP was a
surprise to the KMT, which later announced that a cabinet-level Labor
Commission would be added to the Executive Yuan.

Since the party-versus-party competition between the KMT and
the DPP in the 1986 supplementary Legislative Yuan election was a
historical turning point for Taiwan's democracy, it is useful to conduct
a thorough analysis of factors related to the intensity of the competition so as to understand the dynamics of Taiwanese politics more
completely. This chapter first reviews Taiwan's socioeconomic development after 1949 and relates the changes at that time to the more
recent social and political changes. Second, it analyzes the growth of
the Taiwanese opposition movement and the DPP to illustrate the
nature of the electoral competition between the KMT and the DPP.
Finally, it estimates a township-level regression model to assess the
social, demographic, economic, and political factors that strengthen
competition between candidates of these two parties. Attention centers on the hypothesis that the socioeconomic development of an area
stimulates the intensity of local party competition.

## Socioeconomic Development after 1949

In 1949, on the eve of its final exodus from mainland China, the KMT
began a program of land reform in Taiwan. The program, originally
proposed by Dr. Sun Yat-sen in the Three Principles of the People,
had earlier been unsuccessfully tried by the KMT in mainland China.
The land reform introduced to the Taiwanese included a farm rent-
reduction program, a public land sales program, and a land-to-the-
tiller program.[2] The social and economic impact of land reform on
Taiwan's later development is significant. Living conditions were
improved for the majority of farm households, the traditional local
power structure was reshaped, landlord-tenant relations were effectively transformed, and landlords were no longer the sole authority
in the countryside. Modern organizations, such as political parties,
farmers' associations, and schools, were introduced or strengthened
in the countryside. These organizations encouraged participatory
democracy, elections, and compulsory education and made available
such products as fertilizer, radios, bicycles, and farm machinery. All
these changes served to link the Taiwanese countryside more closely
to the cities and transformed the countryside in the process.

After the military collapse on mainland China, the Chinese
Nationalist government was eager to keep Taiwan more stable in the
early months of 1950. The outbreak of the Korean War in June of that

year brought U.S. military and economic aid to Taiwan, which helped maintain military stability in the Strait of Taiwan. U.S. aid played an important role in Taiwan's economic development during the 1950s and 1960s. The estimated total amount of such aid from 1950 to 1968 was about $1.5 billion.[3]

The government's economic policies in the 1960s were designed to promote rapid industrialization in order to change the predominantly agricultural economy into an industrial one and also to develop labor-intensive light industries. The achievements have been extensive and deserve careful review. Table 4–1 presents indicators of social and economic development, including economic, health, transportation and communication, and educational development, since 1952. These four aspects reflect the major socioeconomic changes that have occurred in Taiwan during the past four decades, although improvement did not become rapid until the mid-1960s and accelerated in the late 1970s and early 1980s.

The first four indicators are indexes calculated with their 1952 figures as 100. The GNP increased significantly in the 1960s and in the 1970s. In 1986 it was seventeen times as large as in 1952. Taiwan also experienced rapid increases in per capita income in the 1970s and 1980s.

One important feature of the economic improvements is the development of a more equitable distribution of income. The income share of the poorest 20 percent of families increased from 7.7 percent to 8.6 percent from 1964 to 1979, while the income share of the richest 20 percent decreased from 41.1 percent to 37.5 percent.[4] The case of Taiwan is one of economic development that has improved the living conditions of the majority of the people more significantly than has been experienced in less-developed countries.[5]

The land reform program probably had a substantial effect on the sizable increase of agricultural production in the 1950s and 1960s. The agricultural production index more than doubled from 1952 to 1970, then increased a little more than 30 percent from 1970 to 1986. Before the general industrialization took place in the 1960s, Taiwan was basically an agricultural society, and government policy emphasized the development of the agricultural sector. The land reform program and other agricultural policies encouraged farmers to find high-yield, low-production-cost crops to raise on their newly owned land. When industrialization first spread in the late 1960s and early 1970s, a significant number of rural residents, especially young adults, moved from farms to urban areas to work in factories, and some eventually left the rural areas permanently. The government was unable to cope with the problems of agriculture while focusing

## TABLE 4-1
### Indicators of Social and Economic Development in Taiwan, 1952–1986

|  | 1952 | 1960 | 1970 | 1980 | 1986 |
|---|---|---|---|---|---|
| Economic Indicators |  |  |  |  |  |
| GNP index[a] | 100.0 | 179.1 | 448.7 | 1,128.7 | 1,711.2 |
| Per capita income[b] | 100.0 | 137.2 | 263.1 | 546.4 | 755.0 |
| Agricultural production |  |  |  |  |  |
| index | 100.0 | 142.5 | 230.5 | 289.4 | 301.4 |
| Industrial production index | 100.0 | 242.1 | 1,104.5 | 3,910.1 | 6,000.0 |
| Health Indicators |  |  |  |  |  |
| Death rate per 1,000 |  |  |  |  |  |
| population | 10.0 | 7.0 | 5.0 | 5.0 | 4.9 |
| Life expectancy, females[c] | 60.7 | 66.7 | 71.2 | 74.1 | 75.8 |
| Child mortality rate per |  |  |  |  |  |
| 1,000[c] | 26.0 | 14.0 | 5.0 | 3.0 | 1.9 |
| Population per health and |  |  |  |  |  |
| medical facility[d] | — | 9,919.0 | 13,187.0 | 1,624.0 | 1,608.0 |
| Population per physician[d] | — | 1,661.0 | 2,240.0 | 1,323.0 | 1,077.0 |
| Transportation and Communication Indicators |  |  |  |  |  |
| Automobiles per 1,000 |  |  |  |  |  |
| persons | 1.0 | 2.1 | 7.0 | 38.8 | 77.1 |
| Telephone subscribers per |  |  |  |  |  |
| 1,000 persons | 3.0 | 5.2 | 17.0 | 130.0 | 232.7 |
| Education indicators |  |  |  |  |  |
| Illiterates age 6+ (%) | 42.0 | 27.1 | 15.0 | 10.0 | 8.1 |
| Primary graduates enrolled |  |  |  |  |  |
| in junior high (%) | 34.0 | 51.2 | 80.0 | 97.0 | 99.7 |
| Females having at least attended junior high |  |  |  |  |  |
| school (%)[c] | — | — | 14.3 | 34.3 | 46.6 |

a. Adjusted for gain or loss due to changed terms of trade; 1952 = 100.
b. Real income at 1976 market prices, adjusted for gain or loss due to changed terms of trade; 1952 = 100.
c. Data from *Taiwan-Fukien Demographic Fact Book* (Taipei: Interior Department of the Republic of China, 1963–    ).
d. Figures for years before 1971 are provincial, county, and city health and medical care facilities and their numbers of beds. Figures for 1971 and subsequent years include all public and private hospitals and clinics and their numbers of beds.
Sources: *Taiwan Statistical Data Book* (Taipei: Republic of China, 1981); and *Taiwan-Fukien Demographic Fact Book*.

on industrial development. Labor shortages, inefficient agricultural mechanization, insufficient chemical fertilizers, underpriced agricultural products, and other problems all delayed further improvement in agriculture in this period. The limited acreage of arable land in Taiwan is, of course, a fundamental problem of agricultural production.

The real growth of industrialization in Taiwan started after 1960. Industrial production increased 2.5 times from 1952 to 1960, more than 15 times between 1960 and 1980, and more than half between 1980 and 1986. The cessation of American aid in 1968 might have had a serious negative effect on industrial development had foreign and overseas Chinese investment not poured into Taiwan. The increase in the industrial production index probably reflects not only the successful efforts by the government to attract foreign investment but also the effective economic policies implemented during this period. The land reform movement, for example, through the program of purchasing land with nationally owned company stock, forced some landowners to become industrialists. The policy of emphasizing light industries such as food processing, textile production, electronics assembly, and furniture and shoe manufacturing in the early stage of industrialization also put Taiwan in an advantageous position since it had a large and well-educated labor force to work in these labor-intensive industries. The export processing zones in Kaohsiung, Taichung, and Keelung successfully attracted foreign and overseas Chinese investment in the late 1960s and 1970s.

Substantial improvement of living conditions brought the death rate down from 10 per 1,000 in 1952 to 4.9 per 1,000 in 1986 (a favorable age composition was an important factor in decreasing the crude death rates), and female life expectancy increased during the same period from 60.7 years to 75.8 years. Although crude death rates leveled off after 1970, female life expectancy still increased moderately in the early 1980s. The child mortality rate (under age four) showed an even more impressive drop from 1952 to 1986 than the crude death rate. Starting at a relatively high 26 per 1,000, the rate declined steadily to 5 per 1,000 in 1970 and 1.9 per 1,000 in 1986. These improvements are probably a result of better nutrition and increased health services provided by personnel from both public and private institutions. Data on improvements in these areas are also shown in table 4-1.

Both automobiles per 1,000 persons and telephone subscribers per 1,000 persons increased moderately before 1970 and very rapidly after that year. Automobile ownership, which was 1 per 1,000 in 1952 and 7 per 1,000 in 1970, increased to 38.8 per 1,000 from 1970 to 1980 and doubled in the first six years of the 1980s. A similar trend occurred in the number of telephone subscribers, which increased from 17 to 232.7 per 1,000 from 1970 to 1986. It is the economic development of the past sixteen years that has dramatically increased the numbers of automobiles and telephones. Modern communication and transportation systems are now generally available in Taiwan and had a major effect on daily life.

Education improved significantly from 1952 to 1986. The proportion of the population age six and over classified as illiterate decreased from 42 percent to 8.1 percent during this period, 80 percent of the decrease occurring between 1952 and 1970. Both the proportion of primary school graduates enrolled in junior high school and the percentage of females having attended junior high school significantly increased after 1970. These improvements are apparently a result of the 1968 extension of compulsory education from six to nine years, which caused most primary school graduates to enroll in public junior high schools and provided an opportunity for higher education to females who might otherwise have been forced to conclude their formal education with elementary school.

Social and economic development in Taiwan in the thirty-six years from 1950 to 1986 can be divided into three stages: the first stage is characterized by the land reform movement and the government's efforts to rebuild the agricultural sector in the 1950s; the second stage is distinguished by the establishment and expansion of labor-intensive light industries in the 1960s; and the third stage is defined by the general improvement in various aspects of social and economic life in the 1970s and 1980s. After 1960 two socioeconomic trends emerged. In the 1960s these changes occurred slowly, whereas in the 1970s and 1980s the pace accelerated and the changes diffused throughout the island. Important policies such as the extension of compulsory education and the establishment of export processing zones that were implemented in the 1960s had significant effects on social and economic development in the 1970s.

What are the social and political implications of the socioeconomic changes for the emergence of Taiwanese democracy in recent years? First, Taiwan has made the transition from an underdeveloped country to a newly industrializing society. As early as the end of the 1970s, many Taiwanese felt that the society was ready to establish a democratic political system that would be in accordance with its economic prosperity.[6]

Second, by the early 1980s Taiwan had successfully trained a well-educated generation that was occupying important positions in society. These persons learned basic concepts of Western democracy in school or during graduate study outside Taiwan. Much of this foreign influence, as expected, came from the United States.

Third, the growth of nongovernmental sectors of the economy has fostered a new elite class composed of young entrepreneurs and intellectuals who are independent of the government and the ruling KMT. These include professors, journalists, businessmen, lawyers, doctors, and full-time politicians in their thirties and forties.

Fourth, rapid economic development has resulted in a number of negative externalities. Problems of environmental pollution suddenly became unavoidable and extremely urgent in the early 1980s. Workers also began to express the feeling that they had been exploited by both local and international capitalists during previous decades. Moreover, workers believe that martial law prevented them from organizing independent unions or striking to protect their interests. The demands by workers for a better environment, improved workplace conditions, and an improved quality of life have added new dimensions to the Taiwanese political arena.

Finally, the seemingly endless conflict between the KMT in Taiwan and the Chinese Communist party in mainland China during the past forty years has led the Taiwanese to develop a more mature political attitude on these issues. The KMT political myths based on the Taiwan–mainland China conflict are no longer widely accepted. Their questioning helps the young, well-educated, and affluent generation develop a new and independent view on the future of Taiwan and the relationship between Taiwan and mainland China.

### Taiwanese Opposition and the Democratic Progressive Party

Before the founding of the national opposition Democratic Progressive party, local factions were the only political forces competing with the ruling KMT. The Taiwanese opposition, which includes a variety of factions from across the island, is also referred to as Tangwai, or non-KMT politicians, although these factions are quite distinct political groups. Among them local/family factions, such as those of Yu Teng-fa of Kaohsiung County, the late Hsu Shih-hsien of Chia-yi City, Su Tung-chi of Yun-lin County, and Hsu Hsin-lian of Tao-yuan County, and other more independent opposition leaders, such as Huang Hsin-chieh, Kang Ning-hsiang of Taipei City, and the late Kuo Yu-hsing of I-lan County, all represent different political groups with diversified local interests. Of course, the factional character of the Taiwanese opposition is mainly the result of KMT policies, including localized elections, strict media control, and restrictions under martial law on such citizens' rights as free assembly. These policies successfully prevented the emergence of strong and unified opposition parties and islandwide opposition leaders.[7]

Despite suppression by the KMT, opposition leaders tried in the 1950s and 1960s to organize formal opposition parties. The most famous case was that of Lei Chen, whose trial for organizing the Chinese Democratic party in the fall of 1960 ended in Lei's arrest and a sentence of ten years in prison. Lei, a veteran member of the KMT and the chief editor of *Free China Magazine*, was very active in the 1950s in organizing the opposition party with local politicians such as Li Wan-chu and Kao Yu-shu. The KMT authorities decided not to tolerate such political activities and accused Lei of Communist espionage. Lei's case is typical of KMT political suppression of opposition leaders. This strategy was quite effective during earlier decades.

Nevertheless, rapid socioeconomic changes and the growth of young political elites in the early 1970s altered the nature of the Taiwanese opposition. With the support of these local/family opposition factions, urban-oriented opposition politicians with grass-roots support dominated the new wave of opposition in the early 1980s. The goal was to organize a formal national opposition party. The founding of the DPP in 1986 reflected the collective success of opposition politicians, including *Formosa Magazine*, the Tangwai Central Supporting Association for the 1983 Supplementary Legislative Yuan Election, and the Tangwai Public Policy Association. All these organizations had paid a very high price for their previous efforts.

The new opposition party is less centralized than the KMT and apparently less troubled by intraparty factionalism. Factions are generally organized by political interests, geographic connections, and ideology, especially perceptions of the future of Taiwan. For example, the Club of Editors of Tangwai Magazines, a radical coalition of young opposition activists, is one of the leading factions and plays a crucial role in the daily operation of the DPP. The political line of this unique club has led the DPP toward street-demonstration strategies and emphasizes the policy of Taiwanese self-determination.

The leaders of the DPP understand very well, even as they did before the formal founding of the party, that the survival and growth of the party rely heavily on its relentless challenging of the legitimacy of the KMT. Therefore, they stress such issues as the holding of full-scale reelections for the members of the three parliaments and the selection by popular vote of the provincial governor and city mayors of Taipei and Kaohsiung. Other emotional disputes involving labor relations, nuclear energy, environmental pollution, and imported agricultural products have also been seen by the DPP leaders as opportunities to promote their popular support against the KMT.

Only two months after the formal founding of the DPP, the newly organized party faced its first battle against the KMT in the 1986 supplementary Legislative Yuan election. Its performance was clearly better than that of the previous quasi-party opposition organizations, although intraparty conflicts still existed. The most important achievement of the DPP, however, was to legitimize its role in competition with the KMT. With the 1986 election the DPP earned its position as the most important opposition political party in Taiwan.

## Party Competition and Democratization

In a competitive democracy political parties compete with one another in elections for opportunities to form governments. Parties participating in political competitions are expected to accept the legitimacy of their major opponents and the constitutional system.[8] Since the outcomes of party competition determine the future ruling party in a democratic society, it is important to study this phenomenon. Anthony Downs developed an economic theory of democracy that emphasizes a spatial model of electoral competition.[9] His theory is grounded on a basic assumption: both voters and politicians are rational in elections. This assumption, however, has produced serious disagreements among scholars. Downs's spatial model, which emphasizes the policy issues adopted by candidates in party competition, apparently neglects nonspatial characteristics of candidates.[10] Factors such as campaign strategy and ethnicity can easily become important variables in determining election results.

Seymour Martin Lipset studied data for forty-eight societies and found that, although advanced economic development does not necessarily lead to democracy, it is rare to find a stable democracy in societies that are not economically advanced.[11] Gerhard Lenski also found that advanced industrialization is often associated with political democracy.[12] The exception is Communist societies. The totalitarianism of these societies has made them highly resistant to democratization, no matter how economically advanced they are.[13] Since economically advanced societies always contain an urbanized and literate population that expects some participation in the political process and the large middle class in these societies also tends to pursue political stability, political democratization is more likely to occur in economically advanced societies than in societies with large and impoverished populations.

Studies on the relationship between urbanization and party competition in the United States provide evidence for the link between economic development and democracy. County-level studies by Heinz Eulau, Phillips Cutright, Douglas Gatlin, and Frank Sorauf suggest some support for this hypothesis.[14] But others have found no significant relationship between urbanization and interparty competition.[15]

Similar findings on the link between development and the growth of opposition parties exist for East Asian countries. Results of a study of South Korean opposition voters, for example, indicate greater support for the opposition among urban voters, students, and intellectuals than among rural voters.[16] Richard Samuels argued that the rise of the Japanese opposition parties in local elections in the 1960s and early 1970s was mainly the result of the opposition's manipulation of such social issues as urban problems and environmental pollution.[17]

The changing political relationship between the KMT and the opposition in the early 1980s has had a tremendous effect on the democratization of Taiwan. The opposition began not only to challenge the ruling status of the KMT through elections but also to attack the legitimacy of the KMT by denouncing the KMT government and its leaders. Earlier signs of change emerged in the 1980 election. The opposition candidates won a substantial portion of both votes and legislative seats in the 1980 supplementary Legislative Yuan election. Scholars considered this outcome a movement toward a multiparty democratic system that would eventually revitalize functions of the legislative body within the Nationalist Chinese government system.[18] Furthermore, a study by Sheng Shing-yuan of the electoral competition between the KMT and the Tangwai Central Supporting Association for the 1983 Supplementary Legislative Yuan Election found that socioeconomic development had a significant and positive effect on the intensity of local political competition.[19] Although this quasi-party opposition organization did not function successfully as a party and the result of the election was not favorable to the opposition, Sheng's findings are very useful to the current analysis.

Studies of voters' behavior in Taiwan have found that mainlanders are more likely than Taiwanese to support the KMT.[20] But among Taiwanese, Hakkas seem to be more conservative than Fukienese in their attitudes toward democracy and related political behavior.[21] Young voters tend to vote for opposition candidates, older voters to support KMT politicians.[22] The overall trend of the opposition demands for democratization seems to coincide with the rate of economic development, although the KMT started to respond to these demands only after the late 1970s. The focus of this chapter is, however, on analyzing party competition at the township level to test the developmental hypothesis. Party competition is considered a measure of democratization, and the hypothesis is that the level of competition between the KMT and the DPP can be predicted by the socioeconomic development of an area.

The electoral competition between the KMT and the DPP constitutes an important stage in the development of democracy. Although the earlier discussion has shown that the growth of Taiwanese opposition is closely related to the island's socioeconomic development, results of previous studies of other countries indicate that development factors such as urbanization and education are associated with party competition. This study uses ordinary least-squares regression to test the hypothesis that socioeconomic development has a positive effect on party competition between the KMT and the DPP.

An index of local socioeconomic development, which is composed of the percentage of residents commuting to urban centers, the percentage not involved in agricultural employment, and the percentage who have attended high school, is used to test the developmental hypothesis. This variable measures the overall development experienced by local residents. Development may be expected to foster opposition power and increase the competition between the ruling party and the opposition. The DPP nomination strategy variable is constructed to control for the effect of the non-spatial factor. Townships where the DPP has adopted an aggressive nomination strategy may be expected to experience an increase in the intensity of electoral competition between the KMT and the DPP. The unemployment rate and demographic factors, such as the percentage of young voters, the percentage of mainlanders, and the percentage of Hakkas, are included to control for their influences (see appendix A for variable construction).

### Findings

Table 4–2 shows the multiple regression results of the party competition analysis. The correlations, means, and standard deviations for the variables are presented in appendix B. Except for the variable percentage of Hakkas, all independent variables are statistically significant. Townships with higher socioeconomic development, a higher unemployment rate, more young voters, and fewer mainlanders are more likely to experience an increase in party competition. The coefficient of determination ($R^2$) for this regression model (.3652) explains a substantial portion of the variation in the dependent variable.

Examination of the regression coefficient for the index of socioeconomic development reveals that this variable has the hypothesized

TABLE 4–2
MULTIPLE REGRESSION ANALYSIS OF THE DETERMINANTS OF PARTY
COMPETITION BETWEEN THE KMT AND THE DPP IN THE 1986
SUPPLEMENTARY LEGISLATIVE YUAN ELECTION
(N = 330)

| Independent Variable | Level of Party Competition | |
| --- | --- | --- |
| | B | Beta |
| Index of socioeconomic | .0521* | |
| development | (.0090) | .3993* |
| Aggressive DPP | .2117* | |
| nomination strategy | (.0331) | .3274* |
| Percentage of unemployment | 1.8550* | |
| | (1.0287) | .0831* |
| Percentage of young | 1.9354* | |
| voters | (.4338) | .2532* |
| Percentage of mainlanders | − .6753* | |
| | (.1539) | − .2602* |
| Percentage of Hakkas | − .0183 | |
| | (.0600) | − .0159 |
| Constant | − .7738 | |
| $R^2$ | .3652 | |

NOTE: *Denotes $t$-statistics > 1.64. Standard errors are in parentheses.

effect on party competition: the higher the level of socioeconomic development of an area, the more intense the competition between the KMT and the DPP. Since this index is composed of the percentages of local residents commuting to urban centers, involved in nonagricultural employment, and having attended high school, the assumption is that the combination of these components will reflect overall socioeconomic development. Theoretically, people who live in areas with high socioeconomic development not only enjoy a better quality of life but also can expect a more competitive and democratic political process. This kind of expectation can result in more intense competition between the KMT and the DPP. From this analysis of the 1986 supplementary Legislative Yuan election, the pattern of party competition in Taiwanese townships is quite clear. When other factors in the regression model are controlled for, the variable of socioeconomic development suggests greater party competition. Moreover, the relative strength of the standardized coefficient for the level of socioeconomic development is the most important one in the regression model (see beta values in table 4–2).

Why would socioeconomic development be so important in increasing party competition? Areas with higher proportions of local residents commuting to urban centers are located either in or close to highly urbanized regions. In Taiwan urbanization means better access to information, especially information regarding democracy. The attainment of higher education can also accelerate the development of democratic attitudes. And, of course, more nonagricultural employment implies a further diversified occupational structure. Persons with these kinds of experiences can be expected to be more open to and sophisticated in accepting party competition. This finding supports the fundamental hypothesis of this chapter that socioeconomic development will bring about party competition.

The nonspatial variable of the DPP nomination strategy proves to be an important predictor. Townships where the DPP has had an aggressive nomination strategy experience a higher level of party competition. While the KMT might respond with intensified campaign tactics, the aggressive DPP policy seems to have an independent effect on party competition. This finding implies that the intensity of electoral competition, after other social, economic, and demographic factors are controlled for, depends on strategies adopted by the political parties involved in the election.

The unemployment rate is also a significant factor in the regression model and has a positive effect on party competition. Since unemployed persons often blame the government for creating unfavorable economic conditions, they tend to place their hopes on the opposition in elections. Although unemployed workers might not be able to understand the complex economic process, their votes for the opposition and the unpleasant environment of areas where unemployment is high will inevitably increase party competition between the KMT and the DPP.

Voters between the ages of twenty and thirty-nine are the generation raised during the relatively affluent periods of the 1970s and early 1980s. Their unique socialization experiences, which include substantial exposure to the Western concept of democracy and modern mass media, probably give them quite different perceptions of Taiwanese politics from those formulated by older generations. Thus they are less likely to accept a one-party political system. Previous research findings also suggest that young voters tend to support opposition candidates in elections and thus increase party competition.[23] The positive and significant regression coefficient for the young voter variable in table 4–2 provides empirical evidence supporting this hypothesis. Young voters are clearly associated with the competition between the KMT and the DPP. They generate a more competitive political environment for these two parties.

Provincial differences are important in Taiwan because Fu-kienese, Hakkas, and mainlanders are dissimilar in their language, social traditions, and political beliefs. Mainlanders are, in general, strong supporters of the KMT.[24] This factor will certainly reduce the intensity of competition between the KMT and the DPP in areas with a high proportion of mainlander residents. The Hakkas can be classified as a minority group in Taiwan, since their numbers and economic and political influence are less significant than those of the Fukienese. This minority status influenced Hakkas to become strong supporters of the KMT in the past, and their voting record suggests that party competition will not increase in areas with a significant Hakka population. Table 4–2 contains negative regression coefficients for both the mainlander and the Hakka variables. The percentage of Hakkas variable is, however, not significant. The significant effect of the percentage of mainlanders is that their almost uniform support of the KMT works against party competition.

During the past forty years the major tactic adopted by the KMT to maintain power has been to stress the potential threat to Taiwan's security from mainland China and the Taiwanese independence movement. Mainlanders appear vulnerable to such tactics. They do not like Chinese Communists, although they are even more concerned about their fate if Taiwan should become independent. This fear of independence may spring from a belief that native Taiwanese would have full control of the government. The KMT leadership has skillfully manipulated the minority feelings of KMT mainlanders and led them to believe that the only choice they have is to spare no effort in support of the KMT. Therefore, it was expected that mainlanders would show strong support for KMT candidates in elections, and it is not surprising to see that the mainlander variable has a negative effect on party competition.

## Summary and Conclusions

This study has examined the determinants of party competition in Taiwan. Since Taiwan's socioeconomic development is closely related to the growth of the opposition in the past twenty years, the major hypothesis was that areas with higher levels of development have experienced more intense political competition. This hypothesis was tested with areal-unit data by controlling for the DPP nomination strategy, local economic conditions (the unemployment rate), the age structure (the percentage of young voters), and the provincial composition (the percentages of Hakkas and of mainlanders) in a regression analysis.

The results indicate that the socioeconomic development variable is not only a significant predictor of the intensity of party competition but also the most important variable in the model. Socioeconomic development facilitates the development of a more diversified social structure that allows political opposition to grow. While stronger opposition groups will inevitably intensify electoral competition, this finding supports the hypothesis regarding the relationship between socioeconomic development and party competition. Other variables in the regression model have the expected results and, except for the percentage of Hakkas, have statistically significant effects on party competition. The greater the DPP nomination strategy, the unemployment rate, and the percentage of young voters, the greater is the intensity of party competition; greater percentages of mainlanders and Hakkas reduce party competition.

Finally, the basic assumption of this study is that the founding of the DPP is the result of social and economic development in Taiwan during the past four decades and that the intensifying party competition between the KMT and the DPP across the island is associated with the local level of socioeconomic development. The findings of this chapter strongly support this hypothesis and show that when the DPP nomination strategy, the unemployment rate, and demographic variables are controlled for, socioeconomic development is the most important predictor of party competition between the KMT and the DPP.

### Appendix A: The Data Set and Definitions of the Variables

This areal-unit analysis of the determinants of the variation of party competition between the Kuomintang and the Democratic Progressive party in the 1986 Legislative Yuan election requires a complete township-level data set for both the independent and the dependent variables specified in the model. The definitions and sources of the variables are as follows:

1. Level of party competition
   Measurement: The percentage of votes received by the DPP divided by the percentage of votes received by the KMT.
   Source of data: The 1986 *Taiwan Supplementary Legislative Yuan Election Report.*
2. Index of socioeconomic development
   Measurement: The sum of the 2 scores for the following socioeconomic variables—percentage of local residents commuting to urban centers, percentage of adults aged 15 + working in non-

agricultural sectors, and percentage of adults aged 15+ having attended senior high school or higher.

Source of data: The 1980 *Taiwan Area Census* (Taipei: Population Census Office of the Executive Yuan, 1982).

3. DPP nomination strategy

Measurement: Townships where the DPP had nominated more than 40 percent of all posts are classified as areas with an aggressive nomination strategy. Townships where the DPP had nominated less than 40 percent of all posts are classified as areas with a passive nomination strategy. Forty percent is selected as the cutoff point because the DPP received an average of 30 percent of popular votes in the 1986 election.

Sources of data: The 1986 *Taiwan Supplementary Legislative Yuan Election Report;* "The DPP Nomination in the 1986 Supplementary Legislative Yuan Election," *China Times,* December 7, 1986.

4. Percentage of unemployment

Measurement: Percentage of unemployed adults aged 15+.

Source of data: The 1980 *Taiwan Area Census.*

5. Percentage of young voters

Measurement: Percentage of voters aged 20–39.

Source of data: The 1986 *Taiwan-Fukien Demographic Fact Book.*

6. Percentage of mainlanders

Measurement: Percentage of mainlander residents.

Source of data: The 1980 *Taiwan Area Census.*

7. Percentage of Hakkas

Measurement: Percentage of Hakka residents.

Source of data: The 1980 *Taiwan Area Census.*

## Appendix B: Correlation Matrix, Means, and Standard Deviations for Observed Variables

|  | X1 | X2 | X3 | X4 | X5 | X6 | X7 |
|---|---|---|---|---|---|---|---|
| Level of party competition (X1) | 1.000 | | | | | | |
| Index of socioeconomic development (X2) | .386 | 1.000 | | | | | |
| DPP nomination strategy (X3) | .363 | .031 | 1.000 | | | | |
| % of unemployment (X4) | .105 | −.007 | .219 | 1.000 | | | |
| % of young voters (X5) | .400 | .564 | .006 | −.118 | 1.000 | | |
| % of mainlanders (X6) | .061 | .639 | −.039 | .060 | .284 | 1.000 | |
| % of Hakkas (X7) | .109 | −.035 | .451 | .102 | −.213 | −.141 | 1.000 |
| Mean | .333 | −.390 | .324 | .042 | .546 | .107 | .152 |
| Standard deviation | .303 | 2.325 | .469 | .014 | .040 | .117 | .264 |

N = 330.

# 5
# Taiwan's International Environment

*Martin L. Lasater*

The remarkable progress Taiwan has made since 1986 toward democratizing its political system has been more dramatic than most American analysts would have thought possible. The lifting of martial law, legalization of opposition political parties, removal of most censorship of the media, democratization of the ruling Kuomintang (KMT), invigoration of the legislature, and other steps have captured the attention of political scientists everywhere.

For one of the few times in history, there appears to be a true transition from an authoritarian system of government to a democracy. These steps in Taiwan were initiated in 1986 and 1987 by the late President Chiang Ching-kuo, who died in January 1988. From all indicators his successor, President Lee Teng-hui, will continue the fast pace of reforms.

This chapter examines the extent to which the international environment has contributed to (or retarded) Taiwan's recent moves toward greater democracy. Also discussed are these questions: How likely is the international environment to be supportive of continued democratization on Taiwan? What international changes might alter the course of political developments on the island? What is the relationship between the international environment and other factors contributing to political evolution on Taiwan?

## The International Environment Defined

Nations rarely find the international environment totally to their liking, and for Taiwan the environment is less friendly than it often has been. For purposes of analysis, Taiwan's international environment can be divided into security, political, and economic dimensions.

The international security environment of Taiwan is at best uncertain. At worst it is threatening. A long-term threat to Taiwan's survival as an independent political entity comes from the People's Republic of China (PRC). The KMT and the Communist party of China (CPC) have been competing for control of China for sixty years. Both define China as including Taiwan. Beijing is determined, by peaceful means or by force if necessary, to reunite Taiwan and the mainland under the PRC's central government.[1] There is no indication that Taipei is willing to accept a local government status, as Beijing suggests, under a "one-country, two-systems" formula for the return of Taiwan, Hong Kong, and Macao under PRC sovereignty.

The long-term threat to Taiwan is serious, but assessments of near-term and mid-term threats vary considerably, because PRC leaders face a wide range of incentives not to attempt to reunite China by force. It can be said with fair confidence that for the next five years Beijing will be deterred from using force against Taiwan because of several key constraints. These include Beijing's hope that a peaceful resolution of the Taiwan issue can be found; Taiwan's own substantial military force; friendly ties between the United States and Taiwan, codified in the 1979 Taiwan Relations Act; weaknesses in PRC power projection capabilities; the necessity of a peaceful international environment for the success of the Four Modernizations; Beijing's interests in maintaining friendly relations with the United States, Japan, and other Western nations; and its interests in avoiding military actions viewed as threats by its non-Communist Asian neighbors.[2]

These constraints weave a complex but effective web to deter a use of force against Taiwan by the PRC. But from Taipei's point of view the deterrence is uncertain and therefore lacks credibility. The reason is that, of the various constraints against Beijing, the only one under Taiwan's control is the readiness of its armed forces. Even that element of deterrence is limited because of Taiwan's restricted ability to produce its own advanced weapons.[3]

The political dimension of Taiwan's international environment is also uncertain. In the normal diplomatic sense Taipei is isolated. The Republic of China (ROC) is recognized by only twenty-eight governments, and its diplomatic status is still uncertain. Of great concern to Taiwan are recent trends toward improving relations between the PRC and Taiwan's most important diplomatic partners, the Republic of Korea (ROK) and Saudi Arabia. Beijing and Seoul are rapidly expanding their trade and other nondiplomatic relations. ROK President Roh Tae Woo has openly called for improved relations with the PRC. The most significant sign of cordial relations with Saudi Arabia is China's unprecedented sale to the Saudis of CSS-2 intermediate-range guided missiles.

Rigorous intellectual exercises are held on Taiwan to try to find a way to improve its diplomatic position. But the outlook is rather bleak because Beijing jealously guards its recognition as the sole legal government of China, of which Taiwan is a part. There is no indication that the PRC will relax its attitude in this regard.

If one considers functional unofficial relations, Taiwan's position is not so difficult. Since the ROC's expulsion from the United Nations in 1971 and especially since the U.S. derecognition in 1979, most nations have worked out means of handling nondiplomatic, substantive business with Taiwan. Taiwan maintains such unofficial relationships with about 135 countries, including most major non-Communist nations. In this area Taiwan's international political position may be improving as greater flexibility and imagination come into play. The most significant example is the recent lifting of restrictions on trade to Communist nations, including from 1989 the Soviet Union, Albania, and the PRC itself.

A similar improvement in Taiwan's international political position can be seen in some international organizations. Taiwan now participates in ten intergovernmental international organizations and some 670 nongovernmental international organizations. Recently Taiwan decided to resume its role in the Asian Development Bank (ADB) but under the designation Taipei, China instead of Republic of China. This decision reflects greater pragmatism and flexibility on Taipei's part, because in the past it rejected participation in international governmental organizations, such as the ADB, unless it could participate under its official name.

Taiwan participates in other international organizations under a variety of designations. The name changes have been necessary to enable both China and Taiwan to take part in the same international activity. The international community has every incentive for this, since Taiwan has all the accouterments of sovereignty except wide peer recognition.

Pragmatism on the part of all concerned seems to be the emerging trend in this area of Taiwan's international environment. Taiwan is demonstrating increased flexibility in accepting designations other than Republic of China in international bodies. The PRC appears to be more lenient in having representatives from Taiwan in the same international forum, except in organizations seating only one representative from each country. In those instances Beijing reserves for itself the right of being the sole representative of China.

Taiwan's international economic environment is somewhat more friendly, even if highly competitive. Taiwan is the world's twelfth largest trading nation, with about $88 billion in exports and imports in 1987, $129 billion in 1988, and $110 billion in 1989. It maintains trading relations with some 164 countries. These relations are expanding, partly because of recent Taipei decisions allowing trade with Eastern Europe. Direct trade with the Soviet Union was established in 1989. Indirect trade with the PRC, generally through Hong Kong, amounted to more than $2.5 billion in 1987, $2.63 billion in 1988, and $3.5 billion in 1989. Although there have been trading difficulties due to lack of diplomatic relations, most of them have been solved to the mutual advantage of Taiwan and its trading partners.[4]

The major challenge Taiwan faces in the international economic environment is the threat of protectionism on the part of some of its major partners, including the United States. Taipei has taken many steps to soothe protectionist sentiment in the United States, including a lifting of most tariff and nontariff barriers to American goods and services and a 40 percent appreciation of the new Taiwan dollar. Given these steps and the attractiveness of Taiwan's products to buyers around the world, it can be assumed that the threat of protectionism will be blunted without undue damage to Taiwan's trade-dependent economy.

Nonetheless, major differences confront Taiwan and its trading partners. Taipei and Washington have been at loggerheads for some time over the issue of opening Taiwan's financial markets and stock market to U.S. institutions and investors. U.S. negotiators have demanded equal access to these markets, while Taiwan has argued that foreign competition must be phased in gradually so as not to overwhelm local industries.

A more long-term challenge is the difficulty Taiwan will have in maintaining its market share against other developing economies. Taiwan's exports need to move up the technological ladder, but that requires a major restructuring of the industrial sector from light to heavy industry. Rising labor costs, growing environmental concerns, the heavy concentration of family-owned enterprises, and cautious domestic investment all pose major problems.

Already foreign investors on Taiwan are looking elsewhere in Asia, for example, in Thailand, to establish their factories so as to gain a competitive edge for their products. Unless Taiwan is able to marshal the determination and resources to restructure its industrial sector—no small task given budgetary constraints for research and development and cultural resistance to large corporations—it may find its exports too expensive for the world market. This would slow the export-driven economy of Taiwan and no doubt cause serious domestic and perhaps foreign difficulties.

To summarize, Taiwan faces an international environment that is extraordinarily challenging. It faces a long-term threat to its security from the PRC, but for the moment it possesses an adequate if somewhat uncertain deterrence. Politically, Taiwan is diplomatically isolated, but it does enjoy substantive unofficial relations with most nations. Economically, its status as a trading nation is well respected and established. To some extent its economic success ensures that it should continue to be accepted as a legitimate international actor in the world community. In all aspects of Taiwan's international environment the United States plays the most important supportive role. Of the security and political threats faced by Taiwan, the PRC is the most dangerous.

## Taiwan's Domestic Political Environment

Chapter 2 details Taiwan's domestic political environment. A few points should be emphasized, however, to explain Taiwan's receptivity to pressures for democracy coming from the international environment.

First, the KMT was established in 1912 as part of a Republican revolution against the Ching dynasty led by the KMT founder, Sun Yat-sen. Sun suggested that the government of the Republic of China be organized along both Western and traditional Chinese lines. This is reflected in the five branches of the government: executive, legislative, judicial, control, and examination. Sun theorized that the ROC would go through three stages of development: military dictatorship, political tutelage under the KMT, and constitutional democracy. This indeed has been its development on mainland China and then on Taiwan. From its very founding, therefore, the governing ideology of the KMT sanctioned democracy as an eventual goal for the ROC.[5]

Second, the ROC has traditionally divided the world into democratic and Communist camps, with itself firmly allied on the side of democracy. This world view served Taipei's interests in attempting to isolate Beijing during the 1950s through the 1970s, but it also contributed to Taiwan's self-image as a democratic country.

Third, the Western democracies have educated hundreds of thousands of Chinese students in the ways of Western political thought since the 1800s. Many of the closest advisers of President Chiang Ching-kuo in his step-by-step implementation of political reform have been trained in the United States and Western Europe. President Lee has a Ph.D. from Cornell University. In any given year more than 20,000 graduate students from Taiwan are studying in American universities. As a result, much of Taiwan's intellectual elite takes for granted the correctness of concepts such as democracy and human rights.

Fourth, even though the people of Taiwan were inexperienced in democracy before 1950, they have been able to observe the different results of Communist and democratic systems. The economic success stories of Asia are found not in Communist countries but in countries practicing some form of democracy. These observations reinforced Taiwan's belief that its future well-being depends on a democratic form of government.

Because of these domestic factors, the government of Taiwan is sensitive to international pressure to increase democracy. With few exceptions the question on Taiwan has been *when* to implement political reform, not whether the goal is democracy.

### Influence of the International Environment on Political Reform

With these observations in mind, it is possible to cite at least five kinds of influence of the international environment on the development of democracy in Taiwan.

1. The challenges Taiwan faces in its international security and political environments have made it very sensitive to the effects of democratization on its relations with the United States and the PRC. In both cases the incentives to become more democratic are stronger than the incentives to remain authoritarian.

In the case of the United States, the judgment has been that more democracy would lead to stronger United States support. The administration of Ronald Reagan quietly urged Taiwan to lift martial law, legalize opposition political parties, and improve human rights. Recent moves toward democracy in the Philippines and South Korea highlight the urgency of these private administration appeals for more democracy on Taiwan.

Although it is difficult to quantify, there has been a relationship between the growth of democracy in the Philippines, South Korea, and Taiwan. All three countries maintain close military, political, and economic ties with the United States. All three were governed by strong leaders whose authoritarian style of leadership was increasingly at odds with their societies. When the Corazon Aquino government came to power in February 1986, there was immediate speculation that similar democratic revolutions might occur in South Korea and Taiwan. The opposition in both countries took heart at the Philippine experience and increased the pressure for democratic reform. Similarly, President Chun Doo Hwan and President Chiang may have learned from the negative example of President Ferdinand Marcos and elected voluntarily to permit greater democratization in their countries. The effect was that in 1986–1987 both South Korea and Taiwan experienced relatively peaceful democratic revolutions that completely changed the political climate in the two countries.

Complementing the private urging of the Reagan administration for greater democracy on Taiwan and the intangible influence resulting from the Aquino revolution in the Philippines, pressure has been mounting from Congress and the media to liberalize Taiwan's political system. It is no coincidence that Chiang chose to announce the lifting of martial law to *Washington Post* chairman Katharine Graham in October 1986. Nor is it an accident that Representative Stephen Solarz in his several hearings on implementing the Taiwan Relations Act inevitably centered testimony on human rights in Taiwan. Solarz frequently argues that if Taiwan becomes a democracy, the United States will feel a greater moral obligation to come to its assistance in an emergency.

In the case of the PRC, democratization on Taiwan may strengthen Taipei's hand in dealing with the sensitive issue of reunification. Certainly, the international community is less likely to press a democratic Taiwan to join the Communist mainland than it would a Taiwan under an authoritarian regime. There may also be something to Taipei's claim that democratization will help make Taiwan a political as well as an economic model for the PRC. Taiwan's success in political reform contrasts sharply with Beijing's limited success in this regard. To some extent this favorable comparison enhances Taiwan's international image at the PRC's expense. As a bargaining strategy, democracy might unify the interests of the mainlanders and Taiwanese on Taiwan. Should this be the case, Taipei would present to the PRC a much stronger united front in any possible discussions over the future of Taiwan.[6]

2. The international economic environment has indirectly influenced the development of democracy on Taiwan by helping to create a strong, educated middle class. This has occurred as Taiwan's export-driven economy has produced phenomenal growth. Taiwan's 20 million inhabitants produce a $100-plus billion economy. Per capita GNP in 1988 was $6,000—the fourth highest in Asia—and the distribution of national wealth is one of the most equitable in the world. The ratio of the income of the lowest 20 percent of the population to that of the highest 20 percent is about 1:4.

As a middle class has emerged on Taiwan, demands have increased for a more open society. The middle class expects the KMT and the government to be more accountable for their actions. Members of this class generally approve of political checks and balances, including opposition political parties and meaningful elections. The middle class, therefore, has been an essential lobbying force for the development of democracy on Taiwan.

3. Rather than succumbing to a siege mentality, Taiwan has used

its success in dealing with international challenges to build up a healthy self-confidence. This confidence has enabled Taiwan's leaders to proceed with rapid democratization, despite genuine fears on the part of some that national security or social stability might be adversely effected. The United States can take a certain amount of credit for this process, because Washington's policies have contributed greatly to Taiwan's self-confidence. Policies that have been especially useful in this regard include efforts to provide Taiwan with adequate defensive equipment and technology, to support Taiwan's participation in international organizations, to maintain an open U.S. market for Taiwan's goods, and to encourage U.S. investment in Taiwan's industries.

4. The international environment has influenced the development of democracy on Taiwan by supporting political competition between the KMT and opposition political parties. One of the demands of *tang-wai* opposition to the KMT has been for greater democracy. This demand has been supported in the United States, where members of the Democratic Progressive party (DPP) and other opposition representatives have generally received a sympathetic response. The international support given the *tang-wai* has included financial contributions, political advice, and strong appeals for the lifting of martial law and the legalization of opposition political parties.[7]

5. Finally, the international environment has contributed to the development of democracy on Taiwan by providing several models of representative government. Taiwan's educated elite has been widely exposed to Western political systems. Moreover, Taipei has sent trained political scientists to various democratic countries such as the United States, Great Britain, and Japan to inquire into the mechanics of representative government. Unlike other third world countries in which events have outraced political institutions, Taiwan has experienced a democratization that has to a remarkable extent been planned and implemented by design rather than by accident or reaction.

### Changes in the International Environment

If the international environment remains roughly as defined, democracy will take firm root on Taiwan. The first elections on the island were held in 1950, and elections have increased in frequency and political relevancy—if slowly—ever since. Most people of Taiwan are convinced that a democratic system is best for their country and want to see the recent reforms succeed and be expanded. A survey of 1,111 people conducted in early 1988 revealed that 72 percent approved of President Lee's becoming chairman of the KMT and nearly 50 percent felt that democratization would be accelerated under his administration. The only difference between mainlanders and Taiwanese reflected in the poll was that mainlanders preferred a gradual restructuring of Taiwan's parliamentary system to reflect greater democracy while Taiwanese wanted a more rapid democratization.[8]

Progress toward democracy might be set back and replaced by an authoritarian regime under certain conditions. Three scenarios come to mind.

First, the PRC might take over Taiwan by force and impose Communism on the island. This might occur if the PRC decided to attack Taiwan and overwhelmed its defenses, the United States did not intervene on Taiwan's behalf, and the PRC decided to communize Taiwan rather than allow its present system to exist under the one-country, two-systems formula.

Beijing has said it would use force against Taiwan under several circumstances. These were summarized by Chinese scholar Huan Guocang: "If Taibei leaned toward Moscow instead of Washington; if Taibei decided to develop nuclear weapons; if Taiwan claimed to be an independent state; if Taibei lost internal control as a result of the succession process; or if Taibei continued to reject reunification talks for a long period of time.' "[9]

Second, Taiwan's military leaders might stage a coup and establish a military-dominated government. A military coup might occur if a severe threat to national security emerged from Taiwan independence elements or the PRC, the armed forces felt the civilian leadership was not responding adequately to the threat, the Taiwanese rank and file in the army supported the coup, and strong support for the coup was found within elements of the KMT. Once the crisis had passed, the military would be under strong pressure to return the government to civilian rule. Given the high professionalism of Taiwan's military officers, there is little likelihood of this scenario's occurring, except under the most severe conditions where military leaders became convinced that national survival required their intervention.

Third, the KMT might reimpose a civilian dictatorship. This might occur if a national emergency arose because of a PRC threat or because the opposition paralyzed the political process, a consensus on the move was found within the KMT leadership, and the armed forces supported the KMT decision. Again, once the reason for the dictatorship had subsided, pressure would mount for democracy to be reestablished.

Given the enormous efforts of the KMT to liberalize Taiwan's political system over the past few years, such an occurrence seems highly unlikely. The one factor that gives such a scenario credibility

99

is the confrontational politics occasionally engaged in by the DPP and other opposition political parties. Democracy is a delicate political system, requiring some agreement on the "rules of the game" to conduct government business efficiently. For democracy to work on Taiwan, the opposition must not destabilize the society in its search for power.

The possibility that any of the three scenarios will occur is remote. The circumstances under which they might occur fly in the face of current trends. The PRC is not posing an immediate military threat to Taiwan; independence for Taiwan seems to be losing its appeal; most elements of the DPP and other opposition parties seem willing to work within the political system; the military is less inclined to become directly involved in domestic politics; United States–Taiwan relations are as strong as ever; the KMT is moving toward greater democracy; and the situation on Taiwan remains highly stable.

In the influence of the international environment on these scenarios, the key factors seem to be the attitude and action of the PRC and the United States. If these countries maintain their present policies—as their individual interests would seem to dictate—then the likelihood that any of the three scenarios will occur is slim.

### Relationship of the International Environment and Domestic Factors

There is a complex relationship between international and domestic factors in the process of democratization on Taiwan. On the one hand, the international environment provides ROC leaders with several democratic models. This has been very important at certain stages, especially in the formative years on mainland China and during reconstruction on Taiwan in the 1950s.

In addition to providing models and training for democracy, the international environment puts pressure on Taiwan to democratize more quickly. This pressure assumes several forms, the most important being U.S. appeals to liberalize the political system. Even subtle pressure from the United States is a powerful force for democracy because of Taiwan's heavy dependence on the United States for defense, political, economic, and moral support.

Another international pressure for democracy stems from Taiwan's competition with China. The PRC has enjoyed a positive image as a result of Deng Xiaoping's pursuit of "peaceful reunification," the Four Modernizations, and improved relations with the West. The need to counter the PRC image with that of a more progressive and successful Taiwan plays some role in Taiwan's democratization. If statements by officials are any indication, the desire to make Taiwan a political as well as an economic model for the future of China is one of the most important reasons for the recent liberalization of the political system.[10]

As important as these international pressures are, the determination to pursue democracy resides mostly within the people of Taiwan. It is doubtful that outside pressure alone could force Taiwan's leaders to democratize the political system. In the 1980s the international environment supports this process and may occasionally influence the pace of reforms, but the commitment to democracy has long existed on Taiwan. Both the international and the domestic environments of the ROC contribute to the development of democracy, but the influence of the domestic environment is the stronger.

# PART TWO
# South Korea

# 6
# Political Developments in the Republic of Korea

*Daryl M. Plunk*

A new political era has dawned in the Republic of Korea (ROK). In mid-1988, tensions between the government and its political opponents reached a fever pitch and resulted in the June upheaval that threatened not only the vitality of the Chun Doo Hwan administration but also the nation's very stability. But in a remarkable turnaround, the Korean government made drastic concessions to the opposition, which led in December of that year to the first direct presidential election in sixteen years, the first orderly transition of political power in modern times, and the adoption of a new and more democratic constitution. Although the Korean people are well known for the great strides they have made in national development over the past four decades, political liberalization has remained the unwritten chapter in their success story. The ROK is now making progress in its political arena commensurate with its achievements in social and economic development.

By almost any yardstick, the ROK is seemingly well equipped for the task of discarding the authoritarian practices and institutions of the past and broadening the base of political participation. South Korea is blessed with the requisite national characteristics that allow for and, at the same time, require democratization.[1] Among these are its highly educated and motivated citizenry, its strong economy, and its growing importance in the international community.

Moreover, given the remarkable transition that took place during 1987–1988, most indications bode well for the eventual success of the continuing democratization process. There remain, however, significant challenges and obstacles. The quest for "national reconciliation" has been targeted as an immediate requirement for domestic political tranquillity. This includes resolution of a variety of contentious issues such as the smoldering personal animosities among the key political

105

leaders, charges of corruption and abuse of power during the Chun years, and an alarming increase in regional frictions in the ROK.

Other more fundamental challenges loom on the horizon. One is the power restructuring mandated by the new Sixth Republic Constitution. The authority of the presidency has been restricted while the national legislature's power has been strengthened, a change that takes on added significance in light of the outcome of the April 26, 1988, National Assembly election.

A number of important institutions will undergo catharsis as they become more tightly woven into the ROK's political fabric. These include the press, political parties, labor unions, big business, and other interest groups. The result will be an unprecedented opening of the government's decision-making process to popular debate. Upon the occasion of his swearing-in ceremony in February 1988, President Roh Tae Woo pledged that from then on "everyone, not just a single person, . . . [would] have a say in what is good for the country."

## The Road to Reform

To understand where the ROK is heading, we will find it useful to consider the whirlwind of political events that unfolded during the mid to late 1980s. In the 1985 National Assembly election, the New Korea Democratic party (NKDP), which was led by the two most prominent opposition figures, Kim Young Sam and Kim Dae Jung, emerged as the largest and most outspoken opposition bloc in the legislature. The key change sought by the NKDP was elimination of the indirect electoral college system embodied in the Fifth Republic Constitution. Charging that the system could easily be manipulated by the government, opposition leaders called for a constitutional amendment allowing for direct election of the next president.

Throughout 1985, the Chun government took a very hard line, refusing even to discuss constitutional reform. Chun said that discussion about such reforms would have to wait until he left office in 1988. In response, the NKDP launched a petition campaign and held a series of rallies advocating constitutional revision. These actions attracted significant domestic support and foreign encouragement. When the ROK government declared the signature drive unconstitutional, for instance, the U.S. State Department spoke out in favor of the universal right to assembly and right to petition the government.[2]

Chun's government bowed to this pressure, saying that it would allow "study" of reforms in preparation for eventual constitutional change in 1989. Not satisfied, the NKDP persisted in calling for revision during Chun's term and was bolstered by support from various social and religious groups. In April 1986, Chun unexpectedly declared his support for any constitutional change endorsed in the National Assembly, saying that if such changes were to win Assembly approval, a new constitution could be in place by late 1987, when the next election was to take place.

Soon, the position of the ruling Democratic Justice party (DJP) solidified into advocacy for a parliamentary system with a strong prime minister elected by the legislature. Many of the ROK's past political dilemmas, the ruling party claimed, were brought about by excessive centralization of executive power. A prime minister could effectively be checked by the Assembly.[3]

As the debate raged on, many South Koreans and foreign observers suspected that the diametrically opposed positions had less to do with democracy than they did with power politics: NKDP leaders felt they could prevail in a one-on-one race while the DJP believed it could win enough Assembly elections either to govern or at least to play a powerful role in a coalition government.

The standoff intensified throughout 1986 with neither side showing inclination toward compromise or even discussion. Hoping to mobilize the sort of "people power" that brought the anti-Marcos opposition to power in Manila, the NKDP took to the streets on several occasions with large political rallies in support of their cause. The government's response was usually to orchestrate massive displays of force, which sent a strong message that it was in control and not in danger of fleeing as Marcos did from Malacanang.

On April 13, 1987, President Chun addressed the country, saying that, since "efforts to amend the constitution by consensus so ardently desired by the public have not made even an inch of headway" and that the ten months left in his tenure were scarcely enough time to "carry out the necessary political agenda and make practical preparations for a change of government," he had decided "to put constitutional change on hold."

At the time the infamous April 13 decision by Chun to end the debate on constitutional revision was considered a monumental mistake even by DJP insiders. While it is true that the Korean people had become disenchanted to some extent by the politicized squabbling between the government and the opposition over the Constitution, Chun nevertheless underestimated the desire of the people for basic reform and a strong voice in choosing the next president. Chun's repeated pledges to leave office at the end of his term were simply not enough.

On June 10, the DJP held its national convention and nominated party president Roh Tae Woo as its candidate for the upcoming electoral college election, a move viewed by many as the anointing of Chun's hand-picked successor. Within a few days, hundreds of thousands of students had taken to the streets in the worst political demonstrations of Chun's tenure. Groping for a way out, Chun met with Kim Young Sam, president of the reorganized main opposition party, the Reunification Democracy party (RDP), on June 24 and offered concessions that Kim dismissed as too little, too late. By then, rioting had become so widespread that many feared the imposition of martial law.

Then came the stunning June 29 televised speech by ruling party head Roh announcing that the DJP had accepted virtually all the opposition's demands. While he pledged to resign if President Chun refused to carry out the reforms, the next day Chun announced his agreement with Roh's plan. The stage was set for constitutional reform and an open and direct presidential election.[4]

There has been considerable speculation over the events and motivations surrounding the June 29 declaration. Revelations later supported the assumption at the time that Roh made the move without the prior blessing of Chun. While Roh continued to harbor doubts that a direct presidential election and other basic reforms would act as a panacea for Korean democratization, it was clear to him that Chun's April 13 blunder so enraged the people that, short of declaring martial law, only a major act of political concession by the government could restore order in the streets. Overlooked by some analysts at the time was that Roh's bold move received strong backing from powerful military figures who urged him to act.

### Race for the Blue House

Despite having been successful in achieving their long-sought demands, rivalry between the two Kims quickly intensified, and in October Kim Dae Jung pulled out of the RDP to form the Peace and Democracy party (PDP). Although a split opposition obviously handed the DJP a valuable advantage, the Kims announced their intentions to run on competing tickets. In fact, during the final days leading up to the December 16 vote, the Kims' attacks upon each other were as strident as those made against Roh.

This undoubtedly contributed to their demise. As late as early December, many, including DJP campaigners, sensed that Roh's candidacy was a long shot as he was being besieged by heated criticism and press coverage of his prominent role in the birth and administration of the unpopular Chun government. The final weeks of the campaign, however, were also characterized by harsh words between the Kims, creating considerable popular concern that divisive wrangling within the opposition might lead to similar strife within the next government in the event of an opposition victory.

Roh went on to win the election with about 37 percent of the total vote while Kim Young Sam and Kim Dae Jung trailed with 27 and 26 percent, respectively. In an impressive comeback from seven years of political limbo, Park Chung Hee-era heavyweight Kim Jong Pil drew about 8 percent of the vote and began his emergence as a significant new opposition force.[5]

Kim Dae Jung and Kim Young Sam continue to charge that the election was rigged by the government, although no one has come forward with compelling evidence to back up these claims. Most observers, however, tend to discount the charges of massive vote fraud, given the lack of proof and the comfortable margin of Roh's victory. More important, the relative calm that has followed the vote and several public opinion polls showing high public confidence in Roh indicate that most Koreans are satisfied with the outcome of the election.

A breakdown of the vote reveals demographic characteristics that hold clues to future trends in ROK politics. A Korea Gallup survey[6] found Roh's constituency typified by older, less educated, and rural sectors of the population. Kim Dae Jung and Kim Young Sam appealed to younger, more educated voters, with Kim Young Sam faring well among white collar voters and Kim Dae Jung attracting many blue collar votes.

More telling, though, was the intense regionalism reflected in the vote. Roh and the three Kims were all strong winners in their respective home provinces, with Kim Dae Jung securing an amazing 93 percent of the vote in his home base of South Chollado. Even Kim Jong Pil, despite years of political obscurity, won a 42 percent plurality in South Chungchung Province.[7]

### The Sixth Republic

A priority of President-elect Roh was to begin building a leadership image in sharp contrast to the rigid and impersonal style of Chun Doo Hwan. The press made much of Roh's promise to be an "ordinary president" for the "ordinary man." During media interviews, he impressed reporters with his casual style and easygoing manner. Roh announced that he would be transported around the capital city not by the American limousine used by Chun but rather in a Korean-made car. At his inauguration on February 25, many of the 25,000 invited guests were "ordinary people including street sweepers, factory workers and housewives," according to the *Korea Herald*. A few days later, "He invited hundreds of people, including cured lepers, to Chong Wa Dae [the presidential compound] and showed them around the vast complex."[8]

All of this amounted to a public relations masterpiece that seemed to make quite an impact. By early March, DJP officials were boasting that public opinion surveys placed Roh's approval rating at well over 50 percent.[9] Beyond these stylistic reforms, the new president set out to establish his preliminary policy agenda. In his inaugural address, Roh pledged to follow "a new chart of democracy and a new compass of national reconciliation." Noting that "growing disparities among social strata and geographical regions have bred strife and schism," he promised economic reform. He promised an end to authoritarianism and the beginning of the "age of the ordinary people."[10]

Roh's first significant political act was the formation of a new cabinet in mid-February. His choice of a university administrator and political novice, Lee Hyun Jae, as prime minister raised expectations that the Roh government would be characterized by fresh faces and a break with the jaded Fifth Republic. Many Koreans expressed disappointment, however, when Roh eventually retained eight incumbent ministers in his twenty-five-member cabinet. The emerging government was dubbed by some the "5.5 Republic." Roh's cabinet choices were, in fact, not really surprising. While many of them had indeed held important posts under the Chun government, they were also some of Roh's closest advisers and staunchest supporters. And while many Koreans have long harbored fears that former president Chun planned to remain a powerful force behind the scenes, ROK political realities dictated otherwise. Once out of the Blue House, Chun soon began to fade into the pages of Korean political history.

Still, undoubtedly stung by the criticism over the cabinet appointments, the DJP announced that 28 of its 160 incumbent legislators had been dropped from the party slate of nominees for the April National Assembly elections. Those cut from the party roster included some with reputations as close Chun allies. The Korean press labeled the purge the "Friday massacre of Fifth Republic men."[11]

The Roh administration moved swiftly to address one of the most explosive political issues: the 1980 Kwangju upheaval. In May of that year, citizens of this southwestern provincial capital demonstrated in opposition to the declaration of martial law and the growing political authority of then General Chun Doo Hwan. Bloody clashes between soldiers and civilians eventually left at least 200 dead. Kim Dae Jung, whose power base includes Kwangju, was later convicted of sedition in connection with the uprising but was granted amnesty by the government after Roh's June 29 initiative. Reemerging as a powerful opposition force, Kim has demanded an investigation of the 1980 tragedy.[12]

One of Chun Doo Hwan's biggest political mistakes was his refusal to allow public scrutiny of the Kwangju uprising. He apparently believed that, in time, the memory of the clash would fade. In fact, the Chun administration's refusal to discuss the incident simply aggravated public resentment, particularly among citizens of Cholla Province, and perpetuated doubts about the official account released by the government. In February, Roh appointed an ad hoc committee of private citizens and directed them to make suggestions designed to soothe the wounds of the Kwangju incident. Responding to the committee's recommendations, on April 1 the government expressed regret over the affair, calling it "part of the democratization efforts of the students and citizens of Kwangju." It was announced that a national commission would be established to offer financial support and medical services to the wounded and to families of the casualties. Government funds would also be made available for construction of a monument in the cemetery where many of the victims are buried. The recommendations did not include a call for an official investigation.[13]

Roh also allowed another previously taboo subject to be the subject of public scrutiny: official corruption. In mid-March, news was leaked to the press that Chun Kyung Hwan, younger brother of former President Chun, was being investigated on charges relating to various irregularities. The younger Chun had served from 1981 to 1987 as head of the Saemaul Movement, a semipublic agency involved in rural development projects. On March 31, Chun Kyung Hwan was arrested along with several of his former aides and charged with influence peddling, tax evasion, and embezzlement. The swift investigation of the Saemaul affair was obviously an attempt by the Roh administration to prove its commitment to clean government. In addition, it suggested to the public that the new government was not going to cover up the excesses of the previous regime. Finally, the anticorruption campaign had the added benefit of ending once and for all any suspicions that former President Chun would wield significant political power behind the scenes, as many of his critics had charged. In fact, Chun reacted to the scandal by publicly apologizing for his brother's actions and resigning from his last two remaining official posts—honorary president of the ruling DJP and head of the governmental Advisory Council of Elder Statesmen.

## National Assembly Elections

These events set the stage for the April 26, 1988, National Assembly elections. Most political analysts generally agreed that the ruling party was on a strong footing and, with most Koreans apparently approving of the new government's performance, predicted that the DJP would easily secure a majority of seats in the 299-seat legislature. The pundits were wrong. In results reminiscent of the presidential race, the DJP received only about 33 percent of the popular vote and 125 of the seats in the Assembly, 24 short of a majority. For the first time since the early 1950s, the ruling party lost its control of the legislature. In another surprising development, Kim Dae Jung's Peace and Democracy party emerged as the dominant opposition force in the Assembly with 70 seats. Kim Young Sam's Reunification and Democracy party captured only 59 spots, despite outpolling the PDP in total popular votes. The RDP and the PDP received 23.7 percent and 19.2 percent of the vote, respectively. Kim Jong Pil's New Democratic Republican party (NDRP) confirmed its status as a formidable new opposition force by winning 35 seats. Since no single party held a majority, the NDRP functioned as an important swing bloc.[14]

It is interesting to note that the ruling party's performance in the recent election was comparable to that of the 1985 Assembly contest. Then, DJP candidates received about 35 percent of the total vote nationwide, just two percentage points above their 1988 showing. Bolstered by a multimember legislative district system that tended to favor the ruling party, however, in 1985 the DJP was able to hold on to a solid 54 percent majority in the Assembly. The 1988 switch to a single-member district plan clearly worked to the DJP's disadvantage. As it did in the December 1987 election, regionalism played a significant role in the Assembly elections. The DJP dominated Roh's home province of North Kyungsang as did Kim Jong Pil's party in South Chungchung. Kim Young Sam took all but one of the fifteen seats in his native Pusan and ran strongly in surrounding South Kyungsang Province. Kim Dae Jung's forces exhibited the staunchest regional loyalty by giving Kim's PDP thirty-one of the thirty-two seats in North and South Cholla Provinces. Except for the PDP's strong showing in Seoul, the new home of many Cholla natives, Kim Dae Jung's party won no races outside his home region in the southwest.

## New Political Rules

Roh Tae Woo's June 1987 concessions cleared the way for a fast-paced reform process, which has drastically reshaped the ROK political landscape and opened a new and unpredictable chapter in Korean politics. The Sixth Republic Constitution, which was hastily written in negotiations among political parties late in 1987, outlines some of the new rules that mandate significant changes in the government's decision-making process as well as other aspects of social and political life in Korea.[15] Major reforms required by the new constitution include:

- stipulation that the armed forces must remain politically neutral
- strengthening of the rights of the accused and restoration of the right of *habeas corpus*
- enhanced press freedoms; prohibition of prior approval and censorship; an end to licensing of the media
- promotion of workers' rights; lifting of restrictions on the freedom to unionize and bargain collectively; establishment of a national minimum wage system

The most significant constitutional reforms change the intragovernmental balance of power, with the National Assembly assuming new authority and the presidency subjected to new checks. Restored are the investigative powers of the legislature. The Assembly is also given the right to pass motions calling for removal of cabinet members, including the prime minister. While such legislative action is technically nonbinding, it is likely that a president could ignore such recalls only at great political peril. Moreover, a president can be impeached by a two-thirds vote of the Assembly.

The tenure of a president is limited to a single, five-year term. An amendment to this provision cannot apply to the president in office at the time of its proposal. Discarded is the chief executive's right to dissolve the National Assembly (despite his right to do so, President Chun never exercised this authority). The scope of the president's power to decree emergency measures is narrowed, and such actions by the Blue House can be revoked by a majority vote of the National Assembly.

Under the previous constitution, the president appointed the chief justice of the Supreme Court with the consent of the Assembly. Other justices were chosen by the chief justice with no input from the legislative branch. The new guidelines stipulate, however, that the legislature must approve all the high court's justices. Moreover, while in the past the chief justice alone appointed all other national judges, lower judges must now be chosen with the consent of the entire high court. These changes should work to enhance the independence of the ROK judiciary.

## Outlook for Democracy

The events culminating in the April 1989 legislative elections re-shaped ROK politics and decision making. Accordingly, some of the nation's institutions will experience a growth of their influence while others must become accustomed to limitations on their power. The Korean press will be central to this evolution. The ROK media, particularly the daily newspapers, have tested the limits of the government's patience for several years and have already become more free and independent from governmental control than most foreign observers realized. For instance, the death by torture of a student at the hands of police in early 1987, which hastened the pace of events leading to the Roh concessions of June, was exposed by a Korean reporter.[16] Also, the media first exposed the Saemaul scandal involving President Chun's brother and subsequently covered the story in great detail.

The press has shaken off virtually all remnants of control by the government, a new-found freedom protected by the Constitution. Gone is the requirement that magazines and newspapers must be officially licensed, leading to the birth of many new publications. Gone, too, is the daily "press guidance" from the government information agency, which had a chilling effect on the reporting and editorial policies of major publications. All this suggests that the Korean media, like their counterparts in the United States and other modern democracies, will achieve the status of a powerful watchdog institution capable of having an enormous impact on public opinion and thus become a formidable political force.

While it is true that the print media are now virtually free from all the limitations previously imposed by the government, the broadcast media present a very different situation. For one thing, one of the two television networks is state owned, and its political reporting has been heavily influenced by the government. While the second network is private, its coverage of contentious political issues is not known for being aggressive. Control and management of the airways in a manner that allows for press freedom and, at the same time, promotes the public interest will certainly arise as a topic of debate on the National Assembly's agenda.[17]

The new vitality of workers and their labor unions will have a profound influence not only on domestic politics but also on the nation's economy. After the June 1987 liberalizations, Korea experienced an unprecedented period of labor strife, during which there were 3,600 wildcat strikes around the country. In most cases, workers demanded the unfettered right to unionize along with double-digit wage hikes. In the new spirit of the times, the government stayed out of the frays, allowing individual companies to deal with the challenges, in sharp contrast to the past when labor activities were often met by riot police. There were great concerns in many quarters that the unrest and resulting concessions would have an adverse effect on economic performance, but the economy in general and ROK exports in particular registered impressive gains in 1987.

Labor disputes continued into 1988 but at a fraction of the intensity of the previous summer's strife. In late April, the Labor Ministry reported that there were about 100 disputes in progress. The unions for the most part turned away from violence and street clashes and opted for more sophisticated methods, many of which they learned during the winter in training programs conducted by American and other foreign labor groups. The workers' efforts have reaped considerable return: ROK wages in real terms rose 18 percent in the year beginning October 1987.[18]

As important precedents are being established, labor and management will continue to test the limits of this new process. Of concern to all Koreans is the well-being of the economy and its ability to remain competitive in international markets. This is particularly true given the ongoing appreciation of the *won* against the dollar, a trend that will make ROK goods more expensive in Korea's largest export market. From September 1985 to September 1988, the Korean currency appreciated 25 percent.[19]

The changes in the economic arena are not limited to labor. In addition to the demands for a loosening of the reigns on workers, the business community is also asserting its rights. On May 3, 1988, Koo Cha Kyung, chairman of the huge Lucky-Goldstar Group as well as head of the Federation of Korean Industries, called for broader "economic democracy." Given Korea's economic vitality and sustained current account surpluses, Koo called on the government to allow market forces and private sector decision making to guide the ROK's economic policies. Specifically, he asked the government to end its tight control over business loans and foreign currency supplies.[20] On the same day, a presidential advisory commission sounded a similar theme. In its report on economic restructuring, the commission noted that economic policy is most efficient when dictated by market forces rather than by government decree.[21]

Central to virtually all these rapid changes wrought by Korea's democratization will be the new and more equitable balance of power emerging within the ROK government. The National Assembly will undergo the most dramatic transformation. Lacking a majority bloc, the ruling party must secure opposition support for even its most modest initiatives. President Roh sent the requisite signals of reconciliation and flexibility by announcing that, for the first time, opposition parties would be offered important Assembly leadership posts, including committee chairmanships. On June 20, 1988, an agreement was reached giving opposition parties nine of the sixteen Assembly committee chairs.[22]

At least for the short term, though, several unresolved and divisive issues will take their toll on relations among the parties led by Roh and the three Kims. All three Kims were purged from political life when the Chun forces took power in 1980 and may believe they have scores to settle. This may be particularly true of Kim Dae Jung, who at one time was under a death sentence for activities related to the Kwangju upheaval and spent several years in prison during the Chun years. In fact, Kim, who emerged from the Assembly election as the main opposition leader, soon took the political offensive. He minced no words and referred to the Roh government as a "military regime," which "lacks legitimacy."[23] True to campaign pledges made to his constituents in Cholla Province, Kim pushed for a full-scale investigation of the Kwangju incident. In August 1988 a national special committee was formed to investigate the 1980 bloodshed. Other items on Kim's agenda included the release of all those still imprisoned for their political activities and an end to the domestic operations of state intelligence agencies.

Another National Assembly investigative body was convened in July 1988 to focus on the allegations of corruption during the Chun administration. Evidence clearly suggests that the government supported and even encouraged the initial investigations that led to the arrest, conviction, and imprisonment of, among others, Chun's brother and the former mayor of Seoul on corruption charges. The investigations will no doubt result in future revelations and indictments.

The October 2 closing of the Seoul Olympics marked the end of an uneasy political ceasefire that had existed for several months between the Roh government and its critics. A month later, the future of former President Chun had become the rallying point of renewed violent student demonstrations around the nation, a development that prompted opposition politicians to step up their demands for a full accounting by Chun. While some called simply on the former leader to apologize for the actions of his imprisoned brother and others from his administration implicated in wrongdoing, others pressed for a criminal investigation of Chun himself.

By November, ruling party officials were working behind the scenes to ask Chun's assistance in defusing the crisis. Roh loyalists worried that public discontent over the previous government's actions would eventually take its toll on Roh's popularity. On November 8, DJP sources leaked word to the press that Chun would be willing to surrender all his estimated $5.7 million in assets, although it remained unclear whether Chun would admit to any personal wrongdoing.[24] (That he did later, in 1989.)

In an interview with the *Wall Street Journal* in early May, 1988,[25] the new president said he intended to hold the opposition to an agreement not to seek revenge against the former first family. Roh felt a strong compulsion to protect his mentor, who, his supporters believe, for all his faults, greatly contributed to the nation's development and lived up to his promise to leave office at the end of his term. In the event of a frontal assault on Chun by the opposition, Roh would have to walk a fine line between loyalty to his friend, on the one hand, and fulfilling his anticorruption pledges, on the other. Therein may lie the single most difficult challenge for the new president. Getting beyond these sensitive issues is not likely to be a smooth process.

## Conclusion

Adding to these strains is the alarming rise of regionalism in ROK politics. Results of the presidential and National Assembly elections suggest that none of the major political parties enjoy broad national support but rather find their cohesion in loyalties to favorite sons. The influential *Dong-A Ilbo* newspaper in Seoul lamented this "most painful" reality, noting "the nation's division into four major areas."

With the passing of time and the institutionalization of functioning democracy, these fierce loyalties centered on regional power bosses should fade, and Korea could experience a realignment of its political parties. Eventually Korean voters ought to base their affiliations more on considerations of issues and political philosophy. Stripped of their regional biases, the Korean electorate is much more homogeneous than the current divisions suggest. A vast majority of the people share basic values such as support for capitalism, staunch anticommunism, a desire for a strong national defense, and support for close relations with the United States and other Western bloc allies. Despite the considerable attention given by the foreign press to the growing radicalism of some dissident groups in the ROK, most Koreans have no taste for extremism. Hence, once regional strains and other divisive characteristics that have developed over the past four decades of confrontational politics have begun to fade, it is quite conceivable that Korea will gradually move toward a situation like Japan's in which a single party dominates the political scene.

Finally, as the Korean people achieve greater input in their nation's decision-making, it will be necessary for them to be well informed about the world around them. The ROK must continue to cope with a hostile power on its northern border and, at the same time, to open the sensitive topics such as north-south relations, reunification policy, and close military cooperation with the United States to more public debate. Koreans will inevitably begin to reevaluate some of their popular notions about foreign policy, security affairs, and international trade, which are deeply rooted in outdated historical perceptions. The ways in which many Koreans view the world today remain strongly influenced by years of ROK underdevelopment and dependency, and their rapid progress toward achieving the coveted developed-nation status has not yet completely reshaped these old perceptions. For instance, although the ROK has become one of the world's most important trading powers and has begun to achieve substantial annual current account surpluses, Korean popular sentiment wrongly perceives U.S. demands for import liberalization as an insensitive attack by a powerful bully upon a helpless weakling. In the realm of international trade as well as in political and military relations with key allies such as the United States, Koreans must learn to accept both the privileges and the responsibilities that accompany the ROK's emergence as an important international player.

After years of turmoil and false starts, democracy is on the move in the Republic of Korea. The year 1988 was pivotal for the ROK. It began with the country's first orderly transfer of power and the implementation of a new and democratic blueprint for government. The year ended with the Seoul Olympic Games, giving a boost not only to the ROK's national development but also to its international stature and prestige. Basic conditions and trends influencing the ROK's political culture today bode well for Korean democratization.

Of course, institutional reform alone will not guarantee the success of Korea's transition to a more open political system. While over the years some have called for the "restoration" of democracy in Korea, the fact remains that Koreans have experienced precious little democracy. Since 1948, the ROK's chaotic history has seen little but authoritarianism and the politics of confrontation. After all, democracy is not simply a political system spelled out in a detailed constitution: it is also a process that allows differing views to achieve consensus on important national issues. Therein lies democracy's challenge for the ROK.

# 7
# Economic Developments in the Republic of Korea

*John T. Bennett*

As a framework for an analysis of democracy and economic development in Korea, two questions were posed: First, how will economic developments and possible changes affect recent and potential future gains for democracy in Korea? This question pertains both to current trends and to future developments, perhaps as yet unrecognized. Second, what generalized relationships exist between democratization and other variables affecting Korea's future?

In addressing the first of these two questions, we must accept the assumptions on which this volume is based: that there is a relationship between economics and democracy and that economic growth, at least that which is widely shared, promotes democracy. The relationship, however, is complex. It therefore makes sense not to address that aspect at the beginning but instead to return to it at the end.

The relationship between economic and political growth needs to be refined in another way. While economic development (or growth) may promote democracy, a pause in growth or even an absolute decline does not necessarily set the clock back. Thus, optimism about the future of Korean democracy is possible even if one concludes that Korea is unlikely to continue to grow rapidly.

## Economic Prospects and Dangers

In 1988 the Korean economy looked as strong as ever. Having grown 12 percent in 1986 and 1987 and seeming likely to continue, the Korean economy faced problems of success. Thus, in the short run, economic growth is likely to continue to provide a favorable context for democracy.

This section examines Korea's economic prospects in light of the major long-term economic dangers that lie ahead, namely:

119

- technology
- markets for exports
- world depression
- global automation
- changes in Korea's employment structure
- breakdown in labor-management relations
- inability to manage the economy

**Technology.** Korea has been able to grow rapidly—at 8.9 percent a year from 1962 to 1987—for a very simple reason: there has always been new technology readily available somewhere that would allow it to invest in a new product that added more value in Korea. While growth has been largest in manufacturing, it has been high in other sectors as well, compared with other countries. Thus, even agriculture grew 3.5 percent a year in the past sixteen years.[1] The ready availability of new technology was also central to the rapid development of the United States in the nineteenth century and in this century of Japan and the high-growth "new industrial economies"— Taiwan, Brazil, and Mexico.

Several points should be made about this phenomenon in Korea:

- In identifying technology as critical, we assume that other elements required for rapid growth have also been present: that labor and management could quickly master the newly acquired technology and that government or the private sector have done what was required to expand and multiply the effect of the new technology on total output. Many examples of failure in this respect can be found, including the Soviet Union today where *perestroika* has been the response to the inability of the country to exploit a great deal of technology to which it has had access.
- The ability to absorb any new technology depends on both the educational system and the job experience of the labor force. Others have remarked that the educational system in Korea rarely teaches job skills per se.[2] It does, however, teach people to read and write, skills that are key to learning other skills. Moreover, the educational system inculcates a code of conduct in Korean society based on the Korean version of Confucianism. This code seems to have played an important role in establishing labor discipline and dedication, making it the labor force that works the longest hours in the world, according to the International Labor Organization.[3]
- Mastering technology also depends, in the Korean case, on management's ability to concentrate on the production process and to ignore marketing problems. This seems to have been accomplished

because of the widespread use of contract manufacture. Contract manufacture, which also played a role in Japan and Taiwan, will continue to be important in Korea where it may account for as much as 40 percent of exports, although no one has made a careful estimate.

• In contract manufacture a foreign buyer comes to Korea to find a supplier that can manufacture cheaper than anyone else. This practice started when the U.S. armed forces found local sources for products cheaper than U.S. imports. This expanded to buying for the worldwide PX system. A complementary explanation is that after World War II, U.S. clothing and footwear manufacturers were having to pay rising wages but had little prospect of improving productivity. Retailers and chains therefore sought cheaper sources abroad.

• From the buyer's point of view, the secret of contract manufacture is to find a foreign labor force whose wages are relatively lower than its productivity. Such relatively high productivity usually exists alongside literacy and probably an ethical system that creates work force discipline. This is important, if one remembers that the Industrial Revolution seems to have had some initial difficulty taking hold in England because farmers were reluctant to go to work at a certain hour and stay until the working day was over.

• Contract manufacture also brings much technology with it. In particular, it frequently includes product technology in the specifications and design of the product (that is, a simple product, such as a man's shirt salable in the American market, has to have a certain appearance, and that style is likely to be different from country to country and is not easily learned in Korea). The technology it brings often requires more sophisticated elements as well, in the specification of materials (that is, the right metal for a tool) and the selection of the best machine to do the job.

• Increasingly, contract manufacture now takes the form of OEM contracts (producing under contract to the "original equipment manufacturer," such products as Delco alternators for General Motors or Carrier air conditioners), where the foreign buyer seeks a Korean source to save money and stay competitive. This phenomenon reflects the growing manufacturing sophistication of Korea, which is no longer simply producing clothing and footwear for name-brand distributors or chain stores. It is fortunate for Korea that this is so, as other countries now have low wage costs and can compete in producing those products.

Will contract manufacture continue to help fuel Korean growth? Probably, simply because rising wages in the developed countries lead them to seek replacement sources abroad. The alternative is to develop technology that lowers costs in the developed countries. As a result, there will be a cast-off technology that the developing country can often obtain at a low price. Its lower wages restore the competitiveness of the cast-off technology. Thus, trailing countries like Korea will still continue to benefit.

If Korea must depend on developing leading-edge technology on its own, however, one must be skeptical about how successful it will be in the short term. Korea has begun to try and has developed a program to promote science and technology, but it is still too small and has produced little so far that can be transformed into marketable products. The secret is not basic science, at which many Western countries excel, but the transformation of basic science into products that embody the new ideas. This is a phase in which the Japanese have distinguished themselves. The Japanese model has not been lost on the Koreans, so one can be optimistic over the longer run that they at least know what they must do.

One need not be discouraged by the lack of Korean technological development so far. For a variety of reasons, including the rising educational level and recognition of the need, one may reasonably expect Korean science and technology to become more productive over time.

In the interim, Korea has also begun to develop technology abroad. It has, for example, contract offices for electronic research in Silicon Valley. This effort has already been responsible for both chip and computer designs that have done very well in the American market.[4]

**Markets for Exports.** While contract manufacture has meant that Korean companies have not had to be concerned with marketing institutions or strategies and have not had to invest time or money in them, this situation is now beginning to change as several of the larger companies have begun marketing under their own brand names. They are following the path taken by the Japanese so successfully, and it appears now that the Koreans will be every bit as good at it, not so much because they are naturally skilled but because they are willing to invest in marketing. Perhaps the best example is Hyundai Motors, which markets in the United States as Hyundai America. It has developed a highly successful distributor network, largely financed by the dealers themselves.[5]

At another level, however, Koreans have rightly begun to worry about their dependence on the American market as it takes 40 percent of their exports. The problem is complicated by the huge U.S. trade deficit, which obviously cannot continue for too many more years. But the more fundamental problem has always existed: as Korean exports bulked larger in world markets, achievement of past levels of growth has become increasingly difficult.

Growing protectionism is widely expected to limit Korean growth, particularly in the American market. While such protectionism may occur, however, the declining dollar is more likely to cause exports to the United States to level off or decline. Protectionism cannot alter the U.S. trade deficit so long as it is being financed by net capital flows into the United States, drawn by the enormous budget deficit and exchange rates float in response to supply and demand.

Two solutions to the problem of long-term growth of Korea's export markets are obvious: switching to third-country markets or to the domestic market. In the foreseeable future, South Korea's domestic market will remain small, both in population (44 million) and in current income ($119 billion in gross national product or $2,861 per capita in 1988).[6] Still, it is growing rapidly and has crossed the line at which domestic expenditures on, for example, housing and cars, will become very important. Thus, at this point, one may reasonably expect that growth in the domestic market will contribute a good deal to offsetting lower growth in exports. Getting the balance right between exports and domestic sales may prove somewhat difficult to manage but is hardly beyond Korea's capacity. In the longer run, reduced hostility between the north and south might also provide a significant increase in demand.

Until recently, rapidly growing exports to non-U.S. markets looked unlikely. Japan's innate protectionism has remained hard to penetrate until the high yen made imports much more attractive. In addition, the high yen has taught Japanese manufacturers a lesson the United States has learned in the years since 1982 when the high dollar left its manufacturers little alternative but to have products and components made abroad or lose market share to foreign competition. While Western Europe looks attractive, though, it is both distant and protectionist, and the elimination of the last internal barriers in the European Economic Community by 1992 suggests that foreigners will have increasing difficulty selling there. Eastern Europe, where Korean marketing is just beginning, also has a great deal of potential, but many issues have yet to be resolved.

Asia, excepting Japan, is already Korea's second largest market after the United States. In this regard, China looms very large. The problem is to find creative ways by which these countries can pay for their imports. One way is through moving production of low-end

123

exports to these countries, as Korea loses its competitive advantage in their manufacture, while retaining the marketing function in the countries that are members of the Organization for Economic Cooperation and Development. Control of both technology and the marketing channels and skilled management will possibly permit Korean companies a significant role (and profits) in the development of this third-party trade.[7] This phenomenon is even now similar to the role Japanese general trading companies often play as a vital intermediary in Korea's exports.

**World Depression.** Another cause for worry on the world scene is the threat of a world depression as serious as that of the 1930s. This possibility may not be entirely independent of the adjustment problem implicit in correcting the American trade deficit, but for analysis it is helpful to think of them as independent.

Such a crash might have several components, including the collapse in the value of securities because debtors find they are unable to pay. It might also include a substantial rise in protectionism, as countries attempt to maintain output and employment by walling off their domestic markets from competitive imports. Although protectionism has increased in recent years, markets have remained sufficiently open that trade growth has not been stifled entirely. Such an all-encompassing system of beggar-my-neighbor policies would be bad enough, but it might be exacerbated by growing unwillingness to share technology and by various restraints imposed on capital flows, because of their effects on exchange rates and the resulting flow of goods.

In such a depression, Korea would be affected primarily by policies that restrict its exports and ability to obtain new technology. It should be able to pay off its foreign debt in the next few years, however, and establish a substantial balance of foreign investments, both in factories and in the portfolios owned by the private sector.[8] Its credit, therefore, would be restored, unless of course potential lenders foresaw that Korea would have difficulty repaying new debt.

Even should the Koreans face problems getting new technology, they are still likely to succeed, just as they did in the past when they were initially refused technology for steel making and for video cassette recorders. More important, at least for the foreseeable future, a large part of Korean exports is tied through contract manufacture to the fate of foreign companies. Thus, attempts by governments to protect their markets from Korean exports become next to impossible without hurting their own companies.

This depression scenario, however, assumes a degree of irrationality that is hard to credit, given what we know about the international financial system and about the economies that make it up. International financial institutions have, moreover, been created to handle such emergencies. In the past few years the evolution of international economic policy coordination among the largest economies is also a significant and hopeful development.[9] Finally, much of the international debt is denominated in U.S. dollars, and the United States is the big debtor in the system, so that it can sell U.S. assets or print more dollars to satisfy the demand.

Ultimately, however, most people will not feel secure from this nightmare scenario because of the oil shocks of the 1970s and the still-possible repudiation of international debt by many third world countries. Many are also aware that the maladjustments in the world economy are very great and that little has been done about them, despite widespread understanding of what needs to be done. This leaves one with a sense of the possibility of surprise. Still, Korea is likely to suffer no more than the average country and to adapt more quickly and successfully than most.

**Global Automation.** As automation technology continues to evolve, one may conclude that low-wage economies like Korea will be crippled and no longer able to export. In that case, their major customers will be capable of meeting all their needs from domestic output. Consider, for example, the possibility of automated garment manufacture. Those developing it appear to be getting closer to success. Already, manufacture of work clothing, which used to be done abroad, has come back to the United States because so little labor is in it.

The view that automation will destroy Korea's ability to export, however, ignores the existence of comparative advantage. While the United States (or Japan or any other country) may have an absolute advantage in producing everything, so long as Korea needs something from the United States, there is an exchange rate at which balanced trade will take place because it is to the advantage of both sides.

That automation will go to such an extreme also suggests that there will be no cost to the output—in which case, all goods can be given away and the quintessential economic problem, scarcity, will have disappeared. In fact, however, other kinds of labor than production employees will have to be paid and will therefore continue as a cost, as will capital.

Finally, one might infer that Korean real wages will drop disastrously because of extensive automation. That too, however, seems unlikely, because Koreans will have access to the same technology. If one foreign technology owner is unwilling to sell, others can almost always be found who are. And as a last resort, Korean scientists should be able to develop a similar technology themselves as their scientific prowess expands.

**Changes in Korea's Employment Structure.** Korea continues to experience two trends that may prove troublesome for its economy in the long run. One is the continued high (20 percent) though rapidly declining proportion of the labor force dependent on agriculture. The other is the high and growing proportion of high school graduates who choose to go to university (currently about 35 percent, as high as any developed country except the United States, where the proportion exceeds 50 percent).

These trends raise the possibility of insufficient jobs for either group. That concern has been the basis on which the Korean government limits university enrollments, not only in total but by professional field.[10] Similarly, the problem of finding jobs for farmers who wish to leave agriculture has been one justification for high farm price supports and other measures to preserve family farms (another justification being equity). Korean attempts to limit college enrollments have not been effective, however. Korean economists and consumers have now begun to question the high prices they pay for agricultural products in a glutted world market, and for the first time Korea faces threatened retaliation against the export of its manufactures if it does not open its markets to outside agricultural products.

The two trends in the labor market are largely offsetting, though. On the one hand, those who worry about the number of college graduates do so because the economy will be excessively rich in intellectuals and poor in manual workers. The drop in the farm population, on the other hand, should initially increase the supply of blue collar workers. The government policy of stimulating manufacturers to locate plants in rural areas is also intended to absorb surplus farm workers.

While conceding that the supply of college graduates is very high and approaches the U.S. proportion, the product mixture can possibly change and match the demand for labor to its supply. Failing that, either immigration or emigration may serve to solve the problem. In the past, Korean professionals have gone abroad when Korean demand for their services was too small. Or, like the United States, Europe, and now even Japan, Korea can import unskilled labor to perform those services its citizens find unpleasant or unrewarding and are no longer willing to do.

Automation and leisure constitute two avenues of adjustment to what really seems a consequence of success. The likely increase in automation just discussed suggests that having a high proportion of white collar workers is desirable.

**Breakdown in Labor-Management Relations.** Recent labor unrest suggests that past patterns of labor-management relations will not survive.[11] One view is that the government used to intervene on the side of management and limited trade union organization, suppressed wages, and prevented strikes. Given Korea's increasingly democratic practices, those approaches are no longer possible.

Even as one must recognize that government has not been neutral in labor-management relations, an overheated economy in the late 1970s and the labor unrest that occurred in the period after Park Chung Hee was assassinated did lead to a cycle of inflation and inflationary wage increases that threatened continued growth. In response, the government adopted wage guidelines and succeeded in stopping the wage-price spiral. But its role left it appearing anti-labor, in an apparent alliance with big business.

At a deeper level, the harmony supposed to exist between management and labor can arguably be said to have been destroyed. Workers want more of the benefits of growth, and many seem to think that trade unions will benefit them. They believe they have been exploited through poor working conditions, low wages, and long hours, and they would like to have an institution mediate between them and management.

Although the evidence is mixed, wages in manufacturing have probably kept up with productivity, and wages in other sectors have probably kept pace with those in manufacturing.[12] Certainly evidence shows that workers' real wages have grown a great deal, most often in response to competition for their services in a tight labor market. The existence of unemployed or underemployed workers in nonmanufacturing sectors of the economy does not change this conclusion; most of those workers cannot be employed in manufacturing because they lack the skills or because they cannot be induced to shift employment quickly enough to prevent demand from raising wages.

At the same time, economics teaches that as wages rise, leisure has greater value. The old days of working an average of fifty-two hours a week have perhaps past, particularly in view of the fact that this average contains weeks that are much longer than fifty-two hours. The problem for workers is to find a new relationship with management that allows them to say no, with some probability of success. Trade unions are known for that ability.

For many years, economists in Korea have been asking how long the work ethic (meaning "worker discipline") would last. It appears that experience has now answered that question. The conclusion that workers' new outlook will raise costs, however, is almost certainly premature. A change in work hours or wage rates will not preclude other avenues for increasing output or productivity, for instance, by using more capital equipment or hiring additional, perhaps part-time, workers. More likely, the changes will force improvements in management that achieve greater efficiency.

Although many have talked about radical politicization of the Korean trade union movement, there is little evidence that it will go very far.[13] Radical leaders have not done particularly well—some have succeeded for a time and were then replaced. Nor have union leaders who were identified with the more leftist political positions survived. Most workers seem to want recognition, better wages, and then better working conditions, including the right to be consulted on changes in the work place—and union leaders have responded to these interests. They give every evidence of sharing the American political tradition—supporting labor's friends. Indeed, in the 1988 National Assembly elections the Federation of Trade Unions supported some fifteen candidates who were identified as labor candidates, but they came from several different parties. Moreover, a legal limit remains on the Korean unions' ability to engage in politics. While they can encourage their members to support a candidate, they cannot support candidates directly or contribute money. It may also be that the authorities will find it inconvenient to enforce the law.

Many Koreans have also begun to ask themselves whether the emerging pattern of labor-management relations will resemble the confrontational mode of the United States or the cooperative pattern of Japan. Management, for example, is described as working hard to reestablish the sense of harmony by, among other things, intense socializing with workers. This approach has even come to the point where some middle managers complain of "soju stomach," resulting from the time spent drinking with their subordinates.

Such efforts seem to be a forced response, unlikely to succeed when the grievances are real. The residue of distrust from the past seven years of government-business "low wage" policy will not be easy to dispel. Thus, one may conclude that labor-management relations will be cooperative much of the time but may be punctuated by occasional outbursts of militant confrontation when workers become impatient. It is as if the Confucian ethic of social harmony prevails except for those occasions when Koreans have accumulated a reserve of outrage at what they perceive as unfair or exploitative—

and explode. This pattern seems much more likely than one in which management continuously and successfully generates a sense of fairness among its workers.

Nevertheless, labor problems seem unlikely to be the source of economic failure, primarily because business cannot pay more than labor contributes. If it does and tries to pass on its costs in higher prices, sales and exports will decline, and unemployment will result, which will take the pressure out of wage demands. At the same time, labor relations will, of course, be continuously influenced by the evolution of Korean democracy.

**Inability to Manage the Economy**. Much of Korea's economic success has been attributed to the sound management of the economy by government technocrats. Many have observed, however, that success will be more difficult in a democratic future because of the need to adjust policy to the conflicting claims of interest groups.

This conclusion assumes that policy must be continuously reformulated in response to constant changes in the economy, arising principally from the acquisition of new technology, shifting market demand, and new foreign competition. Korea has experienced such a need so far, and it seems likely to continue. The adjustment process, however, is often unpleasant for many of those affected. Nobody likes to be forced to move or change jobs or take additional training or see his wages cut, even temporarily. Thus, vested interests in continuing the status quo are always strong.

On the other side, however, are the increasing complexity of the Korean economy and the growing incapacity of the government to intervene to promote or prevent changes. In fact, the government has only a limited ability even to learn about changes before they happen. Senior technocrats increasingly take the view that the analysis of problems and the selection of the right choices have become much more difficult; thus, the probability of failure argues against government intervention in detailed business decisions.[14] The government should rather use macroeconomic policy, mainly fiscal and monetary policy instruments. While some resort to industrial policy[15] will also no doubt continue, it is likely to be less extensive than in the past.

Lower-level technocrats have fought the trend to reduce intervention, responding in part to interest group pressures. In addition, technocrats and their ministries are both interested in retaining power. The evolution often seems painfully slow to outsiders but is hard to stop. Business itself takes varied positions on government intervention. One time it will favor involvement and another, oppose, apparently as it sees itself benefited. In any case, so far business has

129

not taken a principled stand. Over time that may change, probably in the direction of opposing intervention. This seems most likely because other groups will seek government intervention that favors them and not business.

A period of several years may come during which this question of government-business relations, like that of labor-management relations, will be worked out. But interest groups tend to be countervailing and often cancel each other out, making the probability of increasing resort to market solutions quite high. Even within the limits imposed by interest group pressures, however, the Korean government will probably be able to avoid hindering economic growth. Politics will surely play a role in this, but experience will almost certainly drive the government toward less rather than more intervention. Business is likely to reach the same conclusion.

Outside pressure, particularly that of the United States, to open Korea's markets also makes continued government intervention more difficult. American pressure obviously plays a role, though it sometimes seems to be negative, in that opponents of liberalization are able to use such influence to portray changes as concessions to the United States rather than as good for Korea. Both of course can be true, which suggests that the process of applying pressure to open markets will not be stopped easily.

### The Connection to Political Development

The connection between economic and political development can be approached in several ways. All persuasive explanations depend, whether stated or not, on an underlying theory or model. It would therefore be good to begin by looking at the models that have been suggested.

A second task is to make the connection between economic and political development explicit. One may observe, for example, as so many have in the case of Korea, that economic changes have preceded political development. The problem here is to define political development—which tends to be equated with democracy—satisfactorily. On the face of it, some Koreans are reluctant to concede that the present system is democratic or democratic enough to meet their standards. But if one takes the view that democracy is in large measure a process and provides other broadly defined human rights only to a smaller extent—though these have come to be seen as essential in most Western countries—then Korea may well qualify as a democracy, unfinished but having crossed a qualitative line from authoritarianism. That still leaves the possibility that Korea, like others before it, will continue to improve its democracy. The key word is "its." Just as Japanese political institutions differ from American, so will Korean democracy have indigenous characteristics.

**Hypotheses.** That a relationship exists between economic and political development seems self-evident—but even that could be questioned. In some cases, the relationship is described as unidirectional. That is to say, for example, the state of political development determines economic development. In a sense, this seems obvious—the state of public administration and the legal system clearly affects the economy. In many cases, the "hard state"[16] has been identified as essential to economic development.

Some express equally strong views that the relationship flows the other way. *The Wall Street Journal* stated such a view in an editorial on May 3, 1988, associating Korea's democracy with economic growth.

> You can't sustain economic growth over the long run without relaxing political restrictions. Even Communist China is discovering that it takes economic freedom and a free flow of information for markets to work. When a government starts endorsing such principles, it hands the people enough power to press for political change as well. That is happening today on Taiwan, and that's what has just happened in South Korea.

Many might conclude that such a view reflects what the *Journal's* editorial writers would like to believe, and they remain convinced that the relationship is somewhat more complex. Still, there seems to be a considerable element of truth in it, since *glasnost* and *perestroika* seem to have become a communicable disease among Communist states. This development raises the possibility that the relationship between democracy and economic development may vary from stage to stage or from culture to culture.

Another view is that economic development is actually destabilizing, as social changes not only undermine old forms of government but destroy social cohesion, making the formation of a democratic system largely impossible.[17] One can point to the case of Iran since World War II as an example. This negative view becomes compelling if the process is viewed as taking place in a comparatively short time.

This negative view of the effects of economic development is weakened, however, if one looks at how rapidly Korea has evolved. Opened to outside influences just over 100 years ago, it was then occupied and annexed to Japan in 1910. But if anything, change accelerated thereafter. In the thirty-five-year period of occupation, however, both economic and other influences seem to have promoted the development of democratic values. In particular, both Christianity and nationalism tended to come down against the undemocratic occupying power. This also allied them with democracy, which challenged the right of the occupier to be there.

Rather than depending on unidirectional explanations with possible exceptions, however, we should recognize that political and economic development interact. But how does the interaction take place? The most important connecting elements seem to be the philosophical definition of the individual's place in society and the mutual obligations that people believe should determine the relationship between the individual and society. Such a definition needs to be commonly accepted and to have some altruistic content in its concern for fellow citizens. If the political or economic system then fails to meet the ethical criteria, pressure will grow to change the system. In other words, the political system depends on what the population considers fair and therefore whether its government or government economic policy is legitimate.

Koreans seem to share a common belief in what constitutes a good society. Among the forces influencing their definition of fair political institutions are the educational system, the urbanization of a previously rural society, the spread of wage employment requiring new skills and education in place of static self-employment in farming, the changes in Confucianism under modern influences and of Christianity, and the failure of the old system—the Yi dynasty. This domain, however, lies outside the professional competence of economists and instead seems properly to belong to historians and other social scientists. Several points, though, seem indisputable, and therefore even an economist may be safe in making them.

**Some Observations.** First, the extraordinary belief in equality in Korea alongside the Confucian hierarchical norm seems a contradiction. Nonetheless, that belief remains powerful. In Confucian terms, the argument for equality stems from the existence of mutual obligations between the superior and the subordinate. When, for example, the subordinate's due is not rendered (the most likely case), the social contract is broken and the moral basis of society is violated. In that case, the offended can act to get his due or to retaliate. This same egalitarian value has been strongly reinforced by the influence of Christianity.[18]

Even if one does not accept this description of the philosophical basis for egalitarianism in Korea, one must recognize that its influence is pervasive. The stress that all political parties give to full employment and to the evil of income inequality strikes the outsider as extraordinary. But these are constant political themes with enormous value to Koreans. They are the world's true "ethical Communists"— they would go beyond "to each according to his need," as that would allow the possibility of different needs, and substitute "to each equally." It is no further step at all to "one man, one vote," the ultimate democratic value. The Korean problem is how to put this equality into practice; in this sense, political and economic development go hand in hand.

Second is the now-widespread Korean belief in progress. The enormous economic development accomplished in Korea since 1962 has greatly changed attitudes. The benefits have so far been widely shared, persuading most people that they can continue to participate. The fact that people look forward to a "good life" (a phrase Koreans use very often) suggests that they do believe that things can get better. It is logical to conclude that they should get better and that a government that fails to bring about improvement should be put out of office. Korea's political opposition has made this point repeatedly and apparently with some success, from Park Chung Hee's last years to the present. It is a new and major change in viewpoint that providing economic growth is no longer enough to keep a government in power or prevent it from being forced to share power.

Third, economic growth and the involvement of government in the economy have of course made the emergence of economic interest groups more important in determining how the economic pie is divided. On the one hand, some sectors of the economy now see that policy may affect them adversely in a way they did not understand in the past. On the other hand, these groups offset one another to a degree. Hence, a shared ethical basis for dividing the pie becomes more important.

A fourth important aspect of the relationship between economic and political development in Korea is the influence of the military and the impact of security considerations on political behavior. No one can question that influence. Growth of the Korean economy, however, lightens the military burden. Korean growth in recent years has allowed the military budget to grow even as it drops from about 6 to about 5 percent of GNP.

While the military role has lessened, other social groups have emerged as increasingly powerful political forces. Most clearly important has been the rise of business, particularly big business. While it has often identified its interests as consonant with those of the military, that it less likely now. Business is also less likely to view agricultural protection as beneficial to it, especially when this may involve possible retaliation from the United States against its manufactured goods exports.

Very recently, large business has begun publicly to display a new independence from the government. One of the large company groups, Kukje, was split up several years ago after the owner was forced to sign over his stock to his creditors.[19] He now accuses the government of having illegally forced him to sell because he failed to contribute enough to several quasi-private organizations. The Federation of Korean Industry—the association of large company groups in Korea—has now come out publicly on the side of the former owner and has attacked the existence of these hidden taxes (which were also a key charge in one presidential candidate's campaign).

A fifth observation concerns the emergence of regionalism. Korea has always been thought fortunate in having a high degree of ethnic homogeneity. Yet regional identities and their concomitant, regional prejudices, seem to have dominated both the 1987 presidential and the 1988 National Assembly elections. That produced an Assembly with expanded power and an executive that will have to depend on an Assembly-based coalition to govern. Another result may be decentralization of government through a revival of local autonomous units.

A newly powerful and politically active union movement and political activation of religious groups also seem likely to contribute to the further development of pluralism. Thus, ethically based democratic values and the evolution of democratic practices have begun to reinforce one another in developing democratic processes.

A sixth and final observation concerns the increasing influence of internationally accepted values. Obviously, the growing international interdependence of states increases their influence on each other—for example, if country A does not know or care how country B treats political opposition, country B is free from international peer pressure and can ignore the values the international community holds at any given time. Economic interdependence also enlarges the influence of this aspect of the relationship. One way is the flow of ideas along with goods across boundaries. Another might be the threat of retaliation for "failing to observe universally accepted norms," as stated in some American trade and aid legislation. Foreign pressures can obviously backfire if they can be portrayed as interference. On many human rights issues, however, that charge has not stuck.

Still another way in which the international community makes its influence felt is through professional peer groups. Academics in various fields meet frequently, for example. Many Korean economists in particular have been trained in the United States, collaborate with U.S. institutions on research, and seek recognition from their colleagues by the application of generally accepted professional standards. To the extent that there is a conventional wisdom, it will tend to be adopted across national boundaries. Moreover, values and viewpoints tend to be transferred across professional as well as geographic lines. Thus, what economists think becomes accepted by other social scientists, and what the others think about their professional fields becomes accepted wisdom for economists. Here is another point at which values come into play in judging public policy and government behavior.

## Conclusion

Two basic points are worth emphasizing. First, it seems clear that the Korean economy will face a series of severe challenges over the next several years and in the more distant future. How it will adjust to them is less clear, but one can feel reasonably hopeful about its ability to adapt. That possibility suggests that Korea can continue to grow rapidly, export, employ its growing and increasingly well-educated population as rising wages produce rising standards of living, and take better and better care of its dropouts and less fortunate. Although there will be changes in its economic structure, its performance will continue to be good, both by historical standards and in comparison with other countries. Korea will retain its ability to understand what is happening in the world economy and its stunning capacity to adjust in an appropriate way.

Second, the likely economic outlook seems favorable for Korea's political progress. The relationship between its political and economic evolution is complex. But to the extent that positive economic performance helps the political aspects and vice versa—and the association seems to be high in the Korean case—one may continue to be hopeful about the future. To the outsider, much remains to be done, particularly with respect to local government, the security apparatus, the further increase in pluralistic associations, and greater tolerance of nonmainstream thought. But the growth of democracy seems to be a slow and unending process in other countries as well as in Korea.

What would happen if there were an economic failure—a leveling of growth or an actual downturn? Obviously, this would put pressure on the system. Squabbles over the division of a constant or diminishing pie could well create sharp divisions in society. Assuming that the threat from North Korea continues and that the military remains a powerful institution, it might be tempted to intervene, ending democracy. An alliance of the military and big business springs to mind, as in the case of Nazi Germany. But the longer Korean democracy exists and evolves, the less likely this outcome seems. Given the low probability of an economic downturn in the near future, such a political downturn seems even more unlikely.

# 8
# Sociocultural Developments in the Republic of Korea

*Kim Kyong-dong*

Over the past few decades East Asia has been belying one by one the central predictions of major theories of development and modernization advanced outside the region. In the 1950s and 1960s Japan surprised Western theorists and observers by demonstrating that a non-Western society with a very small domestic material and economic base and little of what had been considered a sine qua non of modern rational capitalism—the Protestant ethic—could achieve economic takeoff in a rational and modern capitalist guise. The earlier version of modernization theory, couched mainly in the language of convergence and conceived in terms of the historical experience of the West, has inevitably been pushed into an awkward corner by this "unique" case.[1]

In the 1960s and 1970s the Four Little Dragons, or the Gang of Four (South Korea, Taiwan, Hong Kong, and Singapore), embarrassed the champions of the dependency and world system theories, which had flourished by offering critical views in an attempt to overcome the earlier modernization theories. These countries, also poor in resources and capital, made enormous strides in economic growth owing to their export-oriented industrialization policies and relatively equitable income distribution—this despite their heavy dependence on advanced industrial countries.[2]

Still, however, many social science observers have kept a secret smile of satisfaction that most of these East Asian societies have been unable to shed their traditionally authoritarian political mantle even in the face of rising standards of living attained through successful economic growth. As it turns out, however, they are breaking out of the old authoritarian mode of social organization and are beginning once again to show the world that they can do other than what Western theories would have predicted.

137

Just as these countries' rapid economic growth has puzzled analysts of development and social change, it has also spurred new theoretical and empirico-historical analysis to seek proper understanding and more adequate explanation. Recent East Asian political dynamics are also surprising observers, who must now find some reasonable theoretical explanation for the phenomena. Thus far these attempts have largely been made within the theoretical framework of views conceived primarily outside the region. But some new insights are beginning to be drawn from ideas within the cultural context of the region. In other words, attempts are being made in East Asia to explain the phenomena by those who have been experiencing them and with whatever schemes they have derived from that experience.

This chapter is conceived in that spirit. Since, however, society and culture embrace such a broad and hazy dimension of human life, the sociocultural aspects of political democratization covered here are necessarily limited to a few distinctive elements. My strategy is to focus on the human element and the principle of social organization, or the who and how, of political democratization and to characterize the dynamic interplay of factors and forces in an effort to explain why certain phenomena occurred as they did. In doing so, I draw on various ideas, some borrowed from Western theories but others indigenous to Korean culture.

The framework is based on the idea of yin-yang dialectics found in the ancient thought of China and elaborated in Confucian scholarship. Political democratization and societal liberalization, the twin goals to which Korea and other East Asian societies aspire, entail dialectical interaction between forces that attempt to retain the power to monopolize decision making and to influence others and forces that try to change the existing distribution of power and influence. This is a good example of yin-yang interaction. Democratization and liberalization in these countries also involve dynamic cultural change due to international acculturation and indigenous adaptive change. Often they tread a path where traditional elements of culture and imported forces meet, clash, but eventually complement each other as both change in a dialectical synthesis. This is also a case of yin-yang interaction.

Lags and imbalances among sectors of society and phases of culture also ensue, causing tension and the need for adjustment or, when they are extreme, severe conflicts shaking the existing order. In all this, "cultural preparedness" and "political selectivity" differentially influence society's ability to change as well as its prospects. These concepts may all be variants of yin-yang dynamics, too.[3]

The major actors in political democratization may be classified into two groups: those in the positively dominant role and those in the negatively dominant role. The former include the political and bureaucratic elite, the technocratic bureaucracy, the military, and the corporate-managerial elite; the latter are largely the intellectuals, including college students, the broad middle class, the working class, farmers, and women. My overview of the historical unfolding of democratization focuses on the dynamic interplay of these forces.[4]

As to the cultural elements relevant to political culture, my discussion is necessarily confined to some of the most salient cases, such as Confucianism, Japanese militaristic-bureaucratic authoritarianism, Western (primarily American) democratic ideals, and more recent Marxist-Leninist ideologies. I refer to the differential influences of these elements in the appropriate contexts. But we must be cautious about the influence of Confucianism. While the influence of the other three may be readily discerned, analysis of the part played by Confucianism is much more complicated and delicate.

In discussing the role of Confucian tradition in political democratization in Korea, we must understand that the version of Confucianism relevant to current political culture is not the celebrated intellectual system entertained by scholars. What are relevant in today's context are the Confucian notion of statecraft as practiced in Korean society and the more vulgarized version of Confucian teachings manifested in the thoughts and behavior of ordinary people.[5]

When we limit our interest to this aspect of Confucian tradition in Korean society, we can make some reasonable inferences. First, the Confucian element of statecraft may have been adopted by the ruling elite consciously or unconsciously, primarily as the rationale for centralized authoritarian rule, but this element must have been reinforced by Japanese influence. Second, the collectivist and hierarchical pattern of thought and social behavior prevalent among the Korean people may have originated, at least partly, in the Confucian heritage. Third, the strong moralistic orientation of Koreans, especially with respect to the political elite and political behavior, has its root in the Confucian legacy. Fourth, the tradition of dissent and protest often practiced by the Confucian officials and intellectuals of the Choson dynasty has been repeatedly honored in the process of socialization in modern times. Fifth, an egalitarian (not necessarily democratic or liberal) tendency that is quite strong and widespread in Korea also has its partial origin in Confucianism.

From these observations we might infer that the first two orientations—of authoritarian statecraft and collectivist-hierarchical behavioral traits—have been used by the political elite in their effort to maintain authoritarian rule and arrest the process of democratization, whereas the other three have been adopted by the forces for democratization in their fight against the ruling elite. The Japanese legacy would have worked to reinforce the former tendency, the Western influences to reinforce the latter.

## The Dynamic Interplay of Forces and Factors

Let us take the colonial period as a starting point. After the Choson dynasty crumbled in the face of Japanese imperial encroachment, sociopolitical movements envisaging a republican form of government emerged among the intellectual leaders who initiated independence movements during the early decades of the twentieth century. Such attempts were almost totally crushed by the colonial authority until the liberation in 1945. The end of Japanese occupation left two contradictory legacies for the subsequent unfolding of political democratization.

The first and more lasting imprint is the militaristic, bureaucratic, authoritarian political culture. This has provided the basic framework of governance for the political and bureaucratic elite ever since and became the root of forces hindering easy democratization. The Syngman Rhee regime had to rely on a politico-bureaucratic elite corps recruited largely from the indigenous bureaucrats and professionals serving under colonial rule. Leaders of the junta of the 1960s also received their schooling or military training before 1945.

The second effect of colonial experience runs counter to the first because of the reaction created by that very experience. Although the people had grown accustomed to militaristic authoritarian rule, they had also accumulated a strong resentment of political suppression and a desire to be rid of it. They had built in their minds and hearts what is called in Korean *han*, a complex emotional state of resentment and regret, caused by acute frustration and injustice and often creating a desire for revenge or a feeling of hatred. Motivated by this sentiment, the people readily came to accept the ideals of democracy implanted by the occupation forces of the United States at the end of World War II.[6]

The yin-yang dialectic between these two opposing forces has operated throughout the postwar history of Korean democracy. The often pathetically keen desire for democracy on the part of the people has been reinforced not only by the formal educational process emphasizing democratic ideals adopted from the American system but by the reaction to the continued effort by the politico-bureaucratic elite of subsequent regimes to maintain authoritarian rule. The more a regime tries to keep itself in power by an iron grip, the stronger and the more intense become the people's demand and yearning for democracy.

In this process, of course, the role played by international acculturation has been important. The ideals of democracy, painted in a somewhat rosier color than the political realities of Western societies, were poured into the naive minds of the Korean people, who had not quite gotten over the experience of colonial suppression. Especially sensitive were the young generation suddenly exposed to an entirely different political culture imported from the outside. This new generation, brought up for the first time in Korean history in an educational system where all instruction was given in *han'gul*, the pure Korean alphabet, and when the American influence was still central, became the student protesters who toppled the autocratic Rhee regime in April 1960.

This experience with international acculturation was painful and frustrating as Korean society muddled through its effort to naturalize the imported culture. The success of such adaptive change depends on a society's ability to absorb the foreign culture with as little internal distortion as possible. The cultural preparedness of the Korean people simplified that task. Of course, the legacy of the colonial days was the most serious hindrance to this adaptive change.

According to a theory of cultural change espoused by Leslie White, any significant cultural innovation must wait until the evolution of culture reaches a point where such change is possible.[7] Without some cultural preparedness, in other words, innovations are difficult or impossible. In the aftermath of several decades of authoritarian colonial rule without any notable experience of democracy, Korea was not ready for democratic practice. Nonetheless, its international acculturation furnished a cultural framework and information useful for the practice of democracy. It may have instigated an overzealous desire for immediate democratization of the entire system. The imbalance created by the gap between the yearning and emotional zeal for democracy, on the one hand, and the general deficiency in cultural preparedness, on the other, caused anxiety, insecurity, and eventually unrest.

The crucial factor that saved the country from prolonged political instability and postponed democratization may have been the political decisions made by the leaders of each regime, especially the Rhee government. This reflects the principle of political selectivity. Important changes in society are often selectively brought about by political decisions made by the elite in interaction with various forces in society.[8] Here, too, we find an interesting case of yin-yang dialectics.

When a regime grows corrupt and resorts to illegitimate means

141

to retain power, the protest from the opposition—and in Korea since 1960 from the students—becomes intense. When a regime fails to make the political decisions needed to save itself and democracy, the counterforces grow stronger and crush the regime. Afterward the dissident forces run wild, and rampant disorder ensues. On the surface various signs of democratization and liberalization appear, but in the eyes of the establishment the situation resembles one of anarchy. A more conservative force steps in to restore order. This force adopts repressive policies, which in turn cause protests by the liberal and radical forces. Thus continues the vicious circle of suppression, protest, repression, and counteraction. This has been the pattern in the four decades since the inauguration of the republic.

Certain lags and imbalances appeared in the course of rapid social change. The most outstanding involves leveling, or equalization, and the reshuffling of social strata. This trend may be traced back to the demise of the old dynasty. Since about the beginning of the seventeenth century, after the seven-year war initiated by a Japanese invasion (1592–1598), the traditional status system had shown signs of disorganization. It was finally abolished legally at the end of the nineteenth century and was crushed by the Japanese introduction of a new landownership system and a capitalist economy. The colonial class system disappeared at the end of World War II. While the society was struggling to reorganize the class system, the Korean War broke out, leaving the entire population poor and deprived. After a period of rehabilitation a new wave of industrialization engulfed the society.

In this historical process of reshuffling and leveling, certain social forces emerged to gain power. The Japan-trained bureaucratic-professional elite gained power initially, and a new element of English-speaking intellectuals joined their ranks under the U.S. occupation and in the initial stages of the Rhee regime. A new class of entrepreneurs emerged during and after the Korean War. The war also enabled military leaders to come to the fore; their lot has improved enormously since the 1961 coups by Park Chung Hee and his junta. Industrialization and the accompanying urbanization naturally shifted a great many people from the farm to the city and from agricultural to other occupations.

When a society goes through such changes in a limited period, people are likely to view social mobility as something that anybody can expect to experience. A sense of egalitarianism pervades the society, as people aspire to move upward. Mass education has contributed to this aspiration among many ordinary people. Egalitarianism combined with the strong aspiration toward upward mobility has become so pervasive that a "popularized elitism" has come to permeate the psyche of the population. Coupled with a widespread belief that most of the regimes have been illegitimate and most wealth has been illictly accumulated, egalitarianism and popularized elitism have bred a cynical attitude toward the elite and mobility. Most people believe that anybody can attain an elite position or upward mobility inasmuch as a next-door neighbor who used to be nobody has suddenly become a member of the elite because of the right connections, luck, or education.

The significance of this attitude is that egalitarian sentiments and popularized elitism have fostered a desire for political democratization, especially among the young. Nevertheless, the political regimes viewed by the people as illegitimate and autocratic have adamantly resisted the demand for democratization. Here lies the first case of lag. Although authoritarianism has prevailed in sociopolitical life since the inception of the republic, authority, particularly the authority of the political and economic elite and institutions, has continuously deteriorated.

The second lag is between the rising expectations and aspirations caused by rapid economic growth and the lack of political democratization. As the economy has taken off and swiftly advanced, standards of living have risen accordingly. This economic progress has raised consciousness and widened and diversified the spectrum of needs. The focus of interest among the people has steadily shifted from immediate satisfaction of basic needs to gratification of more qualitative needs, such as improvement in individual and social welfare, amelioration of the uneven distribution of wealth, political democratization, and leisure and recreation.[9]

The political leadership and the government bureaucracy have been less than responsive to this rising tide of demand for change. Irritation and frustration, not only among the more deprived and alienated strata but also among the better-off middle-class people, have risen steadily. As long as the elite maintained strict law and order when it might have adopted a more flexible political stance, the society was awaiting a moment of explosion. The regime kept floating in a wayward direction until the explosion occurred in June 1987.

It is the dynamics of the yin-yang forces pushing and pulling that had made ensuing events so unusual. The political leadership had to yield to the demand under very abnormal circumstances. The pressure had been mounting for so long with such force that, once the sluice was open, the flow of demands burst out. If there had been a slow but steady response from the government through institutionally legitimate means, if the government had been flexible enough to listen and open channels of communication, the pressure would have been ameliorated so that very little violent reaction would have been necessary.

In this complex process the first generation of political leaders came chiefly from the ranks of former leaders of the independence movement. They had to fight one another ideologically and politically, however, to gain power. In the political struggle through which the new republic was born, the leaders had to rely heavily on the bureacratic elite of the colonial period. Combined, these forces laid the foundation for an authoritarian government.

Although local governments were established and local politicking seemed abundant, the real power rested in the hands of the centrally located politico-bureaucratic figures. This early regime left a legacy of resort to illegitimate, often violent means of retaining power and of rampant political corruption. Military and police force was used to suppress opposition.

The political opposition, consisting largely of factions gathered around political bosses, was unable to gain power and rule. Even when they were given the chance to govern after the fall of Rhee, deep-rooted divisions made it very difficult for them to rule effectively, especially in the face of pressure from the almost uncontrollable political force of the students. The widespread insecurity caused by pervasive instability furnished the "lions" (in Pareto's sense) of the military an attractive excuse for a takeover of the government by force.

The zeal for reform pronounced by the military junta in 1961 was not matched by its ability to make fundamental changes in the system, so that the former military political elite had to mobilize the old hands in politics, the bureaucracy, and the economic leadership. Thus the elite structure remained much the same as before, except that many retired military men found a channel for upward mobility. It was difficult to expect the newly inaugurated regime to be capable of widespread political democratization and societal liberalization, because President Park and many of the men he recruited from the old political and bureaucratic elite had been trained in Japan and because the military culture began to dominate the politico-bureaucratic sphere and to influence the entire society.

Moreover, the new regime that came to power with the promise that the corruption, injustice, and irregularities of the old regime would be wiped out not only was unable to cure such social ills but became deeply involved in and severely tainted by corruption. This was in part caused by the need for great sums of money to retain power but was also an expression of the *han* the new leaders had accumulated under previous regimes, which had alienated them and under which they had suffered relative deprivation. Although the Park regime was able to keep its promise that chronic poverty would be overcome and the livelihood of the people improved through economic growth, this accomplishment alone could not gain full legitimacy for the military takeover of political power and continued authoritarian rule.

Since political protests never ceased, the regime had to rely heavily on force, and authoritarian rule was rigidly enforced. At the peak of political unrest the student protesters were joined by workers, and internal friction finally ended the life of the regime and the person of Park Chung Hee in a secret shootout. The subsequent regime, led by another military junta, unfortunately was not an improvement on its predecessor. The fundamental pitfall of the Chun Doo Hwan regime lay in the Kwangju incident, which involved the massacre of hundreds of people by the armed forces. The regime was unable to resolve the issue of Kwangju and fulfill its initial promise to build a just and democratic welfare society. One reason for its inability to do so may be found in the problem of personnel.

Unlike the Rhee government, the Park government was able to mobilize a well-trained technocratic elite from academia and the bureaucracy, especially in the economic area. The new technocratic elite came from the ranks of professionals and bureaucrats trained mostly in the United States, no longer in Japan. They rarely raised their voices against the authoritarian rule of the regime that they served professionally. They were criticized by the intellectuals outside the government for their lack of sensitivity about the authoritarianism of the regime they served and the demand of the people for greater democracy, despite their training and higher education in countries like the United States, where they had been exposed to liberal democratic ideals and practices. Yet they never attempted to be champions of democracy while they diligently pursued the goal of economic growth.

The Chun regime was doubly hurt in this regard. The technocratic elite kept its stance of political neutrality, but their loyalty declined because of the problem of legitimacy. Many professionals and intellectuals either stayed away from the regime or kept it at arm's length lest they be too closely identified with an antidemocratic government with the scar of Kwangju and the problem of legitimacy still hanging over it. In addition, the involvement in political affairs by former military men changed, mainly because the military had come to claim its own share of Ph.D.'s trained in America and capable intellectuals in the armed forces. In a way the military culture was reinforced, especially around the person and style of President Chun,

145

whereas the society, with sustained growth in the economic sector, was undergoing tremendous change. The regime was not prepared to absorb the mounting demands for liberalization, democratization, and greater social justice created by rapid economic growth.

Under the regimes of Presidents Park and Chun, the political opposition could not win an election, because of both internal and external dynamics. Internally, political parties had not become democratic political organizations grounded in grass-roots support but were engulfed in factional strife around political bosses and their cliques. The regime and the ruling party were also responsible for keeping them in disarray by overt and covert political manipulation and persecution. Under the circumstances professional politicians in the opposition became more radical in their action, projecting an image of fighters rather than compromising politicians. In fact, compromise of any sort came to be identified as political treachery. This orientation did not help the opposition parties to prepare themselves to formulate realizable policies or to govern. The opposition political parties coalesced and parted as their bosses moved about in the political arena, their formation and dispersion not based on any ideological or policy differences.

The more formidable opposition has come from intellectuals and students. Student protest has a long history in Korea. Some observers even refer to the often prolonged and tenacious protests by apprentice Confucianists of the Choson dynasty as the predecessor of current student movements. We do not have to go that far back into history. Students were active in national independence movements before liberation, and at times the conflict between rightist and leftist students during the postliberation period led to violence. The root of the political movement of college students in the past three decades, however, lay in the termination of the Rhee regime in April 1960. This was a genuine protest movement striving toward a democratic political system against an autocratic government tainted by corruption.

As the subsequent regimes ruled by former military leaders became more authoritarian and corrupt, student protest movements changed their political color. In the 1960s they were loosely organized movements rallying against the government for democratization and civilian rule. Their nationalistic sentiments were not yet ideologically well articulated. The so-called Yushin reform of 1972 hardened not only the regime but also the student movements. Their antigovernment activities gained legitimacy in the eyes of many people who mistrusted the regime's attempt to justify the Yushin move, whereby the rigidity of the government had grown and its hidden intention to perpetuate itself had become obvious. Students were joined by activ-

ists among the opposition politicians and in the academic and religious spheres. Student movements became better organized, and
their influence on campuses increased. They even began to stir up
the still dormant working class. This move slowly gained momentum
because the society had grown accustomed to rapid economic growth
and industrialization while the lot of working people had not improved as quickly.

As the spring of 1980 ended with the May 17 coup and the
Kwangju incident, students who had seen democratization as close
at hand were filled with rage and became much more radical. The
most significant change in the student movements in the 1980s was
their ideological shift to Marxism-Leninism and overt anti-Americanism. The sheer number of students expelled from the universities or
even imprisoned became a force in itself, working mainly underground with ousted activist journalists, religious activists, labor activists, and opposition politicians. Student radicals were exposed to
such neo-Marxist theories as dependency and the world system and
to other secretly imported vulgar Marxist works, chiefly from Japan.
Working closely with small publishers, the Marxist element in academia began to publish materials along this line, so as to expand its
influence over students without activist inclinations.

The large majority of intellectuals in the academic, press, and
religious sectors rarely expressed their opinions explicitly or engaged
in political activity, whether they supported or disliked the governments in power. In 1960 many university professors joined the ranks
of student demonstrators to protest the shooting of innocent students. During later regimes, however, surveillance and persecution
became so obvious that most intellectuals remained onlookers. But
there were activists in both camps: functional activists participating
in the government processes and critical activists fighting the government. The functional intellectuals became professional technocrats,
helping the government to formulate and evaluate policy without
questioning the nature of the regime. The antigovernment, critical
intellectuals were fewer but very loud in their voice. Although some
of them initially provided ideological guidance to the student activists, their relationship became more distant as the student movements took on a clearly Marxist color.

The entrepreneurial-managerial elite emerged in the early period
of the new republic in close collaboration with the politico-bureaucratic sector, and the relationship has been maintained in essentially
the same way. The role played by the entrepreneurs and managers in
political democratization has been at most passive, if not negative. By
actively leading the way to economic growth, they have provided a

147

soil for rising aspirations among the people toward greater democracy. Nonetheless, they have not actively sought to persuade the governing elite to pursue democratization. In effect, the industrial sector has aided the elite in its effort to retain power under an authoritarian system. Furthermore, industrialists have been hesitant to promote democracy within their enterprises, particularly for labor.

Labor, for its part, has moved rather timidly on its path to democratization. In the initial phase of economic takeoff, workers had to tolerate whatever treatment they received since surplus labor was abundant. As the economy progressed, labor became differentiated and the orientation of workers diversified. The relatively slow change in income distribution in the face of more rapid change in economic growth has left some labor groups with an acute sense of deprivation, while others, though a minority, have found themselves comfortably in line with the general progress. The relatively deprived element was susceptible to instigation from such outside forces as student radicals and religious groups.

Labor unions have generally been considered handmaidens of the ruling elite, unable to put up a real fight against either management or government. They were rarely organized or operated democratically. This situation has left a gap for interested outside forces to sneak into to influence the consciousness and the behavior of workers. Only since the June declaration has labor become a formidable democratic force in Korea.

Farmers and women have been comparatively passive in the process of political democratization. Both have been conservative forces, even though pockets of protests have arisen among farmers over certain economic issues and movements for liberation among women. These two groups, which are not well organized and have suffered deprivation and alienation most extensively, form a potentially explosive source of social unrest. The extent of frustration in the form of *han* is extraordinary.

## The Current State of Democratization

An assessment of the nature and extent of political democratization in Korea may be helpful in understanding the significance of some of the factors I have mentioned. The earliest indication came in the declaration of June 29, 1987, by Roh Tae-Woo, then the head and presidential candidate of the Democratic Justice party (DJP). This opened the door to a constitutional amendment providing for direct presidential election by a simple popular vote. In addition, the Roh declaration laid out programs of broad liberalization in various sociopolitical areas, including the press, amnesty for political prisoners, and redefinition of the historical meaning of the Kwangju incident and rehabilitation of the honor of its victims. The declaration was made under severe pressure from massive street demonstrations not only of college students and workers but also of middle-class men, who joined out of rage and impatience over the insensitivity and unresponsiveness of the government toward the people's long-held desire for democratic reforms. As Roh himself admitted, he had to succumb to the will of the people, but he felt proud rather than ashamed of doing so.

As many opposition politicans, intellectuals, and student leaders emphasize, Roh indeed yielded to the pressure and will of the people, but he might have been pressured to do otherwise under the circumstances. It is important to note his political selectivity. Although the pressure for liberalization was much stronger, he had to risk displeasing some significant forces around the central power. At stake were not only his own survival and the fate of his party but also the future of democracy in Korea. His decision was crucial, and he should be given credit for his courage and wisdom.

On the surface one might suppose that the major forces Roh was up against were President Chun and his entourage, backed by the military and intelligence communities. Of course, they were major sources of power. But, as Roh and his party soon came to realize, the most formidable force he had to confront was the bureaucracy. After the June declaration and especially during the presidential campaign, the bureaucracy was extremely passive and became a negative element by withdrawing from any active cooperation with the Roh campaign. Roh thus began to be seen by the people, particularly the opposition and the still doubtful intellectuals, as doing little to fulfill his promise to liberalize. The bureaucracy, which was responsible for releasing the grip of control and regulation and for changing rules and laws in the direction of liberalization, was very slow to carry out this task.

The process of constitutional amendment, however, exhibited material signs of democratization in the political arena. The political parties exercised prudent consultation and resorted to compromise rather than confrontation in reaching agreement on the issues related to the amendment. These actions were surprising in light of the past political behavior of those involved.

The openness of the campaign and the tolerance manifested by the power elite during it were unmatched in any previous elections. Nevertheless, openness and tolerance may be only part of the symptoms of liberalization. There were few signs of democratization, and the voters were still prone to fall prey to pecuniary temptation, bureaucratic pressure, or even physical violence. The bureaucracy harmed the ruling party in two ways. First, local officials, overzealously trying to show loyalty to the government party by interfering in the campaign process, actually hurt the party, which wanted to project an image of a born-again democratic political party approaching the campaign fair and square. Second, the bureaucracy was very slow to undertake the significant reforms necessary to realize the democratization programs of Roh and his party.

The opposition parties were not far ahead in their own internal democratization. Their centralized, authoritarian principle of organization and decision making remained intact while their propaganda professed otherwise. None of the parties, in or out of power, has improved in this regard. This was clearly demonstrated by each party in nominating candidates for the general election. Similar to the political parties in their lack of democratic attitudes and behavior were the various groups of politically active radical students. In contrast to their professed ideals of democracy, their principle of organization and decision making has been centralized and authoritarian. Easy resort to collective agitation and unnecessary physical violence became a habit of the radical political groups, professional or amateur.

The response of the economic sector was quicker, but the meaning assigned to such terms as liberalization and democratization varied with status. For the entrepreneurial elite and top management supported by the professional management corps, the terms meant freedom from tangible and intangible control, regulation, and pressure exerted by the government bureaucracy and political elite. These groups claimed that the national economy had grown to a scale and quality that required professional managerial and technical skills the government bureaucracy could no longer effectively provide as it had in the past as "guided capitalism." Large corporations particularly wanted an end to what has been known as quasi-taxation, or donations squeezed out of corporations through elbow twisting by the government and political agents. The term "economic democracy" that spread swiftly throughout industry essentially meant all these things.

The bureaucracy has been timid in achieving the promise of liberalization even in the economic sector. Although many regulations have been revised in this direction, the financial sector still claims that the government has scarcely loosened its grip on such central matters as the selection of top management or the operation of boards of trustees.

Economic democratization signified something else for labor. Labor immediately instigated collective action by workers demanding a popular labor union movement and a leap in wages and salaries in compensation for past "exploitation." The bureaucracy moved fairly quickly to amend labor laws in such a way as to make the formation of unions easier. The major responsibility for resolving industrial conflict was to be turned over to the parties involved, leaving the government out as much as possible. Liberalization meant granting greater autonomy with equal responsibility. Widespread industrial disputes ensued, often entailing severe violence, and many industries began to bleed, some small firms even closing in the face of prolonged strikes and sit-ins.

Universities have been the nursery and in a sense the sanctuary of the political movement of students craving political democratization and societal liberalization. The student movement was essentially responsible for the June declaration. Nevertheless, some radical students were not satisfied with the process of constitutional amendment, presidential and general elections, and other reforms involving the establishment in any form. With this force, small yet vociferous, in their back yard, universities have been striving to gain autonomy from the government in various areas. Here again the bureaucracy has been reluctant to move fast in amending basic laws and regulations, without which the autonomy of universities can hardly be achieved.

Perhaps the press has enjoyed the greatest amount of freedom. Taking advantage of the Roh declaration, the press began immediately to open up. It has enjoyed a degree of freedom of expression unimaginable in the past couple of decades. The kind of material exposed to a general audience and the tolerance demonstrated in the press went so far as to make many people anxious.

The military is an important social force in Korea. Although it has gained political skill since the 1961 *coup d'état*, it has accumulated its own share of resentment among the people, especially the critical intellectuals and the opposition politicians. Since the June declaration, however, the military has remained quiet and neutral in the midst of noisy political squabbles and rampant industrial conflict. Calls for professionalism from both within and without seem to be heeded by the leaders and their surrounding core groups in the armed forces.

This discussion has largely focused on the change or lack of change in the attitudes and relations of the political elite and the government bureaucracy to other important sectors of the society. While the trend is in the direction of greater autonomy for institutions outside government, in some pockets bureaucratic control and inter-ference linger tenaciously. A more serious obstacle to smooth liberal-ization lies in the attitudes of bureaucrats who cling to the authoritar-ian mode they have been used to and attempt to resist change if at all possible.

The resisting force, however, is not necessarily confined to the government bureaucracy. In many other sectors internal forces are running against the tide of liberalization and democratization. This is certainly true in the economic sector, which has been familiar with an authoritarian, familistic pattern of management and industrial relations. Universities and the press also contain conservative ele-ments that offer resistance to reforms.

### The Challenge of the Future

The dynamics of interaction among these social forces changed color so dramatically in 1988 and beyond that the prospects for political democratization are highly uncertain. The most outstanding events since the summer of 1987 have been the extensive and often violent labor disputes that erupted in the aftermath of the June 29 declaration and recurred in the spring of 1988 and the presidential and general elections held a few months thereafter. The implications of these events are so complex that a short summary would hardly do justice to their actual and potential effects on the prospects for political democratization in Korea.

The significance of industrial conflicts may be summed up as follows. First, they strike a crucial blow at the authority of govern-ment and management, both of which have enjoyed an easy authori-tarian rule over the working class but can no longer maintain that privilege. Second, a new role for labor unions is being created from the grass roots, denying the legitimacy of the past practice of forming unions top down and being governed by a labor elite, usually progov-ernment and promanagement. Third, labor disputes and the man-hours lost are hurting business and the national economy, forcing management and the government to change so as to survive and continue to grow.

The presidential election produced a president with the crucial handicap of minority support. It also disclosed the deep-rooted divisive sentiments along provincial lines. The current administration is further impaired by the perception of the people that the Sixth Republic is almost identical with the Fifth Republic of the Chun regime, which was implicated in financial and other scandals. This impression was not dissipated by the formation of a new cabinet or by the general election.

The general election of members of the national assembly yielded unexpected results, surprising not only the ruling DJP but also the opposition and voters themselves. This election had several distinctive features. First, the division along the provincial origins of the electors and the elected was once more clearly manifested. Second, for the first time in the history of parliamentary politics in Korea, the ruling party in the National Assembly does not have a majority, Kim Dae Jung's Party for Peace and Democracy (PPD) having gained the largest share of seats among the opposition parties. Third, a majority of the assembly members are newly elected nonprofessional politicians, and the advance of relatively young candidates is notable. Finally, some radical elements of opposition groups have joined the ranks of the national assembly, opening up the possibility of co-optation into the system.

These results are expected to create a situation in which the political parties must learn to compromise rather than fight to the end. The government party cannot and therefore should not force its will through sheer size. This, many believe and hope, could be a critical turning point in parliamentary politics in the direction of building genuine democratic political institutions and processes. Two major forces may stand in the way. If Kim's party cannot contain the bitter *han* of its members and supporters, especially those of Cholla-do background and the relatively deprived and alienated classes, and cannot behave itself in the parliamentary process, disorder may continue to plague the nation. If such disorder turns into uncontainable turbulence arousing a bleak prospect for the nation, the military may step in once again.

So far the military has kept its calm patiently, even when politicians did not hesitate to criticize and insult it openly during the election campaigns. The military has apparently come to realize that the people will no longer tolerate any attempt to take over the government by force. The societal transformations experienced by the people have reached a point where the military may well stay away from politics and develop into an important social institution and force with a spirit of professionalism.

Not because of a threat from the military but because this is a truly great opportunity for promoting the democratic political process, all political men and their parties should strive to achieve this goal. That is the poignant expectation of the people.

The same is true for the actors in the industrial system. Workers who have sacrificed disproportionately in the process of economic progress must have accumulated their share of *han* and deserve much

153

better treatment socially and economically. Management and the government should try to compensate them as far as possible. Yet at this historical juncture Korea cannot afford the luxury of ceaseless and destructive industrial conflicts. Another coup is out of the question, but instability is not what Koreans need now, not even the workers.

Student radicals are not an exception to this rule. They will continue their protests, with a view to a revolutionary takeover by a proletarian populist force. At least on campus this force is gradually losing support because the majority of students have turned their attention to the internal affairs of the universities and ordinary academic life. This turnabout by the students may stimulate the activists to take more violent action to draw attention and mobilize crowds. Since the past authoritarian governments fostered these radical youths, the society must tolerate such action at least for a time until the movements somehow break down from within.

Thus far the police have ordinarily tried to disperse crowds by means of tear gas. The government may, however, have to show a more tolerant and flexible attitude toward such activities, because the police with tear gas and other gadgets to control protests project a negative image of the old rigid authoritarian regime. The timidity of the bureaucracy about change is one of the most crucial yet invisible obstacles to true democratization. Just as it hurt the Roh campaign, the slow-moving bureaucracy is a continuing resisting force. Once this sector can be mobilized to aid democratization actively, the future of democracy and liberalization in Korea will not be at all bleak.

The Korean people have a susceptibility to collective behavior that may have to be overcome quickly to speed up the process of democratization. It may have originated in the strong emotionalism embedded in traditional Korean culture and must have been further reinforced in accumulating *han* under various historical circumstances. The most recent manifestations of such emotionalism in sometimes violent and destructive collective behavior must be the result of the authoritarian, bureaucratic, and militaristic culture that has pervaded the minds of the people for the past couple of decades. This kind of action may certainly be useful when regular channels of communication are closed, but it is inimical to the dialogue and compromise needed for democratic decision making. Here again, therefore, dissipation of *han* on the part of various sectors and strata of the society is essential, and the role of the government bureaucracy in that task is crucial.

# 9

# Korea's International Environment

*Ahn Byung-joon*

In 1987–1988 momentous changes took place in Korea's political life. As a result, Korea is undergoing a transition from an authoritarian state and a state-directed newly industrializing country to a more democratic state and a high-technology and service economy led by the private sector. On the whole the international environment has been favorable to and has supported these changes and will probably continue to do so.

The theme of this chapter is that changes in Korea's political and economic life have resulted primarily from domestic dynamics while the international environment has played a secondary role in the sense of setting certain constraints. There has been more autonomy in Korea's political development than in its economic development, for the latter has been affected by the growing interdependence of Korea and the Western countries, principally the United States, Japan, and the nations of the European Community.

Politically, Korea is going through a delicate process of democratization as a result of the presidential election of December 1987, in which President Roh Tae Woo barely won with 36.7 percent of the votes, and the general elections of April 1988, in which the opposition won a majority in the National Assembly for the first time. Economically, Korea is experiencing a rising tide of labor disputes at home and of trade friction abroad. Against this background Korean society is asserting its influence over the political system by making diverse demands. Internationally, Korea was host to the Twenty-fourth Summer Olympics in September 1988. This event provided an excellent opportunity to expand its relations with the Communist countries, principally China and the Soviet Union. In its aftermath South Korea began to readjust its political and security relations with North Korea and even with the United States. The state of international relations in 1988 and beyond looked quite promising for making such adjustments.

With these broad generalizations in mind, specific observations can be made about Korea's domestic and international environment. First, Korea's political economy is in transition, shifting from planned development directed by an authoritarian state to a more market-led development supervised by a democratic state. Second, the international environment is likely to reinforce such a transition as the security situation further improves because of the realignment in U.S.-Soviet and other big power relations and Korea's deepening involvement in the increasingly interdependent global economy. Third, assuming that this prognosis is accurate, South Korea will become a leading democratic and industrial country, accommodating many of North Korea's demands and achieving a more equal relationship with the United States. Such eventualities are inevitable, given the rising weight of the Korean economy in the international system and the expression of nationalism in Korean society.

### Korea's Political Economy in Transition

Korea is undergoing a transition between the old pattern of authoritarian politics and a state-directed economy and a new pattern of pluralistic politics and a market-driven economy. The dramatic changes that occurred in Korea during 1987–1988 forced the ruling party and the opposition to practice a kind of consensus politics. At the same time, mounting trade friction with the United States, Japan, and other industrial countries is forcing this newly industrializing country to liberalize imports from abroad and to carry out structural adjustments at home toward a more open economy led by the private sector.

Political changes are prompting Korea to shift from what I call "crisis politics" to "interest politics."[1] The former refers to state-led authoritarian politics that results from crises of security, authority, and legitimacy. The latter refers to society-led pluralistic politics that results from reconciliation of conflicting interests among individuals, groups, and parties. Although this shift can be affected by the international environment, the dominant influences are usually national and hence internal.[2] This is not to deny the impact of Western ideas and especially American influences on domestic political development, for access to them helps sustain the values of competitive politics, the freedom of the press, and an independent judiciary.[3] It merely underlines the fact that the political turnaround in Korea has arisen from a long, complex process that has historical and societal roots.

What is significant about this turnaround is that it may mark an end of a vicious cycle of civilian and military regimes in Korea that is characteristic of crisis politics in the third world and especially in Latin America.[4] The Syngman Rhee regime initially aimed at a constitutional democracy in the American style but turned increasingly dictatorial to remain in power. When this government was toppled by a student uprising in 1960, the Chang Myon government turned out to be short-lived because its parliament-centered system was unable to cope with the rising expectations of political factions and social groups. The government was taken over by another veto group, the military, in 1961. The Park Chung Hee regime, too, tried a constitutional system until 1971; but after Park barely beat Kim Dae Jung (who won 46 percent of the electoral vote in that year), it instituted the so-called *yushin* (revitalizing reform) system to perpetuate Park's rule, precipitating what is known in Latin America as "bureaucratic authoritarianism." When President Park was assassinated by his security aide in October 1979, Korea was gripped by another crisis of authority, as students and dissidents staged violent street demonstrations. The military intervention led by General Chun Doo Hwan in 1980 was instrumental in putting down the resultant uprising in Kwangju and in restoring some measure of law and order. But the Fifth Republic under President Chun was haunted by the question of legitimacy, since the president was elected indirectly by an electoral college while opposition leaders were prohibited from carrying out political activities.

The political evolution begun with the February 1985 general elections seems to have been the beginning of Korean society's assertion of political grievances against the authoritarian states and particularly the military. The trend has been toward an active manifestation of populist protests against the authoritarian system, not only by alienated groups but also by a growing middle stratum of professionals, skilled workers, businessmen, and farmers. In the 1985 elections the ruling Democratic Justice party (DJP) failed to secure a two-thirds majority in the National Assembly, winning only 35.3 percent of the votes. The New Korea Democratic party (NKDP), which had been created only two months earlier by Kim Young Sam and supported by Kim Dae Jung at that time, became the largest opposition party with 28 percent of the votes. In the elections, the NKDP campaigned single-handedly for direct popular election of the president.

Faced with rising populist demands for constitutional revision, President Chun yielded in April 1986 by announcing that he would accept any agreement on this issue reached by the parties. But while the DJP sought to institute a parliamentary system, the NKDP insisted on a presidential system. In December 1986 Lee Min Woo, president of the NKDP, indicated a willingness to consider a parliamentary system provided that the government proceeded with democratization. A stalemate ensued, which might have continued had an incident not occurred that undermined the moral basis of the Chun regime. In January 1987 a dissident student named Park Chong-chul was found dead of police torture. In April the two Kims split from the NKDP to form a new party called the Unification Democratic party (UDP). Because of these two events, President Chun decreed on April 13, 1987, that all debates on constitutional revision be ended.

Turmoil spread in April–June 1987 around the middle stratum's disgust at the way in which the Chun regime was handling the political situation. Soon after President Chun's announcement on the constitutional debate, for example, a cover-up of police involvement in the torture of Park was disclosed. Notwithstanding the public indignation at this incident, President Chun designated Roh Tae Woo, one of his longtime military associates, as the DJP's presidential candidate. Perceiving that an amorally tainted government might succeed in passing leadership in a "legal" manner, students took to the streets to demonstrate against the Chun-Roh ruling circle. For the first time many onlookers from the middle stratum began openly to cheer and sympathize with the students.

Perhaps the only way in which the government might have quashed the mass uprising was to call in the military, but three factors worked to prevent this. First, many members of the middle stratum of society and even of the military came to share the view that the military could no longer cope with the political situation, let alone manage the highly complex economic situation. Second, the fact that Korea was to sponsor the Olympics was a powerful constraint on military intervention, for imposition of martial law might well jeopardize Korea's right to stage the Olympics. Third, the United States came out strongly in opposition to any military action. In a speech in New York in February 1987 Assistant Secretary of State Gaston Sigur called on Korean leaders to "civilianize" politics, and he made repeated statements thereafter to discourage martial law or military intervention.[5]

Against this background Roh made an important pronouncement on June 29, 1987. He not only accepted a direct presidential election and the restoration of civil rights to Kim Dae Jung but also promised other measures of democratization. Once this much was granted, it was easy for both parties to reach agreement rapidly, perhaps too rapidly, on a new constitution and a new presidential electoral law. That paved the way for the presidential election in December.

Nonetheless, despite sensing that they now had a chance to assume power after so long a period, the two Kims failed to agree on which of them should be their party's candidate. In October 1987 Kim Dae Jung formed a new party, which he called the Party for Peace and Democracy (PPD).[6] The two Kims therefore divided the opposition vote, and Roh was elected with 36.7 percent of the popular vote. The Kims defeated themselves, Kim Young Sam obtaining 28 percent and Kim Dae-Jung 27 percent, while another candidate, Kim Jong Pil, won about 8 percent.

Roh's supporters consisted mostly of organized interests, elderly persons, and people in the lower income brackets, encompassing the bulk of the middle stratum. Kim Young Sam secured more support from white-collar workers and students, and most of Kim Dae Jung's support came from the two Cholla provinces and from alienated workers and students.

In the National Assembly elections of April 1988, however, Roh risked his gains by accepting a single-member-district electoral system, expecting that it would replicate the outcome of the presidential election. Indeed, the DJP was somewhat complacent in assuming that it would again be the majority party simply by taking advantage of the divisiveness of the opposition. Similarly, the Reunification Democratic party (RDP) thought that it would at least be the largest opposition party, as it had been in the presidential election. But the PPD nominated many new faces with popular appeal in Seoul City, and Kim Jong Pil also designated many former officials as candidates.

The Roh regime failed to generate innovative policies and decisive leadership after it assumed office in February 1988. The composition of Roh's first cabinet disappointed many people who had pinned high expectations on his commitment to recruiting new and competent leaders. In a similar vein the DJP's candidates for the elections fell short of the degree of public confidence necessary for a national mandate. Moreover, the revelation of a massive scandal involving Chun Kyung-hwan, a younger brother of Chun Doo Hwan and former head of the *Seamel* (New Community) Movement, further tarnished the DJP's campaign just when opposition parties were calling for a thorough investigation of corruption by the former president and his family.

Unlike the presidential election, the general elections had no clear-cut issue at stake. There was more involvement of money and more corruption. It appeared, therefore, that the voters cast their ballots on the basis of emotion and mood. In determining the outcome of these elections, regional sentiments and protest counted for more than other factors. The DJP failed to gain an outright majority, winning only 125 seats in the 299-seat National Assembly with 34.0 percent of the popular vote. Surprisingly, the PPD became the largest opposition party, with 71 seats and 19.3 percent of the popular vote, by securing its support mainly from the Cholla provinces, where all its candidates were elected, and Seoul City, where it won 17 of 42 seats. The RDP won only 60 seats even though its popular support was 23.8 percent, larger than that of the PPD. The New Democratic Republican party (NDRP) under Kim Jong Pil won 35 seats, with 15.6 percent of the popular vote.

Fragmentation of the vote was thus discernible; all four parties remained regional. The DJP's support was concentrated in North Kyungsang Province and Daegu City; the PPD's exclusively in the two Cholla provinces; the RDP's in Pusan City, where Kim Young Sam was a candidate, and in South Kyungsang Province; the NDRP's in the two Chungchong provinces, where Kim Jong Pil's candidates were elected. In May 1988 all three Kims were reelected presidents of their own parties, giving rise to the "one Roh and three Kims era" in Korean politics.

A central message of the 1988 elections seems to have been that the parties must practice consensus politics, either through coalition building or by lining up together on issues. Since the National Assembly is empowered to exercise an extensive range of investigative powers and to take votes of confidence on cabinet members, the government and the opposition-controlled assembly can easily find themselves on a collision course. Should they fail to accommodate each other, they may cause immobilism or another series of crises. The political instability resulting from such a situation might well invite another military intervention, which would restore the previous cycle of crisis politics. If both sides learn to compromise and reach consensus for the public good, however, they will make vital contributions to institutionalizing a working Korean political democracy.

It should be clear that democratization in Korea resembles neither another Philippines nor another Brazil. The Philippine case of people's power was a society-led change made possible because the Ferdinand Marcos regime failed totally and collapsed. The Brazilian case was a state-led democratization in which the military was able to agree with a united opposition on gradual civilianization. Unlike the Marcos regime, the Chun regime did not fail totally; the economy was booming. As a result, the middle stratum was growing as a stabilizing force. Unlike Brazil, Korea had neither a tradition of negotiation between the military and the opposition nor a united opposition. In the sense that the ruling party could get its presidential candidate elected and that the opposition could win a majority in the legislature, Korean democratization seems to be a product of compromise between state and society.

In the general elections in 1988, communal emotions and regional sentiments provided a link between political parties and the electorate. But this politics of redeeming resentment (called *han* in Korean) will be difficult to sustain. Invariably, as Korean society diversifies, crosscutting interests will emerge to link parties with the electorate. When parties can grow their social roots by successfully articulating such associational interest, they will become practitioners of interest politics in a truly pluralistic political system.

In shedding light on Korea's economic development, it is important to highlight the important role of the state. The state has been directing economic planning and policy, as in Japan and Taiwan, through its control over banks and credit. In cultivating human resources and in promoting export-oriented development, the state has taken initiatives and created an incentive system through tax benefits and subsidies. Korea resembles Japan and Taiwan in this regard by approximating a capitalist developmental state.[7]

The activation of socially based populist demands for welfare, the demands of business for autonomy from interfering state control, and the pressures emanating from the United States for market opening are all compelling the state to relinquish much of its control over the economy. The consequence of this change will be a devolution of power to the private sector, including business, labor unions, and consumers, and an increasing internationalization of the Korean economy.

In many ways the Korean economy is in a transition between a state-led developmental capitalism and a market-led welfare capitalism. Democratization and internationalization are making this shift inevitable. Already significant changes are emerging. For the first time in Korea's modern history, presidents of the Korean Association of Small and Medium Industries and of the Korean Chamber of Commerce and Industries were directly elected through a competitive process. Instead of capital accumulation mostly within the state sector, savings by households and companies are being encouraged. To reduce the high dependence rate of trade (the portion in GNP deriving from trade), reaching over 70 percent in 1987, efforts are being made to increase import substitution. By lessening automatic approval of bank loan applications and other privileges of conglomerates, the new government is trying to disperse the concentration of capital and assets away from a few huge corporations. Most important of all, severe restrictions on labor unions and their collective action are being lifted.

Until the 1987–1988 events, methods of making macroeconomic policy and managing labor disputes amounted to a kind of corporatism, for the state tightly regulated the economy. Economic plans placed priority on industrialization, especially on exports, over agriculture and domestic demands. But with democratization they are placing more emphasis on agriculture and on small and medium industries, since both the ruling party and the opposition promised in the elections to do so.

By any indicator, as shown in table 9–1, Korea's economic performance has been spectacular. The economy has grown 8 percent per annum over the past two decades. The government plans to sustain this rate to the end of the century.

The challenge to the Korean economy is how to tackle the serious dilemma inherent in the political need to enhance economic autonomy and facilitate welfare at home and at the same time to meet the requirements of internationalization. For example, Korea imports machinery and other intermediate goods from Japan and turns them into manufactured goods for export to the United States. Yet the recently agreed-on increased imports of beef and cigarettes from the United States are causing anti-American sentiments among Korean farmers. While the Korean economy is being incrementally integrated into what Robert Gilpin calls the "Japanese-American economy"

TABLE 9–1

MAJOR ECONOMIC INDICATORS, KOREA, 1962–1987

| | Per Capita GNP (U.S.$) | Growth Rate (%) | Saving Ratio (%) | Inflation Rate (%) | Current Account (U.S.$ millions) | Exports (U.S.$ millions) |
|---|---|---|---|---|---|---|
| 1962 | 87 | 2.2 | 3.3 | 8.3 | 33 | 41 |
| 1970 | 252 | 7.6 | 17.9 | 15.9 | −623 | 835 |
| 1980 | 1,589 | −4.8 | 22.9 | 28.7 | −5,321 | 17,505 |
| 1985 | 2,047 | 5.4 | 30.0 | 2.5 | −887 | 30,283 |
| 1987 | 2,826 | 12.3 | 36.7 | 3.0 | 9,854 | 27,281 |
| 1962–1970 | | 8.7 | | | | |
| 1971–1980 | | 8.0 | | | | |
| 1981–1987 | | 8.8 | | | | |

SOURCE: Compiled from *Monthly Bulletin of the Bank of Korea*.

(*nichibei keijai* in Japanese), paradoxically its opening is fanning the flames of nationalism.[8]

Economic development in Korea is therefore more dependent than political development on changes in the international order. But undertaking structural economic adjustment will entail both costs and benefits for democracy and industrialization, which will be determined through the political process. In this manner politics will affect economics, and vice versa.

## Korea's International Environment

From the inception of the republic, Korea's fate has been decisively influenced by its international environment. Located at a strategic point where the interest of four major powers—China, the Soviet Union, Japan, and the United States—intersect, the Korean peninsula has long been a major concern for global, regional, and local peace and stability. While the international security situation was tense during the cold war and especially after the Korean War in 1950, the Communist bloc and North Korea posed a threat to South Korea's security. Hence Seoul's international environment at this time was almost synonymous with its security relationship with the United States. As the cold war yielded to détente, however, South and North Korea set out to compete in their struggle for security, prosperity, and prestige in the international community.

Whenever U.S. global and regional interests in deterring Soviet adventurism were in accord with South Korean local interests in deterring North Korean adventurism, Korea's relations with the United States were warm. Whenever they diverged, those relations became strained, as they did during the first administration of Richard Nixon and the administration of Jimmy Carter.[9] During the administration of Ronald Reagan, too, Reagan adhered to the security-first policy; but he also refrained from interfering unduly in Korea's domestic politics and thus improved bilateral relations. The Reagan Doctrine of distinguishing totalitarianism from authoritarianism was also applied to Korea. Beginning in 1985, after U.S. relations with the Soviet Union turned businesslike and particularly after people's power in the Philippines succeeded (with some American help) in 1986, the Reagan administration became bolder in encouraging democratization and economic liberalization in Korea.

From the Korean vantage point, all three authoritarian rulers since 1948—Rhee, Park, and Chun—could delay democratization and liberalization by citing the importance of national security and economic development. In so doing, they could easily and with reason invoke the imminent danger posed by the North Korean military threat. But they also used security and unification issues to preserve their own power.

As long as the Korean peninsula remains divided, it will be difficult for South Korea to disengage itself entirely from the United States. Whenever serious conflict threatens or occurs, it is bound to affect not only the United States but all the other major powers. Maintaining a local balance of power on the Korean peninsula is thus vital to maintaining a regional balance of power in East Asia and the Pacific.

The realignment of big power relationships enables both the United States and South Korea to take more relaxed views of security and to be concerned more with political and economic issues. Insofar as economic relations are concerned, Korea has become a middle power to be reckoned with. Seen in this light, Korea's security, economic, and political environments in the 1980s have improved substantially, benefiting democracy and development at home. Korea's security relations with the United States have made steady progress since Reagan put a halt to the troop withdrawal plan in 1981. Seoul's economic cooperation with the United States and Japan has also improved steadily, despite trade friction. Most important, Korea was successful in attracting 160 countries to the 1988 Summer Olympics, decisively winning the diplomatic race with North Korea. Moreover, reforms and open-door policies of China and the Soviet Union have made it possible for South Korea to develop trade and sport cooperation with them, despite North Korea's adamant objections.

The reduction of tension and ideological conflict resulting from the realignment in big power relationships has thus had a positive effect on the Korean security situation, for no power wants another military conflict in Korea that may force it into a confrontation with the others. Especially when the Soviet Union under Mikhail Gorbachev also professes to be interested in improving relations with all other major and minor states, it is difficult for it to cause a military conflict in Korea. Moscow's arms control agreements with Washington, its withdrawal of troops from Afghanistan, and the normalizing of its relations with Beijing further reinforce this trend toward supporting peace and stability on its borders. Much the same can be said of China.

Korea's trade friction with the United States, Japan, and the European Community strains its economic relations. But Korea is the seventh largest trading partner of the United States, producing surpluses of $10 billion in 1987, $12 billion in 1988, and $6.5 billion in

1989. It is the third largest trading partner of Japan, gradually narrowing its current account deficit as a result of the appreciation of the yen. For these reasons Korea can strike a hard bargain with its trading partners. The growing interpenetration of investment, trade, and technology makes it inevitable for Korea and its partners to coordinate their macroeconomic policies in their common interests.

The loss of hegemony by the United States is posing a number of difficult problems for its allies. As the economic resources necessary for it to support a large-scale military establishment decline, its international authority is bound to fall commensurately.[10] Once this becomes generally understood, the United States will have no choice but to seek a strategy of "discriminate deterrence."[11] As long as it can no longer provide such public goods as security, international liquidity, markets, and resources free of charge, it must ask its allies to share the burden of providing them. Being an ally, South Korea is also being asked to join in burden sharing by helping to finance the stationing of U.S. troops in Korea, keeping sea lanes open in the Persian Gulf, and even helping the Philippines financially.

These requests, however, along with the pressure for market opening, are becoming the occasion for the expression of increasingly open and vociferous anti-American sentiment. It will be extremely difficult for any Korean government to meet Washington's demands fully. Some university students are already seizing on these demands in their slogans against the United States, depicting American troops as mercenaries. Closely related to these issues is the question of Washington's operational control over the Korean army in time of conflict. But as an American study report suggested, transferring such control to the Korean government during peacetime is a matter that can be negotiated to the satisfaction of both sides.[12]

Despite the easing of tensions in the East Asian region, North-South Korean relations have continued to be strained. One graphic demonstration of this was the blowing up of a Korean Air flight in November 1987, as Kim Hun-hui, one of the North Korean terrorists involved, revealed in January 1988. But with the advent of democratization in the South, a final source of hope for taking advantage of the political situation was lost to Pyongyang. Seoul's new domestic strength and international prestige place it in a better position to deal with some of Pyongyang's demands, including calls for political and military talks, even those addressed over Seoul's head to the United States. Roh's July 7, 1988, statement initiating South Korea's new *Nordpolitik* (not isolating Pyongyang but trying to induce it to join the international community) was but the first step in a newly confident and assertive South Korean foreign policy.

165

Substantive North-South negotiations began in late 1988, after the Olympic games. They were buttressed not only by the American policy of favoring direct talks but by the Soviet and Chinese participation in the Olympics, the broadening of trade with Moscow and Beijing, and the U.S. and Japanese attempts—however tentative and careful—to open channels of communication and trade with Pyongyang. Thus all outside parties favor some form of direct dialogue between Seoul and Pyongyang as the best means of reducing tension on the Korean peninsula.

As the economic center of gravity shifts to Asia and the Pacific and Korea's economic power grows, Korea has expanded its trade with China, the Soviet Union, and the East European countries. Korea's trade with China reached about $2.5 billion in 1987, over $3 billion in 1988 and $3.2 billion in 1989. That exceeded the volume of China's bilateral trade with the Soviet Union. Korea's trade with the Soviet Union amounted to about $200 million in 1988 and about $600 million in 1989. In 1989 Seoul set up trade offices with Hungary and then moved to full diplomatic recognition.

If the view is correct that the "territorial state" seeking to expand power by fighting has declined while the "trading state" seeking to expand economic relations through trade has prospered, Korea is a good example of the latter.[13] In the age of nuclear missiles and destructive conventional weapons, making war does not make economic sense. Relatively "declining" powers like the Soviet Union and the United States may have come to understand this. Should this trend of putting more emphasis on economic issues in international relations continue, Korea's influence is likely to grow. Korea is likely to expand even further its economic relations with relatively "rising" powers such as Japan and China.[14] Seoul has programmed $500 million to be used as foreign aid to developing countries over five years as part of its new Overseas Development Fund. As an advanced newly industrializing country, Korea is in a position to offer others its financial assistance and developmental experience.

On balance, the international environment in 1988 was evolving in a manner favorable to Korea's development toward political democracy and progress toward becoming an advanced economy.

## Whither Korea after the Olympics?

What are Korea's prospects after the Olympics? Before and during the historic occasion, all opposition leaders indicated their support for the games and moderated their political struggle accordingly. For example, Kim Dae Jung made it clear that he favored undertaking the National Assembly investigation of Chun's abuse of power and of the

Kwangju incident only after the Olympics. Although it is difficult to make accurate predictions about the political situation, one can be cautiously optimistic about the prospects for incremental transition toward a more pluralist system of politics and a system of welfare capitalism led by the private sector. Internationally, Korea should become one of the ten leading industrial powers as measured by trade volume, exceeding the United Kingdom and Italy by the year 2000, as forecast by the *Times* of London.

The most important political challenge for the government and the opposition is to dispose of the negative legacy of the Chun government without causing another crisis of authority and legitimacy. Since political forces, including those that previously fought their battles outside the system, are finally represented in the National Assembly, it may be possible for them to find a way to survive together without sinking the boat. They have an incentive for building a consensus one way or another, for the cost of not doing so is high.

The economic task ahead is to sustain steady growth while meeting the rising expectations of labor and the mounting demands from abroad to liberalize trade. The growth rate may well hover around 8 percent, in contrast to the 12.6 and 12.3 and 12.0 percent recorded in 1986, 1987, and 1988 respectively. In 1989 it did drop, to 7 percent. Given the high levels of savings and technology, Korea's economic prospects look brighter than its political prospects. Its economy should be able to generate enough growth to meet the requirements of redistribution and reinvestment. That was the pattern in Japan.

The foreign policy of Korea will undoubtedly exhibit more self-confidence and independence toward the United States. Its security relations with Washington in particular will have to be readjusted to reflect the changes in its internal and external settings. Initiatives for establishing a working relationship with the North will be made by the South, just as West Germany did with the East. These departures could be used to transform the current stalemate into a relationship of coexistence and coprosperity in which each side not only stops trying to gain at the other's expense but attempts to assist the other through diverse channels of communications, including economic and humanitarian means.

By no means did the Olympics bring a magic solution to Korea's problems. But if the picture drawn here comes close to the reality (a not unrealistic prophecy), Korea will no longer be on the periphery but will be one of the centers of the international community, as President Roh asserted in his inaugural address. At a minimum, political and economic obstacles to Korea's joining the Organization for Economic Cooperation and Development will disappear. One thing stands out: Korea will remain a vital member of the West in East Asia and the Pacific in promoting security, development, and stability.

PART THREE
# The Philippines

# 10
## Political Developments in the Philippines

*Carolina G. Hernandez*

The end of dictatorship and the revival of democracy in the Philippines ushered in an era of transition whose end or eventual outcome is by no means assured even more than four years after Corazon C. Aquino assumed power in February 1986. Laying the institutional infrastructures for a functioning democracy took almost two years, given a restive and divided military, political destabilization from loyalists of the deposed dictator, and inherited problems including the twin Communist and Moro insurgencies, a ravaged economy, and a corrupt bureaucracy. The near completion of political institution building with the local elections in January 1988 demanded that government move on to solving these inherited problems, which still threaten the survival of democracy in the country.

In the 1960s and 1970s, a major rationalization for the institution of authoritarian regimes in the third world was the need to achieve economic development, a process that was claimed to be much more efficiently accomplished under authoritarian than democratic regimes. Hence, the trade-off between democracy and development had significant persuasive effect among many developing societies. The Marcos leadership similarly used this trade-off to rationalize martial law and dictatorship. Fourteen years under this regime, however, did not vindicate the trade-off: instead of bringing about economic growth, social equity, well-being, and progress, the destruction of democratic political institutions and the suppression of human rights facilitated the rape of the national patrimony by a select few and at the expense of the great masses of Filipinos.

Unlike South Korea and Taiwan, where economic development was achieved within an authoritarian political system, in the Philippines people found themselves losing on both counts: they lost their democratic institutions and rights, and they became less developed

171

than their northeast Asian counterparts. Having destroyed democracy in 1972, the Philippines suffered economic decline within the
decade thereafter. The gross national product (GNP) slid from an
annual average of 6.6 percent in the 1970s to 4.7 percent in 1980, 3.6
percent in 1981, 2.8 percent in 1982, and 1.4 percent in 1983 and sank
below the black line to −5.3 percent in 1984[1] and even lower in 1985.
Poverty grew from 49 percent of the population in 1971 to 59 percent
in 1985;[2] in 1983 the upper 20 percent of Filipinos controlled 57
percent of total family income, while the poorest 30 percent survived
on less than 6 percent.[3] Foreign debt ballooned from about $1.6
billion in 1971 to over $26 billion in 1986.

This economic disaster, which partly fueled the opposition to the
Marcos regime, joined with other forces to explode in the popular
revolt of February 1986, as the dictatorship was toppled and redemocratization began. What is the future of democracy in a country in
deep economic difficulties, with two continuing insurgencies, and a
military whose role needs to be reduced and subordinated to civilian
political authority? How was Philippine society transformed from a
democracy to a dictatorship? What are the implications of the political
developments that took place under dictatorship for the process of
redemocratization in the country and for the future of democracy
itself? What are the factors that determine the future of democracy in
the country? These are the key questions this chapter seeks to
address.

The first section discusses the political development and changes
that took place during the dictatorship to provide the historical
background for an analysis of present trends and future prospects.
In the second section the political developments and trends evolving
after February 1986 and the ways they were shaped by the past are
discussed. An analysis of the factors determining the future of
democracy in the Philippines follows in the third section. The conclusion deals with democracy's future prospects in the country.

## The Destruction of Democracy

The imposition of martial law in September 1972 marked the demise
of democracy in the Philippines. Formally established in 1936 under
American colonial rule, American-style democratic institutions were
systematically destroyed under the pretexts of a threat from the
insurgencies by the Communists and by the Filipino Muslims in the
south and the need to establish a "new society" in the country.[4] In
fact, the new Communist party of the Philippines and its armed
wing, the New People's Army (NPA), established only in 1968–1969,

had a mere 300 members, hardly posing a threat to the country's security at that time.[5] The Muslim insurgents, organized under the Moro National Liberation Front (MNLF) in 1970, did not go into battle until after the imposition of martial law itself.[6] Martial law and dictatorship actually abetted the growth of both insurgencies.

With martial law came the arrest of opposition politicians led by the late Senator Benigno "Ninoy" S. Aquino, Jr., the ban on all political parties and political activities, the suppression of the press, the suspension and curtailment of civil and political liberties, and the dismantling of the Congress of the Philippines. Military courts took over the dispensation of justice until the instruments of martial law had been effectively put in place. Military tribunals remained in existence until 1986, although most of them were disbanded in the late 1970s.

In January 1973, a new constitution was proclaimed to have been overwhelmingly ratified by special citizens' assemblies created for this purpose.[7] They approved the charter, not by secret ballot as required by the operating rules of the 1935 Constitution, but by a mere show of hands. In spite of the infirmities of the procedure, the Supreme Court, once the authoritative and revered arbiter of legitimacy issues, ruled that the 1973 Constitution was not validly ratified by the Filipino people but in the same breath stated that there was "no judicial obstacle to the new Constitution being considered in force and effect."[8] Such an ambivalent ruling by the highest court in the land provided the legal legitimization of martial law.

From 1973 onward, political power became increasingly centralized and concentrated in the hands of one man. To control society, the Armed Forces of the Philippines (AFP) was used as the implementer of martial law. Operating on the principle of civilian supremacy over the military at all times, the AFP obeyed the orders of the civilian political leadership and, in so doing, became the partner of the civilian-led dictatorship from 1972 to 1986. Its highest ranking officers were consulted on the decision to impose martial law. All but one, the Vice Chief of Staff General Rafael Ileto, supported the decision. (Ileto was sent to Iran as ambassador, the first of several officers to become diplomats in exile under martial law and dictatorship.)

Because all the political institutions under the old constitution (except the presidency) were destroyed or put in suspended animation, the military was made to assume various roles that had been performed by civilian agencies: judicial, management, developmental, and even political. With the ban on political parties and the dismantling of Congress, the military became the dispenser of political patronage. Its traditional defense and law-and-order roles expanded with the imposition of a nighttime curfew and the execution of numerous presidential decrees, letters of instructions, general orders, and other kinds of executive directives. Its socioeconomic program, begun in earnest in 1966 during Marcos's first term of office, expanded. The enlarged role of the military enhanced its position in the political order, providing it an unprecedented opportunity to develop a political function.[9]

Marcos may have deliberately prepared the military for precisely this kind of role as early as his first term of office. His first state-of-the-nation address included his plan to improve the training and equipment of the AFP and to expand the Socio-Economic Military Program (SEMP), one that had been on the books since 1958 but that became institutionalized only after he assumed office. His first four-year economic plan averred the need to harness the military for national development purposes quite explicitly. It stated:

> The Armed Forces of the Philippines, with its manpower, material, and equipment resources plus its organizational cohesiveness and discipline, possess a tremendous potential to participate in economic development which should be exploited to the maximum. Such participation becomes imperative considering that the problem besetting the country is socio-economic rather than military and that the resources available to solve this problem are scarce and limited.[10]

The training curricula at the Philippine Military Academy and at the service schools were changed to include social and behavioral sciences. The prescribed career development pattern for officers was similarly revamped to include, as another criterion for promotion, the acquisition of a graduate degree from civilian educational institutions in such fields as business administration, economics, public administration, and political science. This training considerably increased the capability of the officer corps in dealing with nonmilitary functions.

It was also during his first term of office that the AFP's engineering expertise was upgraded through an expansion of its First Engineering Brigade and the establishment of a second brigade out of American military assistance. This assistance was extended in exchange for Philippine participation in the Vietnam War through the Philippine Civic Action Group to Vietnam.

Centralization of power was the rationale behind the integration of police forces throughout the country into a single National Police Force, which was placed under the direction of the chief of the Philippine constabulary, himself a military officer. This effectively removed administrative control and supervision of the police from local executives and placed all armed units of the government under the president in his capacity as commander in chief of the armed forces through the mediation of the military hierarchy.

In the early 1980s, further centralization of power occurred with the elimination of the defense minister from the chain of command, making a direct link between the president and the military through the chief of staff of the AFP. Furthermore, the major service commanders were effectively bypassed through the organization of Regional Unified Commands, composite units at the regional level under commanders directly responsible to the chief of staff instead of their own major service commanders.

The expansion of the military role necessitated increasing the size of the AFP. From 55,000 men in 1972, it grew to 180,000 or 250,000 by 1985, if the Integrated National Police and the Civilian Home Defense Forces were included. It consumed the largest share of the budget in the 1970s, at the expense of education and other social services.

Control over society also required the suppression and control of the media, accomplished through various decrees defining the limits of what could be published, broadcast, or televised. Monopolization of the media by the government and by Marcos's cronies—individuals closely associated with Marcos who served as frontmen in the effort to control the economy—also contributed to that suppression. Stories critical of the first family, the military, duly constituted authority, and Philippine society and culture were banned. "Envelopmental" journalism bought off many journalists,[11] who espoused the government cause in exchange for financial and other rewards.[12]

To ensure dictatorial control beyond martial law, several amendments to the 1973 Constitution were introduced in 1976. One of them was Amendment 6, which authorized the president to exercise legislative power even after the end of martial rule and the election of a regular legislature, if in his view it was necessary to do so. This gave him unlimited legislative power and thus rendered the legislature, elected in 1978 and in 1984, a virtual rubber stamp.[13]

In the revival of political parties during the elections for the Interim National Assembly in 1978 Marcos's Kilusang Bagong Lipunan (New Society Movement) dominated politics. Severely handicapped by political suppression since 1972 and by lack of access to material and political resources, as well as by internal divisions and leadership rivalries, the two traditional parties could not effectively compete with the New Society Movement. Control over the entire electoral and political process also ensured the movement's domination of politics. This control was facilitated by an active election boycott after 1978 by leading opposition groups convinced of the futility of electoral exercises under a dictatorship.

The requirement that justices file undated letters of resignation and that judicial positions be filled with either close associates of Marcos or advocates of Marcos's political enterprise compromised judicial independence. Thus it was that the judiciary supported the government position in cases filed before it by opposition groups contesting the legality or constitutionality of acts undertaken during martial law and dictatorship.[14] Judicial affirmation of legitimacy facilitated the acceptance of martial law by people who were much influenced by legalese.

As martial law and dictatorship progressed, the two insurgencies also grew. The New People's Army expanded from 300 members in 1972 to an estimate topping 26,000 and a presence in 60 percent of the country's seventy-three provinces and in 20 percent of the *barangays* (smallest political units) by 1985. The Moro National Liberation Front tied up over 60 percent of the military's fighting force at its height in the mid-1970s. The rebellion damaged industry, agriculture, and private property and exacted a heavy toll on the civilian population in Mindanao. It required international mediation by the Organization of Islamic Conference to halt the war through the conclusion of the Tripoli Agreement in 1976 promising regional autonomy to thirteen provinces with a significant Muslim population. Martial law failed dismally in halting the advance of the Communist movement in the Philippines, though it temporarily suppressed the Muslim insurgency. Communism thrived amid growing poverty and repression in the Philippine countryside.

The assassination of Ninoy Aquino in August 1983, as he returned to the Philippines from a three-year exile in the United States, signaled the beginning of the end of dictatorship. His assassination while under military custody forced former political fence sitters to come to grips with the reality that the dictatorship had become so venal it would stop at nothing standing in the way of its purposes. The assassination triggered massive public protests and demonstrations at levels never before seen in Philippine political history. Significant in this development was the active participation of the middle and upper classes of Philippine society, professionals, and businessmen, including most of the Catholic hierarchy in the active opposition to the continuation of dictatorship.

Within the military, a group of young officers banded together in the Reform the Armed Forces of the Philippines Movement and came out openly for military reform and a return to the professionalism in reaction to the implication of the military in the plot to assassinate Senator Aquino.[15] Their spiritual advisers were Vice Chief of Staff General Fidel V. Ramos, widely perceived as a professional, and Defense Minister Juan Ponce Enrile; the loyalties of these two close associates of Marcos were under suspicion.

Deepening economic crisis, erosion of political legitimacy, and fear of the eventual triumph of the Communist insurgency all combined to set the forces for change in motion. Even the United States shifted its policy of outright support for the dictatorship to continued support conditioned by demands for economic, political, and military reforms.[16] These pressures eventually succeeded in pushing for the holding of presidential elections calculated to give Marcos a fresh mandate one year ahead of the 1987 schedule.

Opposition groups other than the hard left decided to participate in the February 1986 elections. The strategy was to deliver a massive majority vote to Marcos's opponents to make it difficult for the dictatorship to manipulate the results and to make electoral engineering so patently obvious as to destroy the credibility of the managed outcome. After much bargaining and intercession of the clergy it was agreed that Ninoy Aquino's widow, Cory, would lead the opposition ticket. Her running mate was Salvador H. Laurel, chairman of the largest political aggregation, the United Democratic Opposition, and scion of one of the most prominent political families in the country.

### Recent Political Developments in the Philippines

The early presidential elections proved to be a fatal mistake for Marcos. Massive electoral frauds triggered popular disenchantment even among those who voted for him. They galvanized opposition efforts to bring down the dictatorship through civil disobedience. They also fueled the popular support for the military mutiny that might have been launched to ensure the survival of the military leaders but that was nevertheless popularly perceived as an important breakthrough in the struggle against the dictator. These and other developments in February 1986 brought the dictatorship down, and the era of democratic reconstruction began.

President Aquino was thus installed in power by a popular revolt. Although she must have been the legitimate winner in the February elections, the determination of the dictator to hold on to power cheated her of that victory.[17] Consequently, what initial opposition to her presidency there was came largely from forces still loyal to Marcos. She gained the support of the majority of Filipinos, however, as indicated by the general agreement most Filipinos expressed on the political tasks she undertook to rebuild democracy in the country.

177

**Political Institution Building**. During the two years after the February revolution political institutions have been constructed to provide the basis for a functioning democracy. A new constitution, drafted by an appointed body, was ratified by a record 80 percent of the electorate in February 1987. It provided for a presidential system of government with a bicameral legislature; mechanisms for separation of powers and checks and balances; public accountability including recall, civilian control over the military, and ways to secure the national patrimony and economy for its citizens and against foreign exploitative interests.

The ratification of the new Constitution also legitimized President Aquino's assumption to power, as its Transitory Provisions set the tenure of the incumbent president and vice president to 1992. Curiously, the challenge posed by the opponents of the Constitution—Marcos loyalists, traditional politicians who lost power after the popular revolt, and former Defense Minister (now Senator) Enrile— to the effect that "a vote for the Constitution is a vote for Cory" validated her mandate to rule when the charter was overwhelmingly ratified by 77 percent of the electorate. In fact, it was President Aquino's popularity that led to the Constitution's ratification, since while only 32 percent of the electorate read the document, an overwhelming majority approved it.[18]

Popular support for the government was once more demonstrated during the legislative elections. Aquino-endorsed candidates swept the polls. Indeed, if the Commission on Elections, the body in charge of electoral administration, had been more efficient in discharging its responsibility, it is probable that twenty-three of the twenty-four senatorial seats would have been won by her candidates.

Nevertheless, while the legislative elections proved her tremendous popularity, they also previewed a major problem that needed to be sorted out if government programs and policies were to be successfully developed, adopted, and implemented: President Aquino did not have a political party that could effectuate policy formulation and implementation. Her coalition was a motley camp composed of traditional politicians opposed to Marcos, businessmen, political activists, the religious, and professionals. There were also several political parties and other groups joined only in their desire to defeat Marcos and to obtain political power long denied them by the dictatorship. The coalition thus had no common political and economic ideology out of which a common platform and program could have been formulated; neither did these groups have a consensus on power sharing.

Political competition from within the coalition surfaced soon after

February 1986 over issues such as the appointment of local executives and the sharing of key government positions and agencies. This competition also became evident in the legislative elections, which saw the breakup of coalition unity over the choice of candidates for the House of Representatives. It was easier for President Aquino to decide on a common slate of senatorial candidates, since these positions were elected nationwide, than it was to come up with agreed-upon candidates for the House of Representatives. The drive for political base building preparatory to future elections, especially the presidential election slated for 1992, therefore proved too power-ful for coalition unity to be preserved. Candidates supported by various members of the coalition vied against each other, splitting proadministration votes in the process and resulting, in a number of instances, in the election of opposition candidates.

This was repeated in the January 1988 local elections with greater ferocity and unstated bitterness among coalition members. In the effort at base building, they competed in mending political fences with various politicians, including those closely identified with Mar-cos. The two leading groups identified with President Aquino—the PDP-LABAN (Philippine Democratic party–*Lakas ng Bayan* coalition led by Senator Aquilino Pimentel and the president's younger brother, Jose "Peping" Cojuangco) and the *Lakas ng Bansa* (People's Power formerly led by her brother-in-law, Paul Aquino, and, after the local elections, by House Speaker Ramon Mitra)—supported candi-dates closely identified with Marcos. So did the Liberal party wing led by Senate President Jovito Salonga. Politics as "addition" became the name of the game once more.[19] Among the outcomes of this competition were the election of some opposition candidates at the local level, the restitution of old Marcos associates in local government positions, and relative disenchantment among individuals who hoped for a new sort of politics to develop after February 1986.

Two other restored democratic institutions were the free press and the judiciary. Freedom led to the revival of the tradition of a vibrant and near-licentious press. Some twenty-five dailies now com-peted for the country's 5 million readership. Their exuberance, un-derstandable after fourteen years of suppression, could nevertheless injure the fragility of the transition. The press also needs to restore a sense of social responsibility, much compromised among many prac-ticing journalists during the period of "envelopmental" journalism.

Judicial revamping was accompanied by the removal of undesir-able elements in the court system. The leadership promptly restored the tradition in the Supreme Court that its most senior justice serve as its head. Thus, Claudio Teehankee, twice bypassed by Marcos for

179

his too independent spirit, was appointed chief justice at last. The performance of the judiciary in the delivery of justice will be a crucial factor in the survival of democracy, because lack of justice has been a key factor in the apathy and alienation from government masses of Filipinos experienced during the dictatorship. In fact, injustice, more than poverty, could very well have been the major cause of Communist growth during this time.

The only remaining tasks in political institution building lay in the election of *barangay* officials and genuine bureaucratic organizations. The latter involved the rationalization of the bureaucracy, the inculcation of a real sense of public service, public accountability, and professionalism among its personnel and the limiting of graft and corruption, which had become institutionalized during the past regime. No doubt *barangay* elections will be easier to accomplish than the other gargantuan tasks. Yet these could be a major determinant in the survival of democracy for the simple reason that government programs aimed at bringing about socioeconomic and political stability can be effective only with an efficient, enlightened, and publicly trusted bureaucracy. Finally, the harder task of institutionalizing these democratic political structures and the processes associated with them lie ahead.

**The Institutionalization of Civilian Control over the Military.** One of the most difficult tasks confronting the government was institutionalizing civilian control over the military. The transformation of the military from a civilian-subordinated institution to a partner of government during the previous regime was a key problem in this regard. It is never easy to clip power already enjoyed by any group or institution.

The observance of civilian supremacy in the postdictatorship period was complicated by the mutiny of some groups in the military. This was one of the precipitate factors in the popular revolt against the Marcos regime and the ensuing installation of a new government committed to democratic reconstruction. Instead of acknowledging the military's subordinate role in the popular revolt, there appeared a belief that the military provided the new government the power to rule. As such, some of its members expected the right to equal partnership in the new order.

As a consequence of this perception, some in the military felt betrayed when an equal role was denied them. The dismissal of Defense Minister Enrile in November 1986 amid a military plot against the government was a bitter disappointment for his followers in the military. This might have triggered their attempt to wrest power through the coup attempt of August 28, 1987, even as they capitalized on festering military resentment stemming from what they felt were legitimate grievances. These included low salaries for the enlisted ranks; inadequate supplies, clothing, and housing; outmoded equipment; deprofessionalization; contempt for men in uniform among key officials in the first Aquino cabinet; and uneven government policies regarding national reconciliation, human rights, and the insurgency.

Other groups in the military remained committed to Marcos. Hence, the first four military attempts against the government in 1986 and 1987 were undertaken by Marcos loyalists in the military. As each of these attempts failed, however, these groups became increasingly marginalized, and they eventually ceased to pose a serious threat to the government.

From August 1987 to early 1990, there have been two further military attempts against the government, despite the fact that the government took steps to redress many of the soldiers' grievances. The issue of overstaying generals, whose tours of duty were extended by Marcos, had been effectively addressed through their retirement. This unclogged the promotions channel and restored the badly shattered morale of the officer corps.

Military pay scales were upgraded several times before August 1987 and once more afterward. A more even policy on human rights violations covering offenses committed by both military and insurgents was also developed. The failure of the peaceful route to end the insurgencies, a route initially opposed by the military, led President Aquino "to unleash the sword of war," making her approach more compatible with military perspectives on the matter. To be fair, however, as early as April 1986, she stated that if the policy of peace through national reconciliation failed, she would take a tougher line on the insurgencies.

The new Constitution also addressed institutionalizing civilian supremacy by restoring the controls of civilian political institutions over the military. The president remained the commander in chief of the armed forces, and military appointments and promotions were subjected to these two branches of government. In addition, explicit provisions constraining the military's participation in politics were crafted into the Constitution.

Severe limitations on the emergency powers of the executive reduced the probability of a civilian-military political partnership akin to what evolved during the past regime. Unlike the 1935 Constitution, the new Constitution prohibited the commander in chief from declaring martial law and suspending the writ of *habeas corpus* indefinitely. In addition, the commander in chief cannot extend the emergency unilaterally beyond sixty days; legislative and judicial determination of the emergency is mandated by the new Constitution.[20]

The Constitution also prohibits military involvement in any partisan political activity except voting,[21] as well as appointment of active duty military personnel to civilian positions in the government, including government-owned corporations and their subsidiaries.[22] It mandates the separation of the police forces from the military, in recognition of the distinction between the police function of law and order and the military function of external defense. Administrative control and supervision of a national police are assigned to a civilian national police commission, although the authority of local executives over police forces operating within their jurisdiction in accordance with law is also recognized.[23]

The Constitution prohibits the extension of tours of duty of retirable officers, limits the tenure of office of the chief of staff to three years, mandates disbanding paramilitary forces that could be inconsistent with the concept of a citizen armed force prescribed for the country, and addresses other corporate interests of the military by providing adequate pensions and care for verterans and their families.[24] In short, the new charter, if fully implemented, provides the basis for institutionalizing civilian supremacy. The remaining question is the ability of the government to overcome military opposition to reform along the lines prescribed by the Constitution.

In this regard, the continuing threat of the Communist insurgency stands in the way of dismantling the paramilitary forces perceived necessary to the military's counterinsurgency program. The government awaits enactment of specific legislation to implement these constitutional directives. It is important that this task is undertaken while officers remain who are committed to the principle of civilian supremacy. Many who rose from the ranks during the Marcos years, acquired civilian-oriented skills, and were exposed to a prominent military role could resist the notion of civilian supremacy. This is why it is important to institutionalize civilian control before the military hierarchy becomes completely dominated by this sort of officer.

**The Establishment of Political Stability by Addressing the Twin Insurgencies.** Over military objection, President Aquino pursued a policy of peace through national reconciliation by releasing political prisoners and initiating peace talks with both the CPP/NPA through the left-wing umbrella organization of the National Democratic Front

(NDF) and the Moro leadership. A ceasefire forged with the NDF in December 1986 collapsed in January 1987 amid the violence of a farmers' demonstration over agrarian reform.

The talks were bound to fail, given the difficulty of acceding to the front's demands of power sharing and immediate dismantling of Philippine military bases used by American military forces. Having boycotted the elections and having been absent from the popular revolt against Marcos in February 1986, the NDF could not realistically expect the government to share power with it. Its demand on the bases would require a reversal of President Aquino's commitment to honor the bases agreement until its expiration in 1991 and to keep her options open at that time.

The chief gains of the peace talks and the ceasefire were the achievement of a moral authority on the part of the government to adopt a tougher approach to the insurgency and the limitation placed by the ceasefire on the NDF's ability to engage in united front activities. The constraints on political participation must have been a consideration in the left's disengagement from the peace talks, as well as the concern that life in the lowlands could seduce the non-ideologues among them to abandon the armed struggle. The NDF was also pessimistic that anything substantive could emerge from the talks.

In the case of the Moro insurgency, the revival of its leader, Nur Misuari, who had been on the way to political oblivion, might have been an error on the government's part. The Moro front was relatively subdued during the closing years of the Marcos regime, partly because of internal division and competition over leadership, the weariness of the people over a war that had taken a heavy toll, the cooptation of some of its leaders by the Marcos government, and the reduction in international support for its cause. Misuari was revived with the peace initiatives of the Aquino government, which then committed an obvious error by singling Misuari out among the Muslim leadership instead of seeking a broader-based Moro counter-part to the government negotiating panel.

Misuari's demand of the virtual ceding of twenty-three provinces in Mindanao, Sulu, and Palawan to his control, with the front's Bangsa Moro Army as its armed forces independent of the AFP chain of command, was preposterous. The Tripoli Agreement, which Mis-uari signed with the Marcos government in 1976, covered only thirteen provinces, of which only five were Muslim dominated. Such a demand is also contrary to the national policy of regional autonomy within the framework of national sovereignty and unfragmented national territory. Besides these considerations, Misauri's leadership was bound to be contested by such other Muslim groups as those led by Hashim Salamat and the Pendatun and Abbas clans.

As already noted, the collapse of the peace talks led the government to adopt a tougher line against the insurgencies. While these insurgencies continued to challenge the government, a trend indicating that the government might be reversing the growth of the Communist insurgency seemed to be developing. The strength of the NPA had been reduced to about 22,000 from over 26,000 in February 1986. A pattern indicating some erosion of popular support for the movement seemed to have emerged between July 1985 and March 1987.[25] In July 1985 only 26 percent of Filipinos polled disagreed that the NPA network was widespread in their locality, as against 31 percent who did in May 1986 and 42 percent in March 1987. Agreement on the statement that most of the people in their province or city did not sympathize with the NPA increased from 18 percent in July 1985 to 36 percent in May 1986 and 47 percent in March 1987.

Moreover, an increasing number believed that most NPA activities were not justifiable (20 percent in July 1985, 31 percent in May 1986, and 47 percent in March 1987), and that the Communist party should not be legalized (44 percent in July 1985, 54 percent in May 1986, and 71 percent in March 1987). In early 1987, an overwhelming majority (75 percent) believed that the government should be careful and not too trusting in reconciling with the Communist rebels, while 63 percent thought that the National People's Army and the National Democratic Front should not be allowed to endorse their candidates in the elections. Only 17 percent agreed that popular support for the rebels was increasing, and 19 percent believed that the present administration was dominated or too influenced by Communists or radicals.

In October 1987, however, fewer people (34 percent) disagreed that the rebel army network was widespread in their locality, compared to 42 percent in March 1987. But those who agreed with the statement increased only by 1 percent (from 39 percent to 40 percent), the undecided decreased from 14 percent to 11 percent, and those who did not know or did not respond apparently increased from 2 percent to 16 percent.[26]

Popular perception that support for the Communists was increasing rose from 17 percent in March 1987 to 20 percent in October 1987. Notably, however, those who disagreed with the statement declined from 63 percent to just 39 percent in the same period, while the undecided increased from 15 percent to 19 percent and those who either did not know or did not respond apparently increased from 5 percent to 22 percent. Probably escalating violence precipitated by the tougher line adopted by both the military and the NPA made people less willing to express their opinions on the insurgency for fear of possible reprisal from either group. Likely too, many more people were rethinking their positions vis-à-vis the NPA/NDF and the Aquino government in light of the slowness with which much-needed socioeconomic reforms were being introduced and consequently might not have been prepared to state their opinions on matters affecting both camps.

A plurality (42 percent), however, continued to believe that most NPA activities were not justifiable. Interestingly, 40 percent believed that Communist rebels were responsible for many human rights abuses, 30 percent believed it was the military, and another 30 percent believed it was the Muslim rebels.[27]

The military campaign against the NPA resulted in the capture of several high-ranking officials of the Communist party and the NPA at both the national and the regional levels. The consequent breakup of the party's command structure in the Central Visayas region in early 1988 was seen as a major breakthrough in the effort against the insurgents. The capture of the alleged NPA commander in 1986 and the party secretary general and a member of its central committee in March 1988 also caused significant erosion of morale within the hierarchy, even though leadership change did not significantly affect the ability of the rebels to continue the armed struggle.[28]

In mid-March 1988, a news leak reported a secret military intelligence study indicating the reduction of NPA strength to about 22,000 and an estimate that by 1992, the NPA would be reduced to at least half this number. Whether this development will continue is largely a function of the ability of the government to redress festering socioeconomic problems, to deliver social services at the grass-roots level, thereby making government more visible there, and to reform the military toward a more people-oriented and service-dedicated organization. Many see a comprehensive agrarian reform program as a political requirement of a successful counterinsurgency drive. A modified version of such a program was adopted as the government's centerpiece of development.

With regard to the Moro secessionist drive, the major danger lies in the attempt of the Moro front to internationalize the issue by gaining membership in the Organization of Islamic Conference. This organization is composed of countries whose cooperation is important to the Philippines, depending as it does on the oil exports of member countries. Three of the Philippines' partners in the Association of Southeast Asian Nations (ASEAN) are also members of the organization. Their continuing support for the Philippine position on Moro secessionism has been crucial in this international forum.

Another danger lies in the possibility that some kind of tactical alliance might be forged between the Communists and the Moro front. While the likelihood of this alliance seems remote, political expediency has occasioned stranger things in the past. One constraint is that such an alliance might erode grass-roots support for the MNLF, especially among traditional Muslims whose religiosity may run counter to what has been widely propagandized as a godless ideology.

**Return of Traditional Politics and Politicians.** The two elections of 1987 and 1988 witnessed the return of traditional politics and politicians into the political arena. To begin with, the opposition ticket in the 1986 presidential elections consisted of members of two traditional political families, the Aquinos of Tarlac Province and the Laurels of Batangas Province. Moreover, President Aquino comes from politically entrenched families of the Sumulongs of Rizal Province and of the Cojuangcos of Tarlac. She married into the Aquino family, which has also been prominent in Philippine politics for many decades. Some hoped that because she was not herself a politician she would pursue policies and adopt attitudes reflecting the spirit of the new politics. Part of her popularity stemmed from the mold cast for her by Marcos—that of an ordinary housewife.

The results of the two elections after 1986, however, tended to demonstrate the survival of traditional political elites. In the Senate, about three-fourths of its members came from families with a long history of politics. In the House of Representatives, 130 of its 200 members belonged to these families, and another 39 were related to them. Thirty-one members did not have electoral records before 1972 and were not related to these families. Predictably, an overwhelming majority (102) of the congressmen who came from these families or were related to them opposed Marcos during the dictatorship, while only 67 came from families closely identified with the deposed dictator.[29] The return of the traditional elite was not surprising in view of the suppression of genuine political competition since 1972 as well as the domination and control of politics by Marcos. No genuine effort toward recruitment of the political elite was expended during this time. Consequently, traditional politicians simply moved back into the political vacuum left by Marcos and his associates. These elites were in a far better position than other individuals or groups in society to engage in politics. In a manner of speaking, the country was put in a state of suspended animation for fourteen years, after which old elites and political habits resurfaced in the political arena.

In this regard, the predominance of politics at the expense of principles and the focus on personalities rather than on issues survived as well. As already noted, the contest for political allies did not prevent the groups associated with the Aquino coalition from reaching politicians closely linked to Marcos. Among the existing political groups, only the Liberal party led by Senate President Salonga had a coherent program and platform. Yet it was not immune to courting any and every politician of some import regardless of ideology or inclination and inviting them to join the party.

At the same time that traditional politics and politicians returned, new faces emerged. Thirty-one of them out of 200 in the House of Representatives was not discouraging. More significant was the apparent rejection of candidates from prominent political families during the local elections of January 1988. Outstanding casualties in the struggle against the establishment of political dynasties (mandated in the new Constitution) included President Aquino's sister-in-law, who was defeated in the mayoralty race in Quezon City, one of her cousins on the Sumulong side who ran in Rizal Province, and Vice President Laurel's nephew who lost to a relative newcomer on his own political turf. Thus, one finds the political defeat of prominent families, some to relative newcomers, an apparent public rejection of traditional politicians.

Even the left-wing *Partido ng Bayan* (PnB or People's party, alternatively known as Alliance for New Politics or ANP) was able to have two of its candidates elected to the House of Representatives. A number of candidates identified with them similarly won in January 1988, one as vice mayor of Angeles, site of Clark Air Force Base, whose mayor is a well-known advocate of the bases. This moderate success may encourage the Left to consider the electoral road to political power much more seriously. A stake in an open democratic system could facilitate the transformation of left-wing parties into West European types, a process that could augur well for the growth of pluralism and democracy.

### Variables Affecting the Future of Democracy

Our general argument is that democracy's future depends on the ability of the present government to retain popular confidence in and maintain popular support for the present system. This in turn depends on economic recovery, which largely determines: (1) the capacity of the government to address key socioeconomic problems such as poverty and unemployment; (2) its ability to finance programs directed at social equity such as a comprehensive agrarian reform program; (3) the ability of government to provide adequate salaries for the civilian and military bureaucracies as well as for personnel of the public school system; and (4) its ability to underwrite the delivery of basic social services to the grass roots.

Economic recovery will facilitate not only the creation of new employment for the country's 750,000 new entrants into the labor force every year but also upgraded compensation for laborers and improvement of the living standards of the general population. Challenges posed by the Communist insurgency can be better met with these conditions in place, since popular support for the insurgency would decrease if not completely disappear. In the last analysis, poverty and social injustice lie at the heart of popular support for the insurgency. The effective redress of these conditions by the government can break the backbone of the insurgency in a manner far outweighing any kind of military action against the rebels.

A government enjoying popular confidence and support cannot be overthrown by military action. In particular, the Philippine military is well aware of the critical importance of popular support. Having enjoyed popular support in its apparently hopeless mutiny against the Marcos regime in 1986, the military cannot afford to forget its lesson.

The timing of the August 28, 1987, coup attempt by the same elements that mounted the mutiny in 1986 indicates that such a lesson had been learned. The August 28 coup came after a massive transportation strike paralyzing metropolitan Manila in protest of an oil price increase. The coup makers must have interpreted this strike as a withdrawal of popular support for the Aquino government, seeing it as an opportunity to win this support by an alternative group of leaders. They erred in equating opposition against a specific policy with opposition to the government itself. The coup failed to obtain popular backing, and the fence sitters in the military threw their support behind the constitutional order, a position that the majority within the military apparently continues to hold. A similar analysis can be made of the much more serious December 1989 coup attempt.

Effective government performance at the local level is extremely important in generating popular confidence in and popular support for the present system. For most of the population, what the national government does is of small moment in their daily life. The closeness of local government and the immediacy of its impact make local government a more important and relevant institution for them. The effectiveness of the Negros Occidental provincial government in winning popular support and in reversing NPA influence in the province should be a lesson other local governments would do well to learn.

The decisive exercise of political will is similarly important in addressing the sources of social discontent threatening the survival of democracy. The leadership cannot afford to yield initiatives to other groups or institutions in society without losing its credibility and popular support. An indecisive government also tends to tempt the military's appetite for political power. The military ethos is in awe of the decisive exercise of political will and the effective use of political power. A leadership that acts decisively will effectively earn the respect and obedience of the military.

Democracy is said to take root most easily in societies with a large middle class whose population enjoys a fairly high rate of literacy and has a democratic tradition. If education rather than income defines class, the Philippines might in fact have a sizable middle class. It has a highly educated and trained population, able to compete with other nationalities in the international labor market. Its rate of literacy is one of the highest in Asia, and it is one of the few places in this region with a long tradition of democracy. If the theory is correct, these factors are bound to have a positive effect on the future of democracy in the Philippines.

Finally, the lamentable and unfortunate experience with dictatorship has left a deep mark in the collective memory of the nation. This mark finds its expression in the country's new Constitution, which sets severe constraints against executive power at a time when strong powers may be required to address the gargantuan problems inherited from decades of economic mismanagement and political misrule. The framers of the new Constitution must have been aware of this dilemma; yet they chose to place those limitations on executive powers rather than risk another disastrous misadventure with a future dictator. The tragic experience of dictatorship, so recently suffered, should be a powerful influence for democracy within the foreseeable future.

## Prospects for the Future

In 1985, I drafted a chapter for a volume on the Philippines edited by John Bresnan, in which I articulated a positive outlook for a democratic reconstitution of the political order.[30] When the book was finally published after the popular revolt in February 1986, one reviewer thought my optimism about the prospects of democracy in the Philippines was "wishful thinking." The country's long exposure to liberal democratic ideas dating from the Propaganda Movement of the second half of the nineteenth century was implicitly dismissed as unimportant and immaterial in the face of the facility with which martial law destroyed democracy in 1972 amid the apparently silent acquiescence of the Filipino people.

Be that as it may, I continue to maintain a cautious optimism regarding the prospects of democracy in the Philippines. Given the variables that determine the survival of democracy, the balance sheet tends to support this position. This is not to say the situation is stable, but in spite of the flux, important developments augur well for the future of democracy in the Philippines.

For one, the popularity of the present government continues. While satisfaction ratings of President Aquino's performance have declined from the heady but unrealistic levels of 78 percent in October 1986 and 76 percent in March 1987 to 55 percent in October 1987, most recent ratings remain high compared with the popularity enjoyed by other world leaders.[31] The lower rating reflects a more sober and realistic assessment of a people no longer gripped by the euphoria of February 1986 but more in tune with the world of the politically possible in the Philippine context. President Aquino also remains the most popular leader in her country, although her ratings decline.

The concern that many government supporters have expressed over the government's ability to solve economic and political problems does not alter their position that there is no better alternative to the present government and that for all the failings of a democratic regime it is still better than a dictatorship. Even such above-ground left-wing groups as the Socialist BISIG maintained their critical support for the present government, adopting the tactic of criticizing specific rightist policies, tendencies, and elements of the present government rather than opposing the government itself.

In spite of continuing perceptions of instability, an inhospitable international protectionist environment, bearish foreign investment behavior toward the country, a sizable debt service burden, and damages caused by natural calamities, the economy's negative performance began to be reversed in 1986. The economy grew by 1.5 percent in that year, by 5.5 percent in 1987, by 7 percent in 1988, and by 6 percent in 1989. A more positive response from foreign investors could speed up the economic recovery and thereby bolster the country's chances for political stability by winning over grass-roots support for the Communist insurgency through improved socioeconomic opportunities.

An early approval and implementation of a comprehensive agrarian reform, while short of solving the problem of social inequality, could be a symbolic beginning, preempting the seductive attraction of the Communist program among landless farmers and other agricultural workers. Failure to do so could spell the difference between survival and destruction of the democratic infrastructures that President Aquino has diligently constructed during the past four years.

Much international good will for the Philippines remains, a willingness to help the country solve its many problems despite its failure to realize many of the expectations generated by the success of the popular revolt to end the dictatorship. Without international support, economic recovery would be much more difficult to achieve. To harness such support, the Philippines should apply international assistance to the basic socioeconomic problems of the country. International financing for a comprehensive agrarian reform program, which could be extremely costly if it were to work, is a possibility that a number of countries and international agencies could underwrite. A scheme of land transfer that is not confiscatory could erode much landlord opposition to agrarian reform. Clearly, a creative approach is required if the problem is to be solved. This remains a major challenge the Aquino government needs to meet more responsively and effectively.

On the political front, the prospects for pluralism are good, if only for the political ambitions of many politicians who would not be able to yield power to their competitors. They would prefer keeping their own political machinery to fusing it with others whose leaders hold similar ambitions. Consequently, the revival of a two-party system in the country is not likely under present circumstances. Constitutional support for pluralism, embodied in the party list and sectoral representation, would work against the revival of the two-party system. The continued persistence of the above-ground Left to participate in electoral politics and to exploit the democratic space created with the coming of political liberalization, in spite of its disappointment at the outcome of the legislative elections in 1987, is another positive sign for pluralism.

Military support for democracy is likely provided that guarantees for the preservation of its corporate interests are made. An important concern in this regard is the approval of military promotions by the legislature's Commission on Appointments. It would be in the interest of civilian rule for the commission to exercise this power in a more rational and prudent manner. The commission should respect the military's merit system rather than meddling in what is generally regarded as a legitimate area of military competence.

It is also fortunate that officers remain who are committed to constitutional rule, not only among the older generation of officers but even among those who grew up under Marcos. The fact that Philippine Military Academy classes 1958 to 1966 will remain on active duty for a number of years can also facilitate the institutionalization of civilian supremacy.

Whether the newly elected local executives will perform creditably remains a question. Their ability to make government more visible and more meaningful for the ordinary Filipino is crucial to earning popular confidence in the democratic system as well as to obtaining their support. Needless to say, their effect on the competition with the insurgencies for the support of the people is great, if only because government will be judged on the basis of local rather than national performance.

Two other reasons for cautious optimism are the resilience of Filipinos and their unfortunate experience with dictatorship. Resilience will enable them to remain supportive of the present system even if it is slow in responding to the economic problems afflicting the majority. The people's unfortunate experience with dictatorship will make that system extremely unpopular and unacceptable. Having experienced the success of their efforts against a dictator so determined to stay in power will make the people intractable subjects of another dictatorship. These considerations make cautious optimism persuasive for a wishful thinker such as I am.

# 11

# Economic Developments in the Philippines

*Richard Hooley*

Several years have passed since Corazon Aquino was swept into the Philippine presidency in a bloodless coup that captivated the imagination of the world. Aquino took command with the support of a broad coalition of forces. Her supporters included the middle and upper classes, which had despaired of Ferdinand Marcos's ability to manage the economy. They also included a large underclass of rural and urban workers who saw Aquino as their only hope of escaping from the prospects of a spreading poverty. Politicians from several old and new political parties and sociopolitical leaders representing varying ideological perspectives were also among her backers. Finally, elements of the military that found it propitious to accept the help of "people power" when their own plot for a *coup d'état* was discovered by Marcos were also among her followers. All these groups were represented in the original Aquino administration. It is a tribute to Aquino's political instincts that she has managed to continue in power at the head of a coalition so diverse in its constituents' interests and expectations. In the first free elections, held in May 1987, she and her administration won an impressive victory.

In spite of her ability to hold her coalition together, Aquino has been subject to mounting criticism for her apparent inability to administer the rebuilding of Philippine society effectively—particularly its socioeconomic dimensions. A land reform law that she signed in 1985 was passed in the new Congress in 1988; it was a minimal effort. Industrial growth has resumed but at an unacceptably slow pace. Squabbling of her cabinet ministers in public has been commonplace. She has been the target of four serious coup attempts; the last

Dr. Benito Legarda read an earlier draft of this chapter and provided many helpful comments. The statistical computations were performed by M. Ghosh. Any remaining errors or obscurities are solely the author's responsibility.

two, led by a group of young military officers, were nearly fatal to her incumbency. The unmistakable impression is that all is not well with Philippine democracy.

## The Economic Dimension

The economic world in which pre-Marcos politicians operated and that of Aquino are radically different. In the years before 1965 agriculture was expanding rapidly, and industry was growing at heady rates, sometimes as much as 8–10 percent per year. There was a growing demand for both agricultural and industrial labor, so that real wages increased by about 50 percent between the late 1940s and the mid-1960s. The expansion of production and employment and the rise in real wages were at least as important in snuffing out the Huk rebellion in the early 1950s as the much-vaunted superior military strategy of the armed forces.

In the two post-1965 decades, however, the economic environment in the Philippines changed enormously. During the period 1981–1986 agricultural production rose by only 2.3 percent per year while annual industrial growth was a negative 2.7 percent. This produced an annual decline of 0.6 percent in real national income. Combined with an annual population growth rate of 2.7 percent, this produced a per capita decline in aggregate real income averaging over 3 percent per year, or a total of nearly 20 percent for the six-year period. These trends have, unfortunately, been fully reflected in the labor market, where unemployment has grown substantially and real wages have declined by about 3 percent per year. The decline in wage rates and the increase in unemployment and underemployment mean that the Philippine peasant has experienced a decline of at least 30 percent in living standards since the beginning of the 1980s.

Growing unemployment has obvious political implications, which I will explore shortly. Equally important, however, are the ramifications of the expanding national budget deficit. In the pre-Marcos years a budgetary deficit of $200 million (equivalent) was considered large. In her first year in office Aquino was faced with a deficit of close to $2 billion—a tenfold growth in two decades. This has constrained her political maneuverability by severely restricting her freedom of action in public expenditures. In particular, this poses problems in providing leadership for the underpaid military and in efforts to restore a more functional role to the bureaucracy.

From the outset Aquino realized the need for economic reconstruction, and shortly after taking power she asked her economic advisers to draw up a program to restore growth to the economy.

The program that emerged was essentially short term, focused on stimulating domestic demand and production. It provided for the creation of a Presidential Commission on Government Reorganization to carry out the privatization of government assets. The main work of this commission was the dismantling of the Marcos monopolies (such as sugar and coconuts). The economic plan also included a public works program to mop up some of the unemployed labor. These policies received fortuitous support from the improvement in international prices for metals, coconuts, and sugar. In addition, Aquino signed a land reform law that the new Congress specified, passed, and began to implement. In spite of a drought in agriculture, these policies were beginning to take hold as real gross national product registered a 5 percent annual growth rate during 1987. A trickle of foreign capital began to flow back into the country. The military uprising in August 1987 temporarily aborted this short-term recovery, but with peace and stability the recovery continued into 1988 and 1989.

These measures essentially constitute a short-term economic recovery program. Will they significantly alter the longer-term economic prospects of the country? If so, will the emerging economic program assist the continued growth of democratic political institutions?

### Democracy, Dissidents, and Economic Growth

The search for the determinants of democracy is a puzzle that has long engaged the minds of eminent social scientists. What conditions make democracy possible, and what factors allow it to thrive? Why does democracy flourish in England and the Scandinavian countries, while many central European countries experience recurrent crises? Why do democratic processes find it difficult to mature in many postcolonial states, while in others, like Brazil and India, they appear to have taken permanent root? In answering these questions social scientists can be classified into three groups: the behaviorists, the public policy analysts, and the modernization school.

The behaviorists include writers like R. A. Dahl who argue that it is the commitment to democratic values among the political leaders of a country that is important.[1] In a similar vein D. A. Rostow argues that successful conditions for democratic rule depend on the extent to which politicians and the electorate learn to accept the democratic rules of the political game.[2] Carole Pateman emphasizes the role of educational institutions in laying the foundation for democratic processes and ideology.[3] D. Lerner emphasizes the importance of communications systems in overcoming the parochialism of traditional

195

societies.[4] Much has been written on the application of this approach to Philippine democracy, including the nature of political parties and of democratic processes.[5] I will not explore this approach further, however, because it does not focus on the effect of economic conditions on the development of democratic institutions.

Policy analysts take a more eclectic approach to explaining the success or failure of democratic institutions. For example, R. A. Higgott sees the public policy approach as "a way of managing and administering the diffusion of aid . . . and the support of Western-oriented decision-making elites."[6] To achieve results obviously requires policies that are effective and knowledge about the factors underlying them. This appears to have been achieved by policy analysts' rediscovery of economics, as manifest in a cost-benefit framework, and the application of that framework to the question "who gets what at the expense of whom." This approach has been helpful in illuminating the political effects of economic decisions and in outlining the policies most effective for implementing the transformation process.[7] But the approach sheds little new light on the effect of economic conditions on development of democratic political processes.

The modernization school is distinguished by its attempt to develop causal relationships between democratic processes and institutions on the one hand and socioeconomic conditions on the other. Members of this school have a well-established conviction that economic growth provides the material conditions necessary for the development of democratic institutions. Seymour M. Lipset, after studying data for some sixty developing countries, observed a strong correlation between per capita income and the smooth functioning of democratic institutions.[8] He reasoned that per capita income is correlated with such other socioeconomic preconditions of democracy as economic security and higher education, all of which permit the development of "longer time preferences" among the electorate. Gabriel Almond and James S. Coleman, reviewing much the same data as Lipset, came to a similar conclusion.[9] They thought that the rising household incomes associated with economic development are conducive to political socialization and recruitment, interest articulation, and improved sociopolitical adaptation through a smoother, more functional process of rule making and rule application. The Philippines were singled out by Almond and Coleman as "the most advanced and integrated" of the developing democracies. They agreed with Lucian Pye that "the discontinuities between the modern elite subsociety and the mass are much less marked than in other transitional systems."[10] Karl Deutsch shifted attention to the change of political institutions over time in contrast to the static view of their situation at a certain point of time. Irma Adelman and Cynthia Morris set out in quantitative terms the relationship between various political and social variables and the rate of growth of per capita GNP.[11] More recently the connection between democracy and socioeconomic progress has been affirmed by G. Bingham Powell for contemporary democratic systems.[12]

It would be interesting to know how these earlier writers now feel about the contemporary situation in the Philippines. In fairness, however, we should observe that all of them assumed that rising per capita incomes are associated with an income distribution structure that at least does not deteriorate and may even improve somewhat. Today, however, most development economists agree that household income distribution undergoes a U-shaped pattern during the early stages of growth.[13] That is, the share of income going to the lower groups first *falls* and begins to rise only after an extended time.

Had these earlier writers been aware of this income distribution pattern, they would have been more cautious in their assurance of steady progress toward democracy. Lipset observes that stable poverty in a stable socioeconomic environment breeds a docile and conservative peasantry.[14] Presumably, therefore, a steady deterioration of the income distribution structure would be associated with a more radicalized and less docile lower class. In any case, democratic institutions have received a buffeting in recent years, not only in the Philippines but in many other less-developed countries (LDCs), which should prompt some hesitation in accepting a smooth, unidirectional relationship between economic growth and democracy.

Not all investigators have concluded that socioeconomic development inevitably promotes democratically structured political institutions. One group of writers, typified by Samuel P. Huntington, feels that education and mass communication techniques have made the mobilization of public opinion so easy that democratic systems come under extreme pressure to satisfy a greatly increased number of highly vocal groups.[15] The pressure is to produce results for the short term. This implies the deterioration and possible breakdown of the ability of political parties to organize and sort out choices on public questions and public goods of all kinds. It therefore tends to make democracy unstable. In the same vein is the observation that this kind of populist competition will raise public expectations to levels higher than the system can provide for.

Other writers doubt the existence of a causal connection between economic progress and the growth of democratic political institutions. They believe that both are the product of cultural values and behavior

197

patterns springing from Western culture. These writers maintain that economic progress is compatible with a variety of political institutional structures and that the kind of regime is of only minor important at best in shaping the institutional contours of a functionally efficient economy. The consensus of writers of this persuasion is that democratic political institutions result from a number of variables, mostly economic, and that it is not possible to trace a causal arrow from the latter to the former.[16]

We must not overlook Powell's incisive observation that most theorists have assumed that socioeconomic progress and democracy become interdependent only after some development threshold (usually unspecified) has been passed. This is apparently what Mancur Olson has in mind when he says that both extremely rapid growth and economic stagnation can destabilize a fledgling democracy.[17] A broader interpretation of this view might be that economic shocks of sufficient magnitude may destabilize democratic political institutions in early stages of growth. What these shocks consist of remains to be clarified, but the main thrust seems clear enough.

What have we learned by reviewing this literature on the relation of economic development and political democracy? A number of points help specify the nature of the relationship.

• A clear correlation exists between broad measures of economic development like per capita income and democratic political processes. That correlation appears strongest when observed cross-sectionally. Over time the relationship also emerges for individual countries but is weaker.

• This correlation does not, however, conclusively demonstrate causality, and a number of reputable analysts feel that economic growth and democratic political processes are primarily the result of common cultural patterns that occur most frequently in Western societies and are conducive to both.

• A fourth group of scholars point to the possibility of destabilizing democratic political systems by too rapid growth or economic stagnation. This point refers particularly to democratic systems in the early stages of development that have not passed the stability-interdependence threshold. Most analysts in this group have assumed the presence of a monotonic relationship between economic growth and democracy, one in which all relevant economic variables move proportionately with per capita income.

• Few of these writers address the question of income distribution and its relationship to democratic political processes. More specifically, trends toward more equal income distribution and toward rising real income of workers' households would apparently strengthen the public consensus necessary for the development of democratic institutions.

The upshot of this discussion is that economic growth should be broadly conducive to developing democratic processes in early stages of development except when accompanied by economic shocks that disturb systemic growth. One sure possibility is changes in income distribution; if income distribution worsens during economic growth, systemic development backfires. Income distribution is difficult to measure for LDCs, but a proxy is possible. Real wages are a useful proxy, for two reasons. First, the real wage rate reflects the approximate welfare position of the mass of consumers and workers. It does not capture windfall profits going to the elite, as real per capita income does. Second, since periods of falling real wages are usually accompanied by steady or rising real income of the upper-middle class and the elite (as I shall show later), the trend in real wages is a fairly good indicator of changes in the distribution of household income as well as its level.

I therefore plan to organize my investigation of the Philippine economy around the changes in real wages and the relationship of these to measures of discontent with the existing, generally democratic political system. I then focus attention on the prospects for stable or rising real wages, with a view to assessing the outlook for the stability and growth of democracy in the Philippines.

### Income, Real Wages, and the Growth of Discontent

Is there any systematic relationship between sociopolitical discontent, on the one hand, and income level, on the other? I propose two measures of income. The first is real income per capita. This measure hardly needs explanation; it is simply national income divided by total population and expressed in units of constant purchasing power. The second measure is the real wage rate. I have prepared a series on wage rates covering both unskilled and skilled workers, from a variety of government sources such as the old Bureau of the Census (before World War II), the National Census and Statistics Office (NCSO), and the Central Bank. The wage rate data were deflated by the cost-of-living index prepared by the NCSO and, in earlier years (before 1935), by an index of retail consumer prices.

It is more difficult to obtain data quantifying political discontent. Conceptually there is no real difficulty. Political discontent in the Philippines, as elsewhere, has usually led to an increase in strikes, marches, and other forms of social protest and sometimes to the

199

appearance and growth of insurrectionary activity. The number of such social protest events can be measured, as Benedict Kerkvliet has shown.[18] Insurrectionary activity is best measured by the number of persons involved in movements of armed protest.

The difficulty is not in defining quantitative measures of discontent but in finding source material for estimating these activities. There is some material on the extent and duration of hostilities at the beginning of the twentieth century from the work of the Philippine Commission and other government sources. There are scattered references by historians of the prewar period to movements of discontent. There is more material on the scope of the Huk rebellion, as well as that of the New People's Army (NPA). I am not yet prepared, however, to merge all these reports into a continuous series. For the present I am content to define periods of discontent by reference to the existing literature on these social phenomena. For the prewar period I lean heavily on the work of government sources such as the Philippine Commission and on that of Kerkvliet; for the period after 1965 I use generally available but unpublished estimates of the number of persons believed to constitute the core of the NPA.

I have prepared estimates of real national income per capita and the real wage rate from 1897 to 1985. They are shown in figure 11–1. The shaded areas represent periods during which discontent became particularly noteworthy, involving movements of armed protest. We see three periods of major discontent during this century, interlaced with two long periods when discontent was at a minimum.

The earliest period of serious discontent was from 1897 to 1902. This period is characterized by an extremely low wage rate (index value of 47.2 in 1900). The reason for the low rate was the depreciation of the peso (then a silver-backed currency) combined with money wages that increased only very slowly. The depreciation of the peso mirrored the fall in the value of silver, which began in the 1880s and gathered real momentum after 1890.[19]

| Year | Peso Exchange Rate (U.S. dollars) | Year | Peso Exchange Rate (U.S. dollars) |
|---|---|---|---|
| 1874 | 1.005 | 1895 | 0.514 |
| 1880 | 0.899 | 1900 | 0.487 |
| 1885 | 0.835 | 1902 | 0.415 |
| 1890 | 0.822 | | |

The weakness of the peso was exacerbated by a marked deterioration in the Philippine trade balance between 1898 and 1902 due to a particularly poor crop yield in 1902, along with the outbreak of

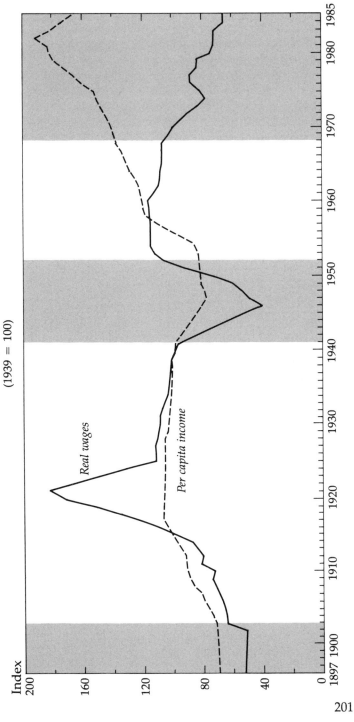

FIGURE 11-1

INDEXES OF REAL WAGES AND PER CAPITA NATIONAL INCOME
IN THE PHILIPPINES, 1897–1985
(1939 = 100)

Real wages

Per capita income

rinderpest disease among cattle herds and the general disruption of internal trade during the War of Independence. The decline in real wages began in earnest sometime during the early 1890s and corresponded closely (but with a small lag) with the outbreak of the Philippine rebellion against Spain (1898), which then continued against the Americans until 1902.

The years from 1903 until the early 1920s were years of substantial growth of real per capita income. They were also years of rapid and virtually uninterrupted growth of real wages. If we put aside the abnormal rise and decline of real wages just before and after World War I, the rise in real wages persisted from 1900 until about 1928. During this period there were no signs of any serious political discontent and absolutely no record of armed uprisings anywhere in the country.

The Great Depression ushered in a period of zero growth in real per capita income, which lasted until the outbreak of war in 1941. In contrast, real wages underwent a period of slow but steady decline during this period. It is also during these years that we see the first signs of popular unrest under the American administration. Kerkvliet indicates low but rising sociopolitical discontent beginning about 1930 and culminating in the appearance of the Kalipunang Pambansa ng mga Magsasaka sa Pilipinas (KPMP) in the late 1930s.[20] These years also saw the appearance of the Sakdalan movement—a rebellion of tenant farmers in central Luzon. These manifestations of protest took place against a background of falling real wages and appear to have occurred with a lag of about half a decade.

The decline in real wages that characterized the 1930s became a downward spiral during the war years of 1941–1945. While we do not have quantitative data during the period of Japanese occupation from 1942 to 1945, we know from well-documented reports that prices entered an upward spiral and that there was widespread hardship. By 1946 real wages had fallen to their level at the beginning of the century. National income per capita fell too, but apparently at a rate somewhat slower than wages. The 1940s therefore saw the sharpest and most persistent decline in wage rates during the entire American period. This, of course, was also the period of the Huk rebellion, by far the most serious and widespread movement of armed discontent during that period.

From 1946 to 1952 real wage rates rose very rapidly, more than doubling in that six-year period. This was achieved by a flood of imported goods that brought the price level down while money wages were being adjusted upward. The upward movement of real wages outpaced the rise in real per capita income—no modest feat considering the previous historical record. In politics this period was marked by the weakening of the Huk movement and the strengthening of democratic institutions. It was the period of the emergence of Ramon Magsaysay (then secretary of defense in the Elpidio Quirino administration) as the government strategist capable of persuading peasants to lay down their weapons and turn away from rebellion. The brilliant results he achieved as secretary of defense and later as president (1954–1957) in bringing an end to the Huk threat were considerably influenced, if not substantially shaped, by the resurgence of real wage rates and per capita income during those years.

Real wages increased throughout the 1950s and peaked in 1960. The retreat during most of the 1960s was moderate—on the order of 10 percent—and reflected the first depreciation of the exchange rate since the end of the nineteenth century. The real wage rate remained reasonably high by historical standards. While the real wage was settling into this static mode, however, real per capita income was growing steadily; so the *relative* real wage rate began to fall during the 1960s, suggesting the beginning of a deterioration in income distribution. Politically the 1960s could be characterized as a period in which democratic institutions continued to function effectively, although the end of the decade saw the first signs of social unrest, including the founding of the NPA.

The 1970s ushered in a new era in real wages and politics in the Philippines. The year 1969 marked the beginning of a decisive downward slide of real wages, which in sharpness of movement and duration of trend eclipsed all previous movements of this century. By 1986 real wages had been falling for a period of eighteen years (twenty-six years from the wage peak in 1960). In magnitude this decline is surely impressive: a fall of 50 percent or more from the peak reached in the early 1960s to a level below that of the 1930s and only a little higher than those of 1897–1903 and 1944–1946. A major reason for the decline in the absolute level of wages was the decline in the value of the peso—from an exchange rate of 4:$1 in the late 1960s to 20:$1 in 1986.

This period is noteworthy for something even more startling. It is the only period in Philippine history in which real per capita income rose consistently over an extended period while real wages were falling. In previous periods per capita income and real wage rates might move in opposite directions for a few years—for example 1918 to 1921. But they have now moved in the opposite direction for most of two *decades*. Hence, in *relation to real per capita income*, the real wage rate is now lower than at any previous time in this century.

What have been the implications of these trends for Philippine politics and democratic institutions? Martial law was declared in 1972, the Congress was abolished, the court system was debased, citizens' rights were violated, and power was substantially transferred to the military. Sociopolitical protest movements multiplied across the country. The NPA grew from a small band of dissidents to a well-organized force of over 20,000 cadres and many more clandestine supporters. We need not dwell further on the disintegration of democratic political institutions since this is amply described elsewhere.[21] Suffice it to say that democratic institutions, in spite of their recent reestablishment, are more in danger today than at any other time in this century.

These observations on real income, real wages, and sociopolitical discontent are summarized in table 11–1.

On the basis of this evidence I feel confident in asserting an inverse relationship between sociopolitical discontent on the one hand and the real wage rate on the other. Second, the relationship between real per capita income and sociopolitical discontent appears to be weak at best. The failure of the real per capita income series to "predict" the present level of discontent appears to be a nearly fatal blow to establishing any useful relationship. Third, the *ratio* between the index of real wages and the index of real per capita income appears to be a most promising indicator of sociopolitical dissidence. It signals the major periods of discontent correctly, in both timing and amplitude. Fourth, there appears to be a lag of three to four years between a change in the trend of real wages and its manifestation in the form of political dissidence—usually unarmed at first and becoming more militant if the trend continues and accelerates.

TABLE 11–1
REAL INCOME, REAL WAGES, AND DISCONTENT IN THE PHILIPPINES,
1897–1989

| Period | Real Wages | National Income per Capita | Discontent |
|---|---|---|---|
| 1897–1902 | Historical low | Low | Yes; armed |
| 1903–1927 | Rising; high | Rising; high | No |
| 1928–1946 | Falling to historical low | Falling; low | Yes; armed Huk movement |
| 1947–1968 | Rising to historical highs | Rising | No |
| 1969–1989 | Falling; reaching historical lows | Rising; reaching historical highs | Yes; armed NPA movement |

## Philippine Labor in Economic Perspective

I take the index of real wages as an indicator of the trend in real income of the rural and urban poor, though fully aware that wage income constitutes only one of a number of income sources for the laboring classes. For two reasons, however, wages are a good index of the major trends in working-class household incomes. First, in family budget surveys most households list wages and salaries as one source of income; nearly two-thirds of households with annual incomes of P2,000 or more list wages and salaries as the most important source of family income.[22] Only in upper-income households (annual incomes over P10,000) and those with incomes under P2,000 do less than 50 percent list wages and salaries as the main source of income. The first group lists business profits as the main source of income; the second includes retirees and small farm households quite distant from local markets, so that production for their own use is their major income source. A second reason for using wages as an index of working-class household income rests in the usefulness of wages as a proxy for other money income sources. That is to say, if real wages decline markedly because of, say, a substantial rise in consumer prices, other working-class household income sources, such as incomes from small retail shops or from small farms, are also likely to show some decline, though not necessarily to the same degree.

The disappointing experience for households of the sharp decline in the real value of their wage and salary income during the past eighteen years has alienated a large fraction of the population. What are the reasons for the disastrous fall in their real income? Why, in marked contrast to the experience of this entire century, has the real wage income of urban and rural working-class households fallen while real national income per capita has risen steadily? Finally, what measures can be taken to reverse these trends, what beneficial effects might be expected, and how soon?

The answers must be sought in the radically changed conditions in the domestic labor market. In the past six years some 5 million young Filipinos have entered the domestic labor market. Not more than 2 million have found jobs in agriculture. Only 150,000 new jobs have been created in the entire manufacturing sector. Where have the remaining 3 million or so gone? Into petty trade and services and into an already overstaffed government bureaucracy. A half million or more have left the country to seek work in Saudi Arabia, Hong Kong, and other countries—this labor market's safety valve. It is clear from the available statistical evidence that the Philippine labor market is experiencing a condition of pronounced oversupply.[23] This accelerated labor supply along with very slow growth in agriculture and industry is primarily responsible for the excess of labor supply that has been driving down the real wage income of the rural and urban lower classes.

Why are agriculture and industry providing new employment at a rate insufficient to clear the labor market? The pace of agricultural growth has slackened in recent years. Gone are the days when land under cultivation increased by 3–4 percent per year, providing a steady expansion of food supplies and steady growth in hard currency exports. As outlying areas such as Mindanao and the Cagayan Valley became more fully populated, the expansion of agricultural land slowed to 2 percent and then to its present 1 percent per year—substantially under the population growth rate of 2.7 percent. As the land resource base tightened, however, Philippine agriculture demonstrated its resiliency by a surge in the value of output per hectare. This has been achieved by increased physical output per unit of land through the use of improved agricultural technology—generally referred to as the green revolution. A second and equally important development has been a shift from lower-value to higher-value crops. The area sown to rice, for example, has been cut almost in half during the past two decades while that devoted to such other crops as bananas and pineapples has increased substantially.

These productivity increases have expanded the domestic food supply and raised export earnings. The problem is that improved farm technology has been accompanied by increased use of nonlabor inputs such as hybrid seeds, fertilizers, pesticides, water, and sometimes (as in fish culture) capital inputs as well. Consequently the traditional increase in demand for agricultural labor has been slowly drying up. The price of this state of affairs has been an increase in tenancy, a steady reduction of agricultural real wages, and a deterioration of the economic situation of both peasants and agricultural workers.

Conditions in agriculture have also suffered because of the drastic drop in the prices of Philippine exports. International prices of sugar, logs, copra, and other agricultural exports have all registered historical lows in the past decade. The loss of the sugar quota of 900,000 tons, largely the result of a major faux pas of Marcos, delivered a nearly fatal blow to the Philippine sugar industry. These adverse developments in the international markets for primary products of the Philippines have had profoundly dysfunctional effects not only on agricultural employment but indirectly on industrial employment as well.

Part of the reason for the slowing of the demand for labor is the recent experience of the industrial sector. Manufacturing has experienced a contraction in recent years. There has been an increase of only 150,000 workers in all manufacturing since 1980. None of this increase came from large firms; all of it is traceable to firms with fewer than twenty employees. The underlying reason for this sad state of affairs is the poor productivity of industry, together with a highly protected environment provided by import restrictions, which has boosted nominal profit rates on capital while reducing real wages by the inflationary effect on consumer prices. As most economists inside and outside the country agree, there is no real chance of getting domestic industry moving without a radical improvement in the efficiency of Philippine industry and a restructuring of the price system.

Underlying the question of the adequacy of the Philippine resource base is population. The population of approximately 58 million implies a density of slightly over 500 persons per square mile, far higher than that of any other Southeast Asian country except Vietnam. Moving past the 500 mark is indeed a crossing of the Rubicon for Philippine society because it puts the country in a select group of East Asian countries—China, Japan, South Korea, and Taiwan—that have densities of 500 to 1,000 persons per square mile. At present rates of population growth the Philippines will have a density of 715 persons by the end of this century, about the same as Japan in 1970.

The main impact of population growth on the economic system is on the labor market. Today 750,000 new workers enter the Philippine labor market each year, and by the year 2000 this will rise to 1.1 million each year. Can Corazon Aquino find jobs for them? Population programs alone cannot provide an answer. First, work force entrants are already determined for the next fifteen years by virtue of the existing population. Second, experience shows that population programs do not work effectively in an isolated socioeconomic environment. They work effectively in an environment of rising workers' incomes and socioeconomic expectations.[24] Unless pressure on the labor markets is relieved so that some rise in real wages takes place, population programs begun now will have little effect on the supply curve of labor even in the distant future.

The contours of the present stalemate in the distribution of the nation's income and product are gradually gaining recognition among the population, including the rural and urban poor; hence the growing support for land reform in the rural sector and increasing strikes and social pressure for higher wages in the cities. These are creating larger political fissures between the rural and urban poor on the one hand and the middle and upper classes on the other. For example, the passage of an effective land reform law was held up in Congress, where a landowner bloc demanded a retention limit of 24 hectares (and possibly higher), while the House Land Reform Committee proposed a limit of only 7 hectares.

Essentially the same kind of situation exists with respect to industrial reform. Filipino tycoons who have made their fortunes in protected markets largely at the expense of low-income consumers (among whom are some of Aquino's closest advisers) are not about to commit voluntary economic suicide by accepting an industrial restructuring program that greatly reduces the rate of return on domestic capital. Yet it is precisely these factors—the closing of the agricultural frontier together with the continued protectionist policies applied to the industrial sector—that have been instrumental in creating the human logjam in the labor market, resulting in skyrocketing unemployment and declining real wages. Obviously, this same policy environment increases profits on capital. Hence I conclude that these labor market conditions are the most important cause of the decline in real wages and the increased income inequality in the country. They are grist for the propaganda mills of the New Left.

The present system has other politically dysfunctional side effects. One of these is the disintegration of discipline in the bureaucracy. Nearly half of the 5 million entrants to the labor force since 1980 went into the services sector. Most of them were taken onto the government payroll. This poses two problems. First, government offices become overstaffed; make-work tasks become increasingly the order of the day and eventually interfere with the performance of functional tasks and efficient operation. The bureaucracy becomes, in effect, the employer of last resort. The more it becomes hostage to its functions as an employment agency, the less it is able to implement the policies of the government. Government policies become ineffective because they cannot be implemented.

Second, the fiscal dimension of a rapidly expanding government payroll at a time when economic growth is at a minimum has become an economic policy problem with particularly burdensome political consequences. The task of financing the bureaucracy has become an enormous dead-weight load in the national budget. In the pre-Marcos years a budget deficit of $200 million was considered large. But in Aquino's first year in office she was faced with a deficit approaching $2 billion—ten times as large. Given the government role as employer of last resort, straightforward belt tightening might translate into political suicide. But failure to deal effectively with this financial hemorrhaging might easily lead to domestic inflation and, eventually, depreciation of the foreign exhange rate and a further and politically disastrous decline in real wage rates. While the roots of this problem are in the Marcos era, it is now Aquino's task to deal with it.

Economic policies to extricate the *tao*—the ordinary Filipino—from his impoverished situation can be set into a potentially effective economic framework. What is much more difficult is to construct a complementary framework of political-administrative policies to implement economic reform. As soon as corrective policies are presented for discussion and action, they expose deep fissures in the country's elite structure. We saw in 1988 a land reform bill become stalled in the new Congress on the retention issue, with factions of the elite on either side of the issue. We witnessed some members of the government and cabinet earnestly trying to lower tariffs and demonopolize the Philippine business environment. But we also saw these efforts thwarted by other factions of the elite who hold powerful positions both in and outside the cabinet.

Early in her administration Aquino realized the need for economic reconstruction and had programs drawn up for getting the economy back on a growth track. The program that emerged was essentially short term, focusing on dismantling the Marcos monopolies and including a public works program to mop up some of the unemployed labor. The central idea was to stimulate domestic demand and production. These policies were aided by the improvement in international prices for metals and coconuts. In addition, Aquino signed a land reform law that was finally passed by Congress. In spite of a drought in agriculture these measures were beginning to take hold—real GNP registered a robust 5 percent annual growth rate in 1987. A trickle of foreign capital held abroad had begun to flow back into the country. Unfortunately the uprising by the military in August 1988 temporarily aborted this short-term recovery process, but if peace and stability return for a time, it may once again get under way.

In any case, these measures essentially constitute a short-term program of economic recovery. Except for land reform they do not get at the more fundamental issues. This is not at all surprising, considering the short notice Aquino's policy makers had to map out a program. Although short-term economic recovery is possible, it is unlikely that it can develop into long-term economic expansion without fundamental reform that deals effectively with the issues of land distribution and agricultural productivity, rural and urban workers' incomes and income distribution, restructuring of the industrial sector, and the national deficit. But it is precisely here that Aquino is having trouble. No tariff reform is planned for industry; in fact some tariffs have been raised since her administration took power. Industrial productivity temporarily turned up after she took office but has resumed its downward trend; and although an effort at legislating agrarian reform is a first step in the right direction, it ran into considerable opposition in the new Congress. In sum, the existing elite, operating within the structures of the existing democratic political process, is having difficulty getting a handle on the economic reforms necessary to win the confidence of the people.

## Summary and Conclusions

In this chapter I set out to assess the impact of present economic conditions on the prospects for continued development of democratic institutions in the Philippines. After a review of data on real income, real wages, and the extent of sociopolitical discontent since the beginning of this century, I concluded that economic progress is indeed related to discontent. The relation is not between growth of aggregate income and discontent or even between per capita real income and discontent but between real wages and discontent. The real wage variable is a proxy for the income of working-class households.

In the Philippines the real wage rate is the product of a quite sticky nominal wage and the cost of living, which depends greatly on the foreign exchange rate. Since the latter is highly volatile at times, real wages can move rapidly in either direction. Because of the stickiness of the nominal wage rate, the foreign exchange rate is the most important determinant over short to intermediate periods. Over the longer run, however, more traditional neoclassical variables play an important role—including the rate of growth of output and factor productivity. These feed on the growth of demand for labor, which interacts with growth in the labor force. The recent dismal showing of real wages reflects the interplay of unfavorable trends in both short- and long-term factors.

In every period during which widespread sociopolitical discontent has been evident in this century, real wages have displayed a significant decline. Real wages have declined first, and after a three- or four-year lag the discontent has become manifest in a variety of protest movements. In the periods of major discontent—at the beginning of this century, from 1940 to 1950, and since the early 1970s—when discontent took the form of armed insurrection, real wages reached historic lows. The present period is, however, unique in the amplitude and duration of the fall in wage rates. It is also the only period in which real wages have declined consistently while real per capita income has increased. I interpret this as a persistent decline in the income of rural and urban workers while income of the upper-middle and wealthy classes steadily increased. The evidence is sufficient by any reasonable historical standards to conclude that democratic institutions are in serious jeopardy if the present situation is allowed to continue indefinitely.

The present sociopolitical threat to democratic processes has its economic roots in the domestic labor market. Each year 750,000 persons enter the Philippine labor market. At present modest growth rates and given the existing farm technology, agriculture can absorb roughly 200,000 additional workers per year. Large-scale manufacturing can absorb less than 25,000—and that under the best of circumstances—given the present industrial structure. The remainder—about 500,000 workers per year—must find jobs in handicraft industries, commerce, personal services, or the government bureaucracy or, when the opportunity presents itself, by migrating overseas. The result of this logjam in the domestic labor market is growth of unemployment, severe downward pressure on wage rates, demoralization of the bureaucracy, and a continual hemorrhaging of the national budget as the government is forced to take on the role of employer of last resort.

It is not beyond the realm of possibility to develop economic policies to deal effectively with this situation. The administration has pushed land reform, but of course this must be followed by policies that ensure that the new landowners have available modern agricultural inputs and sufficient extension services and marketing services, so that agricultural productivity rises as rural equity improves. Of at least equal importance is reform in the industrial sector, consisting of a reduction in trade barriers, particularly of the cascading tariff system that serves mainly to keep the price of consumer goods high (and real wages therefore low). The industrial system must also be changed from one that is a voracious consumer of foreign exchange to one that is a net supplier of foreign exchange. This, of course, implies a shrinking of some industries and an expansion of others, with obvious implications for the wealth holdings of families and elite groups.

Particular attention should be given to raising the productivity of the industrial system. Output per unit of input has been declining for nearly two decades, and the net result is a price level beyond the reach not only of domestic consumers but also of markets overseas. There are a number of reasons for this trend, too numerous to go into here. The ultimate, long-term policy objective is to alter the contours of the economy so that the structure and productivity of the system are consistent with the size and expected growth rate of the labor force.

Democracy is surely at a critical point in the Philippines. The test of democratic institutions (or of any alternative political system for that matter) is whether the leaders of society, operating within the institutional system, can produce an effective strategy to deal with society's pressing issues and get that strategy widely accepted and implemented. Those who argue for a different political system will ultimately have to show that it can produce more effective results. I see no particular advantages in the alternative, more authoritarian systems (other than very short-term advantages). Aquino has, so far, made an important contribution in holding the system together, making a beginning on forming a policy consensus, and, perhaps most important, buying time. The main tasks still remain to be tackled, and the outcome is still far from certain. We dare to hope for the emergence of still stronger economic leadership and a more solid political consensus, keeping in mind that Philippine society has its own special strengths of patience and improvisation and sources of internal resilience, which set it off as a unique, functioning socioeconomic system.

# 12
# Sociocultural Developments
# in the Philippines

*David Rosenberg*

This chapter examines the major social and cultural factors affecting the prospects for development and democracy in the Philippines. Development may be defined, following Joseph Schumpeter in his *Theory of Economic Development*, as follows:

> By development, we shall understand only such changes in economic life as are not forced upon it from without but arise from its own initiative, from within. Should it turn out . . . that the economy . . . is dragged along by the changes in the surrounding world . . . that the economy continuously adapts itself to them, then we should say that there is no development.[1]

Hence Schumpeter made a basic distinction between directed, organic, and autonomous economic change (which he surveyed in Western Europe in the seventeenth, eighteenth, and nineteenth centuries) and the imposed and externally controlled economic change of the colonial or neocolonial periphery. Democracy he defined as "elite competition for mass support," where competition was genuine and mass support was informed and voluntary.

Given these theoretical notions, we can seek to determine how social and cultural factors influence the ability of individual Filipinos to make informed and voluntary choices among competing leaders and the ability of the country as a whole to maintain or increase its organic solidarity and autonomy in response to changes in the domestic and international environment. These social and cultural factors include, in the first case, the degree of equality of opportunity available to individual Filipinos for health care and other basic needs, education, enterprise, social mobility, and political participation and, in the second, the effectiveness of government policies in responding

213

to major domestic changes, such as population pressures, and international changes, such as world market fluctuations.

This analysis is a preliminary attempt to determine how complex social and cultural factors influence political change. First, it briefly reviews political factors influencing development and democracy, in particular, the dramatic transition from the government of Ferdinand Marcos to the government of Corazon Aquino. Second, it equally briefly reviews economic factors, such as growth and distribution of output. Third, it examines social factors, such as the rate of population growth, the distribution of income, wealth, and poverty, and social class stratification. Fourth, it examines government priorities and policies, such as land reform and meeting basic needs, that attempt to overcome obstacles to development and democracy. Fifth, it examines distinctive cultural factors that influence how Filipinos decide "who gets what," such as the tradition of strong families and weak states, the instrumental role of elections in selecting leaders, and the symbolic value of elections in reinforcing social stratification. Sixth, it evaluates Philippine prospects of achieving its national government objectives. Seventh, it offers a summary and conclusion of the analysis. It concludes with some observations on Philippine-American relations.

Social and cultural factors are complex phenomena subject to widespread interpretation, but it is widely agreed that they are all deeply rooted, long-term factors based on slow-changing social structures and cultural values. It is also widely agreed that the Marcos period witnessed a deterioration in these social and cultural factors of development, as evident in high population growth rates, a worsening distribution of income, wealth, and power, and increasing mass poverty. The Aquino government has created a new governmental structure and has made a new commitment to basic economic and social reforms to address these problems. The early momentum for economic and social reform, however, has been stalled in controversies over land reform and local autonomy. Many traditional family-based political dynasties have reemerged to resist these reforms and to resume their domination of national and local politics. As a result, initial political reforms have not been complemented by essential economic and social reforms. Consequently, political pressures—legal and illegal, peaceful and violent—are likely to persist for many years to come.

## Political Factors

On September 23, 1972, the Philippines ended its long experiment with Western-style democracy. On that day, President Marcos proclaimed martial law throughout the country and began a drastic transformation of Philippine political institutions. He rapidly began to dismantle the superstructure of constitutional government that had been transplanted to the Philippines under American colonial rule. Congress was dissolved, civil liberties were sharply curtailed, and the constitution of 1935 was replaced. Marcos proposed a "New Society" to be implemented by a new style of government, "constitutional authoritarianism." He claimed that the loss of civil liberties and representative government was the regrettable but temporary price that Filipinos would have to pay for political stability, economic growth, and social reform. But considerable evidence indicates that Marcos was not willing to implement the policies necessary to achieve these objectives.

Marcos changed the institutions of Philippine government to centralize and personalize his control over the main sources of power and wealth in the country. "Crony capitalism" left deep structural flaws in the economy. The "green revolution" benefited some Filipino farmers but also created a large and durable class of landless peasants and urban squatters. Many lost their traditionally local and conservative orientations and became ripe for radical mobilization. The role of the church changed drastically from staunch supporter of the status quo to constant critic of government. Liberation theology led some in the church into organizing Basic Christian Communities and other social and political action groups to seek redress for popular grievances. Patron-client ties—the fundamental building blocks of Filipino political power—were torn apart. The military became highly politicized and tainted by frequent reports of abuses. A new generation of rebel leaders succeeded in creating a New People's Army to achieve national liberation through armed struggle. In February 1986 Marcos was forced out of power, ending nearly twenty years of rule. Ultimately, his New Society failed because it was not producing its promised benefits of political stability, economic growth, and social reform. Instead, the country was faced with increasing instability, persistent poverty, and more violence than there had been before Marcos.

The People Power movement and the establishment of the Aquino government created an extraordinary opportunity to overcome the social and cultural obstacles to Philippine development and democracy that had been exacerbated during the Marcos years. In its first year the Aquino government averted civil war; it replaced a failing and corrupt dictatorship, with a minimum of bloodshed. It restored a free press. It slowed the country's economic decline. It received a substantial infusion of emergency foreign aid and debt

215

repayment concessions. It ratified a new constitution. It restored the faith and pride of many Filipinos in their country. All this, however, gave the country only a brief respite to plan and implement comprehensive, long-term solutions to revitalize the economy and to reform and retrain the civilian and military bureaucracies.

## Economic Factors

Initially President Aquino pursued a policy of economic recovery, government reform, and reconciliation with Communist guerrillas and secessionist Muslims, despite some contrary views in her cabinet and the military, as well as hostile and sometimes violent objections from left-wing militants and leftover Marcos loyalists.

In its first national development plan, the Aquino government gave a high priority to "(a) alleviation of poverty, (b) generation of more productive employment, [and] (c) promotion of equity and social justice." It aimed to reduce poverty from 59 percent of all households to 45 percent by 1992. The government's *Agenda for Action for the Philippine Rural Sector* gave high priority to an antipoverty focus in rural areas, comprehensive land reform, and the elimination of bias against agriculture. Reflecting this emphasis, the government's Medium Term Development Plan included an increase in investment in agriculture from 9.3 percent of total public sector investment in 1981–1985 to 12.7 percent in 1987–1992.

Economic growth has been slowly increasing through the revival of consumer demand, construction, and manufacturing sales. Many of the benefits of this growth need to be used to rebuild long-neglected transportation and communications systems, power supplies, and other components of the economic infrastructure. Sustained growth requires increased investment, but investment has been slow to increase because of cumbersome regulations and economic nationalist rhetoric. It has been rising, but so has the cost of funds. Debt-for-equity swaps have some limited potential, but investment needs are vast.

The Philippine economy remains vulnerable to fluctuations in the world market. The 8 percent surge in economic growth in the Philippines was due mostly to lower oil prices and higher gold and copra prices. Some export earnings have increased (copra), but the long-term prospects for most traditional exports are poor. It is uncertain how long the commodity price rise of the late 1980s will last. According to many reports, world market prospects are gloomy. What worked for South Korea and Taiwan during the boom years of the 1950s and 1960s may not work for the Philippines in the 1980s and 1990s because of changes in the world economic environment.

216

## Social Factors

**Population and Labor Force.** The population growth rate is perhaps the most basic factor of social change. Estimates of the growth rate vary from 2.5 percent to 3.0 percent a year, among the highest in Asia. This high rate and the correspondingly high labor force growth rate have become problematic in relation to the poor record of economic growth and job creation. The combined result of these factors is that real wages have declined for over two decades. Population growth rates can be expected to remain high.

The outlook for the future is equally difficult. Every year about 750,000 new entrants join a labor force that already contains about 5 million underemployed or unemployed workers. The labor force will be expanding even more rapidly in the future because of the compounding effect of high population growth rates. The new labor force for the rest of the century has already been born; about 16 million new entrants will join it in the next fifteen years. Without major changes in policies, it is not clear where these additional job seekers will be absorbed. Millions of new job seekers have not been absorbed by the formal labor market.

The ability of the economy to generate more jobs deteriorated sharply under the Marcos regime. It has been estimated that each extra 1 million pesos of output resulted in more than 200 jobs in the 1960s, 160 in the 1970s, and only 100 from 1980 to 1986. The capital-output ratio worsened from 4:1 in the 1970s to 11:1 in the 1980s. These data can be explained by capital flight and corruption during the Marcos years, which resulted in chronic unemployment and underemployment. Hence the Philippine economy needs to receive a massive transfusion of investment funds as well as to give a high priority to job creation in the allocation of capital so as to reduce current unemployment and provide jobs for new entrants to the labor force.

**Distribution of Income, Wealth, and Poverty.** Basic needs have not been well met in the Philippines because such economic growth as has occurred has not been widely distributed. Income distribution is highly unequal. It has been estimated that the top 10 percent of the population has more than fifteen times the income of the poorest 10 percent. The income distribution appears particularly unequal when compared with those of some other developing countries in the region, such as South Korea and Taiwan.

Unequal distribution of income is also indicated by infant mortality and malnutrition rates. The infant mortality rate is sixty per 1,000 live births—one of the highest in Asia and six times as high as the U.S. rate. Two-thirds of infants are underweight in their first year of life; they do not get enough to eat. During the early 1980s, on the island of Negros, starvation was widespread among the children of unemployed sugar cane workers. In contrast, while the average Filipino consumes only about 89 percent of the calories needed for adequate nutrition, the country exports about 800 calories per person per day in the form of coconut oil alone.

According to the *1985 Family Income and Expenditures Survey,* nearly 30 million people in the population of 56 million were living in absolute poverty, that is, had incomes that did not enable them to satisfy basic needs. This constituted a significant worsening of the situation from a decade earlier. By comparable definitions, in 1975 the incomes of about 45 percent of families were insufficient to meet basic needs; in 1985 the figure had risen to 52 percent. Given the increase in the population over this period, an additional 12 million persons had been recruited into the ranks of the "absolutely poor." Because of the high population growth rate and the highly unequal distribution of income, mass poverty is likely to increase.

Poverty is concentrated in the rural areas, among small-scale subsistence farmers and agricultural laborers. After twenty years of declining real wages, they are frequent victims of intimidation, extortion, and repression by private armies of security guards and other paramilitary groups. The rural poor have become cannon fodder for both sides in the growing civil war.

**Social Class Stratification.** The stratification of social groups, especially in the rural Philippines, has existed in all historical periods. What is distinctive about current trends is that they reflect a widespread shift to commercial agriculture under conditions of high population pressure, costly and rapid technological change, and polarizing rural social class relations. As a result, Philippine rural society has been undergoing a profound structural transformation that has created a new rural social class system and a new land tenure pattern.

A very few subsistence farmers have become modern, commercially oriented, profit-maximizing agribusinessmen. Some have become modestly prosperous small-scale farmers. A few have found industrial jobs to earn an adequate living through wage labor. Most traditional farm households, however, have been reduced to landless laborers. They own few or no assets or tools and very little or no land. Typically, the immediate cause of their poverty is land alienation due to distress sales, debt foreclosures, evictions, and the frag-

218

mentation of small holdings, especially of insecure farm owners and tenants. Then the rural poor have no way to earn a living except as wage laborers in agriculture, as plantation workers, as migrant workers, or as petty traders, gatherers, craft workers, or any combination of these. They are almost always underemployed, but they cannot afford to be unemployed.

Rural poverty in the agriculture sector is exacerbated by the lack of jobs available at or above a poverty wage. The number of good jobs accessible to rural laborers is not increasing fast enough for the growing population. This can be seen as a result of the high growth rate of the labor force and the relatively low labor intensity of current investment. More and more workers without land of their own and without any other significant assets, capital, or skills are forced to take work that is neither very productive nor very remunerative. Landlessness is one critical aspect of rural poverty; the lack of a good job—on or off the farm—is another.

There are other indicators of worsening poverty. The foreign debt burden of the Philippines soared from $1.6 billion in 1972 to nearly $30 billion in 1986. The Philippines is now one of the most debt-ridden nations in the world. About 40 percent of its export earnings are consumed by interest payments to its foreign creditors. The Philippines is also Southeast Asia's greatest exporter of people. In the United States, Hong Kong, Singapore, and throughout the rest of Southeast Asia and the Middle East, migrant Filipinos have found work in nursing, ship crewing, construction, road transport, domestic service, and entertainment. In mid-1988 about 600,000 Filipinos were awaiting immigrant visas to the United States; visa applications were up 25 percent from the previous year. Almost all are seeking a better life abroad.[2]

The Philippines has fertile volcanic soils, abundant rainfall, extensive fishing grounds, mineral deposits that include gold and iron ores, and a relatively well-educated population. Hence hunger and poverty are vastly out of proportion to the natural wealth of the country. Other countries with much less natural wealth have achieved much more prosperity. The difference can largely be explained by the government's development priorities and performance.

## Government Priorities

The historical pattern of economic growth in the Philippines was not inevitable; nor was it natural. It has been influenced at many points by government policies. Past government policies have exacerbated high population growth rates, declining real wages, an unequal

219

distribution of wealth and income, and the stratification of social classes. These trends have occurred not despite economic growth but because of it. Given the high population growth rate and the highly unequal distribution of income, a higher economic growth rate *of the same style* could create more poverty rather than alleviate it.

Many policies have now been adopted that attempt to correct these earlier policies. In addition, the inequality of ownership of assets could be reduced. Cooperatives or collectives could be formed. Subsidized interest rates for agriculture could be removed so that loans to large-scale, capital-intensive farm operators do not crowd out small-scale, labor-intensive farm operators. The availability and cost of credit could be shifted so that small borrowers could obtain affordable credit and capital intensity would not be encouraged. Research and development could be concentrated on low-cost and labor-using agricultural and craft technology. Assets in the form of useful training could be provided to poor families. Among all these possibilities, there is a widespread consensus that high priorities ought to be given to land reform and meeting basic needs.

**Land Reform.** Land reform is long overdue. The government estimates that 90 percent of the country's agricultural land is in the hands of just 10 percent of the population. Two-thirds of all poor farmers are full or partial tenants. In addition, a growing body of landless agricultural workers lack access to land. The problem is particularly acute in sugar land areas, where large estates are operated with landless wage labor.

There are many compelling reasons for the government to pursue agrarian reform. It can ameliorate a significant amount of rural poverty. It can give the government a large (though poor) base of support in the countryside. It can increase productivity. It can give the government an opportunity to restructure the declining sugar industry. It can increase investment in industry by compensated landowners. Historically, land redistribution has been a prerequisite to sustained development in postwar Japan, South Korea, Taiwan, India, Malaysia, and other developing countries.

Land reform can also reduce one of the major causes of the Communist insurgency. Leaders of the insurgency have said repeatedly that land imbalances are at the heart of their movement. They advocate a "land-to-the-tiller" policy under which they have seized idle or abandoned holdings without compensation. Their message is addressed to the great majority of farm workers who work on land they do not own as low-paid laborers or as sharecroppers who give their landlords as much as half their crop.

The Aquino government has found it difficult to generate the political will or administrative capacity to achieve its stated goals for land reform. Indeed, in very few cases in Philippine historical experience has government successfully implemented a comprehensive land reform program. In very few cases anywhere in the developing world has a democratic government implemented a land reform program for its own people. In Asia land reform has been accomplished in a few cases—postwar Japan, Taiwan, and South Korea—but only with extraordinary external pressure and assistance.

The Philippine government land reform law of 1988 appears to be just as vulnerable as past attempts to procedural delays, legal loopholes, and obstructionist tactics by landlords and other rural elites. If land reform is attempted within an ambiguous scope, at a slow or indeterminate pace, or with qualified funding, it may create numerous conflicts and controversies that may detract from the overall rural development effort.

The government's high-level Agricultural Policy and Strategy Team pointed out in its 1986 *Agenda for Action for the Philippine Rural Sector* that

> the minimum requirements for a successful land reform are: (1) the dismantling of private armed groups (which have been used by landlords to intimidate the peasantry), (2) a democratically-based and non-economically based selection of local officials, whose loyalties would be more to the masses of their constituents than to the economic powers of their areas, and (3) the effective administrative separation of the function of promoting agricultural and natural resource productivity from the function of promoting land justice.

So far none of these "minimum requirements" has been achieved. A land reform bill has been passed by the legislature, but its funding and implementation remain uncertain.

Despite the complexity of land tenure patterns and the political difficulties of any redistribution scheme, land reform is a necessary part of any government strategy for rural development. But it is no longer a sufficient solution, because of population pressures and the growth of the nonfarm rural labor force. Other, complementary policies must be considered. Better rural roads, particularly those linking rural areas to markets, investments in small-scale, communal irrigation, and rural electrification would be highly beneficial. The system of research and extension needs to be improved, so that extension workers can reach poor farmers in remote areas and provide appropriate technological packages suited to their environment.

221

The adaptation of modern technologies by small farmers will require improvements in the system of rural credit as well. Given the scarcity of arable land and the limited labor-absorptive capacity of agriculture, industrial development must also be pursued.

**Meeting Basic Needs.** There is a need to reverse the many government services that discriminate against the poor. The system of government expenditures and taxation has been regressive. Taxes on income are widely evaded, there is no effective capital gains tax, and collection of taxes on real property is extremely poor. While nominal tax rates are high, actual collections are low, so that the tax effort is low in comparison with the efforts of similar countries. The result is a regressive taxation structure in which poor families pay a higher proportion of their income in taxes than higher-income families.

The poor have not been the major beneficiaries of government expenditure programs in the social sectors. The benefits of public education have been greater for higher-income students. In health, most public resources have been devoted to expensive urban-based curative services. Housing subsidies, both in financing loans and in providing shelter, have mainly benefited the upper half of the income ladder. The Philippines spends less than half what other countries at comparative levels of development spend on social services. In some cases, government programs already have extensive coverage (for example, primary education), but the quality of services needs to be improved. Although the majority of the poor have access to elementary education, for example, the educational system is regressive at all levels. In elementary schools poorer students receive lower-quality services. In secondary education there is not only inequality within public schools but also lack of access to the higher-quality private system. Subsidies are highest at the postsecondary level; they go mostly to higher-income students. In areas such as nutrition, health care, and family planning, both the quality and the coverage of services offered need to be expanded. Basic needs can be more easily satisfied by the poor themselves after the bias against them in national policies is removed.

### Cultural Factors

Comprehensive reforms may be essential for development and democracy in the Philippines but is the government willing and able to implement them? What cultural values determine the agenda of Philippine politics? How do Filipinos decide "who gets what, when, and how"? Harold Lasswell's axiom of political analysis directs our attention to the study of the value patterns of a society. The key values are safety, income, and deference. The few who get the most of any value are the elite; the rest are the rank and file. An elite preserves its ascendancy by manipulating symbols, controlling supplies, and applying violence. This is true in the Philippines as elsewhere. While there are many important regional and ethnic variations throughout the archipelago, there are a few widely practiced, distinctive cultural means of political domination, particularly the tradition of political dynasties and the symbolic value of elections in reinforcing social stratification.

**Strong Families and Weak Governments.** Historically, through generations of bitter experience, Filipinos have learned that the state cannot provide most services that the citizens of other nations expect from their governments. In this century the state has collapsed, partially or wholly, at least four times in the midst of war and revolution—during the Philippine Revolution (1896–1902), the Japanese occupation (1941–1945), the postwar Huk Communist revolt (1947–1955), and the People Power revolution (February 1986). After independence in 1946, moreover, the Philippine central government effectively lost control over much of the country to powerful regional warlords. With their economic power and monopoly of local political office, backed by well-armed private armies, the warlords terrorized the peasantry and extracted a de facto regional autonomy as the price for delivering votes to Manila politicians. Moreover, the church, the nation's other leading source of power, has either served the colonial state or remained socially uninvolved.[3]

"What Church and state cannot provide, the family must," observes Alfred McCoy in his recent study of family oligarchies in the Philippines. "It provides employment and capital; educates and socializes the young; assures medical care; shelters its handicapped and aged; and strives, above all else, to transmit its name, honor, lands, capital and values to the next generation."[4] McCoy posits two ethical standards in the Philippines—one for the family and another for the wider world:

> Within the family, Filipinos are honest, loving, loyal, open and affectionate. At home the guard comes down and one can be oneself. . . . Outside the home or compound, the world is beset with violence, duplicity, mendacity and corruption. Open and intimate at home, Filipinos don a mask of excessive politeness that conceals a calculating behavior when they go out into the society at large. Partners will steal, rivals will murder, bandits plunder, allies betray—all

SOCIOCULTURAL DEVELOPMENTS IN THE PHILIPPINES

in a society without government to provide order or assure any redress. In such a chaotic universe, the individual charts his or her course carefully. Each move—in business, politics and government—is done through personal contacts with family, old school chums or ritual kin. All of the passion, power and loyalties diffused in more developed societies are focused on the Filipino family. It commands an individual's highest loyalty, defines his life chances, and becomes his emotional touchstone.[5]

**Political Dynasties.** Philippine political parties are often coalitions of powerful families. Governments can become the private property of the ruling family, as the Marcos era demonstrated. Leading banks are often extensions of family capital (Bank of Commerce was Cojuangco, Manila Bank is Laurel). In the world of elite politics and business dealings, a family name is a negotiable asset for a young aspirant. An elite family's political legacy can be inherited, divided, and disputed. Along with their land and capital, elite families are supposed to transmit character and characteristics through the generations. Although individuals can and do rise through elections, parties and voters seem to feel that a candidate with a "good name" has a certain advantage. A Laurel in Batangas, an Aquino in Tarlac, an Osmena in Cebu, and a Lopez in Iloilo will always poll strongly. Along with the division of lands and jewels, families apportion candidacies for provincial or municipal office among their heirs.

Whether board room battle or presidential election, ordinary Filipino observers often perceive major national events through a family paradigm. Provincial and local politics often seem little more than intrafamily or interfamily battles. The familial aspect of national politics was particularly evident during the twenty years of the Marcos era. Although foreign observers analyzed Marcos's martial law regime in terms of issues and institutions (land reform, insurgency), most Filipinos focused on the family dynamics underlying the power struggle among the leading actors—Marcos, Romualdez, Osmena, Lopez, Aquino, Laurel, Cuenco, and Cojuangco, to cite a few. Although Marcos posed as an institutional reformer battling the vested interests of the old oligarchy, a cynical populace saw the familial basis of his self-interest. Marcos's attack on the oligarchy sprang from a falling out with his wealthy patron, Don Eugenio Lopez. Marcos portrayed his martial law dictatorship as a social revolution from above, but his regime soon lost its populist thrust and became a coalition of rising families (Marcos, Romualdez, Benedicto, and Cojuangco) expropriating the wealth of established elites

(Jacinto, Lopez, Toda, and others). He sought to transform his dictatorship into a dynasty by destroying potential opposition and constructing a ruling coalition of families.[6]

The reaction against martial law, the so-called "EDSA revolution" (named for the boulevard where political marches were staged), and the ascension of Aquino's government all raised hopes for the prospects of a more democratic political system in the post-Marcos era. Aquino came to power in February 1986 with a revolutionary mandate for change and no significant debts to the old political families that had generally been allied with Marcos's (the New Society Movement founded by Marcos) KBL party. After initial attempts at reconciliation with the rebels proved futile, however, Aquino made major concessions to the military and gradually moved into an alliance with traditional regional elites to create a stronger base for her government. Family oligarchies are reemerging through the newly created electoral apparatus.

In the May 11, 1987, elections, 130 of 200 candidates elected to the House of Representatives belonged to traditional political families and another 39 were relatives of these families. Only 31 elected representatives are "new political leaders," that is, not related to the traditionally dominant political families. Several of these ran as "antidynasty" candidates. Of the 169 representatives from the traditional political clans, 102 are identified with the pre-1986 anti-Marcos forces and 67 with pro-Marcos clans. The overwhelming majority of the twenty-four elected senators are from traditional political clans that were prominent in the period before martial law.

According to Resil Mojares, many Filipinos offer a simple reason for the continued political dominance of a few old families: society itself has not changed very much.[7] They may add that the old clans have a built-in advantage; they are already rooted, established, and wealthy, and therefore they have a head start over all the others. Many political clan leaders are recognized for their considerable skill in formulating strategies and alliances in electoral politics. They have the ability and the means to transform the electoral process into an ideological ritual to justify their domination.

**Elections as Ideological Rituals.** Americans introduced elections first in local government. Given the history of Filipino alienation from national government, this ensured the dominance of local issues and local factions in politics. The suffrage requirements effectively limited political participation to the leading families of the town. The provincial elections, which were next introduced, on an indirect basis,

225

established the pattern of family alliances that has since become a distinct feature of Philippine politics.

Under Spanish colonial rule Filipinos had already learned to rely heavily on family and kin to provide for their social welfare. Under American colonial rule the close connection between family and politics was probably strengthened and was projected on a national scale. The national elections of 1907 did not change the situation in its essential aspects. Writes O. D. Corpuz, "A truly national campaign involving genuine national organizations did not materialize. . . . The political organizations which fought out the 1907 elections, therefore, were provincial blocs of the leading families; these blocs were united by the political slogans of the moment into loose national confederations."[8] Provincial family groups became and remain the basic unit of national politics.

Elections have become so deeply established in Philippine political culture that they have become a synonym not only for politics but for democracy itself. They are an exercise deeply inscribed in the Filipino political imagination. During the twentieth century elections (both local and national) have been held once every two or four years. They involve a great mass of Filipinos: over 26 million voters in the country today, virtually the entire adult population. Elections are keenly contested, and voter turnouts are very high. Even under martial law Marcos felt constrained to attempt to achieve legitimacy through a series of plebiscites, referendums, and elections. Since Aquino came to power in February 1986, two national elections and one national plebiscite have been held. In the May 11, 1987, elections, there were eighty-four candidates for twenty-four senatorial seats and 1,899 candidates for 200 congressional seats. In the January 18, 1988, local elections, there were over 150,000 candidates for 16,454 seats. This is an average of three and one-half candidates for each Senate seat, nine candidates for each local government post, and nine candidates for each congressional seat.[9]

Theoretically, an election is the time when society takes cognizance of itself and citizens are most self-conscious, observes Mojares. It is a season of stock taking. Citizens reflect on their collective state and history; they make choices about leaders, policies, and futures. The "democratic space" is visible: incumbents offer themselves for popular judgment; alternative candidates present alternative ideas for government; there is a public exchange of views; finally, the voter weighs his options, enters the ritual inner sanctum of the polling booth, and casts his ballot.

The reality, of course, is not so tidy. In the Philippines, the "democratic space" is greatly reduced by a number of factors. The party system is undeveloped. Elite personalities and particularistic concerns are more important than programs and policies in public debate. Most candidates espouse the same platitudinous objectives. Only those with substantial wealth can organize an electoral campaign. They usually dominate the public space available: public sites for daily rallies, radio broadcasts, newspaper space, wall space for posters and handbills. Various forms of graft, corruption, intimidation, and terrorism are widespread. Through these restrictive factors the electoral process has become the arena for factional competition among traditional elite families.

**The Power of Symbols.** It has often been said that electoral success in the Philippines depends on "goons, guns, and gold." A fourth factor, however, is at least as important. It can be described colloquially as the fourth "g" of "glitter" or "glamour" or more generally as the power of symbols. "It is the way of power to surround itself with an array of things to be believed and admired, credenda and miranda," wrote Charles Merriam in his classic study of political power.

> No power could stand if it relied on violence alone, for force is not strong enough to maintain itself against the accidents of rivalry and discontent. The might that makes right must be of a different might from that of the right arm. It must be a might deep rooted in emotion, embedded in feelings and aspirations, in morality, in sage maxims, in forms of rationalization among the higher levels of cultural groups. The eye, the ear, the aesthetic sense, must be attracted and enlisted also, if whole-souled admiration and loyalty are to be maintained.[10]

The importance of symbols and ceremonies of power has long been recognized in Philippine politics. It is evident in the art of oration, *palabas* (public speaking ability), *pulitika* (bargaining for political support), and in the theatrical spectacles of parades, rhetoric, music, and song in national political rallies at Plaza Miranda and in village plazas throughout the country. Through the use of symbols power seeks to project itself into prestige and prestige to transform itself back again into power. In the Philippines the power of symbols and the role of mass psychology in the construction of power has been studied by Reynaldo Ileto, Mojares, and Richard Kessler.[11]

The manipulation of symbols by elites is useful in explaining recent politics in the Philippines. It explains how Marcos was able to maintain power as long as he did, after years of declining economic performance and increasing opposition. His New Society of constitutional authoritarianism deftly (and cynically) employed both the traditional symbols of *machismo* and *caudillismo*, emphasizing personal leadership, and the modern symbols of the electoral and constitutional due process, emphasizing popular sovereignty.

It explains how Aquino was swept into government by a wave of popular legitimacy, despite the superior economic, organizational, and coercive resources of the Marcos government. She was, in her own words, "just a simple housewife"; but she was also the best-known victim of Marcos's rule, she had no known political ambitions, and she was honest, unpretentious, and deeply religious. As the widow of a martyr she symbolized the suffering of a nation seeking political and spiritual redemption. She not only gave Filipinos a chance to save their country from continued rule by the Marcos government; she also gave them a chance to redeem their self-esteem and national pride. The adroit use of yellow clothing, ribbons, and party banners was a conscious symbolic appeal to unite anti-Marcos forces.

The Philippines lacks a symbol of state that might provide continuity for the national political community. There is no functional equivalent to Emperor Hirohito, King Carlos, Queen Elizabeth, or any transcendent symbol. The closest thing to it is the church. Hence religious iconography played an important role in unifying People Power forces during the Marcos ouster of February 1986. Through mass media and popular media, Aquino's victory became a victory of symbols over "goons, guns, and gold." She became "Saint Cory of the Yellow Revolution."[12]

The persistence and the reemergence of the old dominant political families in the elections of 1987 and 1988 have dispelled hopes about the prospects for development and democracy in the Philippines. As elections restored provincial elites, Aquino restored expropriated corporations to the old oligarchy. The Lopez family, for example, which had been stripped of its wealth and driven into exile by Marcos, has returned to Manila and is rebuilding its national economic holdings and its provincial power base.

Elections are still held but they do not have the symbolic power they used to have. The elections of Ramon Magsaysay in 1954 and Aquino in 1986 were both important in recharging the symbolic power of elections, but neither had much long-lasting value. In the 1984 National Assembly elections and the 1986 presidential election, Filipino voters showed that they prefer ballots to bullets or boycotts, but voter withdrawal and resistance are increasing. Mojares notes that politicians have found that it is increasingly difficult to get the voters out. They have to invest more in the mass media. They have to organize more complicated electoral machines, involving movers, canvassers, ushers, runners, and poll watchers. They have to devise more sophisticated means of intimidation and fraud.[13]

At the same time political mobilization outside the electoral arena is increasing. This is evident in the development of radical trade unions, Basic Christian Communities, various cause-oriented groups, the Moro National Liberation Front, the Muslim Independence Liberation Army, the Cordillera People's Liberation Army, private paramilitary forces and vigilante groups, and especially the "New" Armed Forces of the Philippines and the New People's Army. All these groups want a larger say in national and local politics. They all oppose the control of the traditional family oligarchy over electoral politics. They are all willing to struggle for power in the "parliament of the streets," through "acoustical warfare," or in the underground.

## Prospects

After twenty years of concentrating wealth and power, given the fragile government consensus and threats of political instability, will the Aquino administration be able or willing to pursue genuine reforms for national development? Will it be able to formulate policies to reduce poverty and vigorously implement them according to an explicit timetable? Will it remove the bias in favor of higher-income groups and capital-intensive, large-scale, urban, established enterprises in national policies concerning taxes, credit, investment, housing, education, health care, nutrition, and family planning? Will it be able to overcome pork-barrel politics, the primacy of private gain over public benefit, and other forms of graft and corruption of "public service"?

The Aquino government has considerable support for its political agenda. Aquino still retains a great deal of personal popularity. Many of her early rivals for political leadership have been removed, in particular, Juan Ponce Enrile and Salvador Laurel. The Communist party of the Philippines and the New People's Army have suffered several setbacks. Attempts at military coups have not received popular support. The government has strong support from the church, the business sector, and the international community.

Aquino has not converted her personal popularity or her government's popular support into a more durable form of political organization. She has not formed or endorsed or joined any programmatic political party. Some attempts to do this are being made, however, by many around her, including her brother, Paul Aquino, as well as Ramon Mitra, Raul Manglapus, and Aquilino Pimentel. These political leaders and their factions, particularly LAKAS and PDP-Laban, may evolve into a durable political party.[14]

Aquino's popularity may decrease and her governing coalition may crumble as the government attempts to resolve potentially divisive, even explosive, issues, such as land reform, local autonomy, and the status of U.S. bases. These may all be no-win issues for Aquino in that they may exacerbate inevitable conflicts within her cabinet and among her supporters. For example, National Defense Secretary Fidel Ramos and Foreign Affairs Secretary Raul Manglapus have divergent views on U.S. bases in the Philippines. Compromise solutions—such as the recent land reform legislation—may be inadequate remedies given the scope of the problem.

Philippine prospects are complicated by some unpredictable factors, in particular, the role of the military in the political system and the outlook for revolutionary and secessionist movements. The military has now achieved a major role in national politics. It has acquired a virtual veto over cabinet personnel; it has a major voice in national policies and local affairs, especially with regard to a vague and broadly defined counterinsurgency policy. The military will have a major voice in the next presidential election; indeed, it may even produce a candidate. Ramos has been rumored to have presidential ambitions. Many military officers believe they can govern better than civilians.[15] "There never has been a fully professionalized military in the Philippines," one scholar asserts.[16] Civilian control of the military may be more tenuous now than during the Marcos years. The Aquino government has been unable to reform or remove the remaining repressive instruments in the countryside. Reports of abuse of church workers by military and paramilitary forces persist and continue to swell rebel ranks, especially in Negros and Mindanao.[17]

Despite recent setbacks, Communist party hard-liners are escalating their armed struggle, intent on regaining the momentum lost when Marcos was ousted by Aquino in February 1986. The Communist party and the New People's Army are still well-organized political forces. With enough popular and material support, they would be a formidable rival for government authority. Muslim rebels have also resumed their armed struggle for greater autonomy or secession. Centrifugal forces are also evident in the autonomy movement led by the rebel priest Conrado Balweg and his Cordillera People's Liberation Army in northern Luzon.

## Summary and Conclusion

As a result of the restoration of traditional family-based political dynasties, initial political reforms have not been complemented by essential economic and social reforms. The early momentum for economic and social reforms has been stalled in controversies over land reform and local autonomy. Opportunities created by the People Power movement, the establishment of the Aquino government, and its initial political reforms have diminished. Traditional family-based political dynasties have reemerged to resist proposed government reforms and to resume their domination of national and local politics. Democratic institutions have been revived, but they provide democracy only for the few. Mass poverty remains a massive obstacle to Philippine democracy.

It is difficult to predict Philippine prospects, given all the short- and long-term political, economic, social, and cultural factors. The major assets of the Aquino government are the relatively volatile, short-term factors of personal popularity, public opinion, and commodity prices. But the major problems it faces are the deeply rooted, long-term factors of social structure (inequalities of wealth, income, and opportunity) and cultural values (strong families and weak governments). These problems will be overcome only after many years of sustained, comprehensive effort. It is not clear, however, whether the government's initial reform movement is still getting organized and building up momentum or whether it is running out of steam.

According to historical standards of evaluation, the Aquino government has already greatly improved Philippine prospects over the political decay of the Marcos years. According to optimal standards, however, much more must be achieved in increased investment, output, the redistribution of wealth, power, and opportunity to reduce population pressures and mass poverty. Development and democracy have occurred only where population growth rates have been declining and living standards have been increasing. According to comparative standards, if the Philippines is to attain the progress achieved by South Korea, Taiwan, and the other newly industrializing economies of Asia, then—in addition to these political and social reforms—the government must unite national economic leadership to achieve international competitiveness.

Is the Philippines really like other Asian countries? Will it follow the East Asian models of South Korea and Taiwan? It has often been observed that the Philippine political system is more like Latin America than Asia because of its Spanish and American colonial legacies. The prototypes of the Asian model, Taiwan and South Korea, have achieved sustained improvements in real wages, land reform, education, and other reforms to equalize the distribution of income. They have followed domestic and foreign investment policies to promote competitiveness. They have replaced patronage networks with administrative and military reforms to achieve merit systems. They have had decisive leadership by a coalition of technocrats, modern army officers, farmers, and new industrial entrepreneurs. The Philippines has few of these characteristics of the Asian model. Instead, it possesses many of the traditional Hispanic characteristics: a traditional landed elite dominating key social institutions; a patronage-oriented civil service and patronage-oriented political parties with little ideological or policy coherence (though with much nationalist and reformist rhetoric); industrialists protected from domestic and foreign competition (and therefore an uncompetitive, oligarchic, and inefficient economy); and massive underemployment and poverty. "The result," as William Overholt observes, "is an economy that cannot grow rapidly, cannot employ its people, cannot distribute income fairly, and cannot pay its debts."[18]

These historical, optimal, and comparative standards of evaluation can be summarized by two key indicators: real wages and world market shares. The challenge to the Aquino government is to overcome the Marcos legacy of two decades of declining real wages and decreasing world market shares. Much has already been accomplished; however, much more needs to be done. Major political reforms have been achieved; complementary economic and social reforms have not. Hence political pressures are likely to persist for many years.

## Philippine-American Relations

In the Philippines there is a growing movement for greater independence from the United States and stronger ties with Asian neighbors. Some of this new nationalist sentiment is a reaction to the important role of the United States in providing the Marcos government with material and diplomatic support. The United States supported the International Monetary Fund structural adjustment and austerity programs for the Philippines during the difficult years of the 1980s. It negotiated a new military bases agreement with a major increase in military aid during a period when economic aid and living standards were declining. Apart from a few cautionary statements, it did little in response to the growing corruption and repression during most of the Marcos years. The assassination of Benigno Aquino, Jr., and its political aftermath forced the United States to reassess its priorities in the Philippines.

When she was campaigning for the presidency, Aquino promised to reassess the Philippine-American bases agreement and to pursue closer ties with the Association of Southeast Asian Nations (ASEAN). During her September 1986 state visit to the United States, she said she would keep all her options for the U.S. bases open until the renegotiations. She established a good rapport with President Ronald Reagan and dispelled her suspicions of lingering pro-Marcos sentiments within the White House. But there are potential conflicts over the future of American bases in the Philippines and the nuclear-free status of the country. The new constitution allows for a legislative and popular referendum on the continued presence of U.S. bases in addition to the previous method of renegotiating through executive agreement. Legislation is now being considered to monitor the constitutional ban on nuclear weapons.

Foreign Affairs Secretary Manglapus has repeatedly made the argument that other nations that share in the regional security benefits provided by the United States ought also to share in the economic and political costs of the bases. Countries that border vital choke points or sea lanes ought to be host to some of the military facilities, he argues. Others that derive large economic benefits and trade surpluses under the U.S. security umbrella (in particular, Japan), ought to bear a larger share of the cost of maintaining the facilities. Filipinos are concerned that their country will become hostage as a target in the event of a superpower conflict. Earlier, the United States had been prevented by Marcos from using the bases for combat support during the Vietnam War. In 1985 he also pledged that he would not permit the United States to use Clark Field or Subic Bay to mount an attack against Soviet forces in Indochina. It seems likely that the Aquino government, preoccupied with a Muslim secession movement in the south, will be reluctant to allow the United States to use its bases for power projection to the Persian Gulf or the Middle East. Even within the New Armed Forces of the Philippines, there is considerable distrust of U.S. concern for Philippine security.

The government has a constitutional commitment to achieve a nuclear-free status and has made at least a verbal commitment to the goal of a Zone of Peace, Freedom, and Neutrality (ZOPFAN) for Southeast Asia. Much of this sentiment is part of a trend in which Philippine foreign policy has become more nationalist, more diversified, and more independent over the past two decades. Nationalist groups, many intellectuals, professionals, and government officials, especially in urban areas, as well as the legal left and the underground left, are all highly critical of the bases as a violation of Philippine sovereignty. They will certainly have the prevailing voice in any congressional or popular referendum on the issue. It is unlikely that Aquino would be able to retain her popularity if she campaigned for retention of the bases.

What positive steps can the United States and others take to improve Philippine prospects for development and democracy? The United States, Japan, and other trade surplus nations of Asia can foster Philippine development through economic and technical aid, especially through multilateral agencies in which the Philippine government has a voice. Debt service ought to be recycled into domestic investment to meet basic needs and promote development. Only through this approach will there be any chance for sustained development and repayment of foreign debt. A regional investment trust to recycle the cash and trade surpluses of Japan and other Asian nations into capital-starved countries like the Philippines would generate substantial mutual economic benefits. Japan has already increased its contribution to regional multilateral aid (for example, the World Bank's Emergency Supplementary Assistance Fund) and its bilateral aid (now higher than that of the United States). This trend might also facilitate a wider sharing of regional security costs. It might lead to a Soviet-American agreement on reducing military activities and expenditures in Asia. With regard to its security interests, the United States may have to pursue a multifaceted approach to defuse the highly volatile issue of U.S. military bases in the Philippines. To retain its essential military facilities in the Philippines, the United States may have to relocate some of its military missions. It may have to convert some of its facilities to uses with clear mutual security benefits (for example, joint or shared training facilities). It may have to phase out others. If it does all these simultaneously, it may be able to retain its most important regional defense facilities and still pursue long-term mutual economic interests in trade, investments, and credits.

In giving any form of aid, however, donors should remember the basic lesson of modernization: the inevitability of change. In the Philippines much political change is necessary if there is to be any further social or economic progress. If the United States were to try to retain its military facilities without basic economic and social reforms by the Philippine government, it would become an obvious target for nationalist and reformist opposition groups. As the United States begins to consider a "mini–Marshal Plan" for the Philippines, it may be useful to recall the words of President John F. Kennedy a quarter-century ago at the inauguration of a similar endeavor, the Alliance for Progress in Latin America: "those who make peaceful revolution impossible make violent revolution inevitable."

# 13

## The Philippines in the International Environment

*W. Scott Thompson*

By the time of President Corazon Aquino's accession to office in February 1986, Asian international relations had departed far from their cold war patterns of the previous four decades. This change was especially clear after Soviet leader Mikhail Gorbachev's new approach to the region[1] and the apparent success of China's four modernizations under Deng Xiaoping. The Association of Southeast Asian Nations (ASEAN), almost twenty years old, had also matured into a respected regional group that reinforces the international identity of each of its members. From these changes, one might expect that a new Philippine foreign policy would stress autonomy with respect to the former colonial power, the United States.[2] After all, by nature states maximize independence, and Manila had to bear the burden of a reputation for conducting its foreign policy, from independence in 1946, at the behest of the United States.

As it turned out, the squandering of Filipino resources—human, financial, and political—during the long Marcos dictatorship was so massive that for the first four years of the Aquino regime the United States played the key role in defining Manila's international environment and is likely to continue for at least several more years. The separation from America that a new generation of Filipinos sought had in fact been possible when Ferdinand Marcos launched his New Society in 1972: he had the legislative powers, personal insight, diplomatic skills, and economic momentum to achieve that separation and made it known that this indeed was one of his objectives.[3] But he soon subordinated that goal to simple greed. The chance to distance his country from Washington was lost as he and his family sought to legitimize their regime through a deliberate policy of ingratiating America's elite. Worse, in driving his country into an abyss, at a time when rapid population growth was already straining national re-

THE PHILIPPINES' INTERNATIONAL ENVIRONMENT

sources, he made the Philippines more, rather than less, dependent on its American benefactors.

Inevitably, then, the Philippines hung for at least a decade between the extreme desire of some to "kill the father,"[4] and thus to liberate itself psychologically, and the need to respond to negative American perceptions driving Washington's economic and military aid policies. The dilemma for Filipino nationalists was the more acute because of their long-standing belief that America's main interest in the archipelago, the two bases at Clark Field and Subic Bay, was more target than protection. And in an era of superpower détente, how much more anachronistic to be home to great imperial bases, even if these were the second-largest employer in the archipelago? But for the United States, maintaining these large bases, worth several billion dollars (whose uses had, to be sure, often exceeded expectation in international crises and regional wars), was the prime national objective of American diplomacy toward Manila.

Nevertheless, it seemed likely for three reasons that Manila and Washington would compromise and, in 1991 when the present agreement runs out, extend in some measure the old pact. First is public opinion: although radical sentiment was growing and the chief negotiator would be Foreign Secretary Raul Manglapus, whose anti-bases views were well known, feeling in the provinces was more mixed, where economic spillover from the bases (at least $330 million in payroll annually) was more salient. And it seemed likely that President Aquino, along of course with the military, was disposed toward accommodation.[5] Moreover, the style of Philippine political rhetoric usually hides a more pragmatic and accommodative reality.

Second, views in the region were less ill disposed toward the bases than among Manila's radical circles. In Thailand especially, and also in China, the American presence was encouraged; so too, if less vocally, in Japan and Indonesia. Third, a factor little spoken of, but likely to become more prominent, was the growing role of the New People's Army (NPA). The mess in which Marcos left his country, and the incompetence with which the successor regime started anew, augured ill for defeating the insurgency. Although the Armed Forces of the Philippines (AFP) was encountering some successes—especially in intelligence—in battling the NPA, the trend line was against it; after a meaningful dip in performance at the time of EDSA revolution, NPA successes began moving rapidly back toward their 1985 high.[6] If the elite perceive the threat as more imminent, they are more likely to clutch at American protection.[7] The polity would then of course be increasingly polarized, for it would be precisely the NPA's growth that would embolden the public radicals.

ASEAN, happily, provides the Philippines with ballast for the difficult years ahead. Although little can develop in the way of economic common markets or political integration, given the lack of complementarity in the economies and the geographic and cultural spread of the members, a powerful common mind set has developed among ASEAN elites with respect to their international environment. Few regional groups—perhaps only the Nordic group—exceed ASEAN in effective cooperation at the United Nations, for example. ASEAN has also defused bilateral rivalries and border tensions, like those plaguing Manila and Kuala Lumpur from the start, over Sabah. And it provides an alternative security framework for Manila, as it eventually seeks a new context or use for the American bases. As a Philippine diplomat put it, "The ASEAN partners . . . could give serious thought to the possibility of devising a collective security arrangement under ASEAN auspices and suitable to ASEAN's purposes and principles, in case the Military Bases Agreement between the Philippines and the United States should be terminated by either side in 1991."[8]

The main point, however, is that ASEAN is buoyed by the economic successes of its members, which set bench marks and incentives for the lagging Philippines. Although the other members— save oil-rich Brunei, which has joined major-power donor nations in pledging aid to Manila—can hardly settle Manila's debts, they have provided continuing encouragement. And they have helped strengthen the Philippine hand in its debt-resettlement quest by giving it international support and legitimacy.

Where does Philippine foreign policy go in the 1990s, given the rapidly evolving Asian security equation? Assuming no radical change of pace in the NPA's progress, we can confidently say that Manila will continue to follow, rather than lead, developments. For reasons that are partly obvious already, the country cannot significantly delink itself from the United States. But it is fair, if perhaps unkind, to say that Filipinos, especially in matters of statecraft, are not strategists; they pride themselves on being tacticians.[9] For instance, although talk was always plentiful, they followed the lead of other ASEAN states by a considerable margin in developing ties with both the People's Republic of China (PRC) and the Soviet Union. They have been reactive, looking from a position of injured pride in seeking aid from major donors. They therefore failed to see that success itself is the strongest bargaining point—and failed to understand that the momentum of the EDSA revolution is no longer a sufficient justification for massive aid. And the failures of the Marcos period have run out as an excuse for the economic bottlenecks, preventing the successful conclusion of already commissioned aid-financed projects.

## Economic Development and Economic Reform

In clearing the Philippines of the Marcoses and their cronies, the great events of the EDSA highway stopped short of a revolution, if we conceive that to include significant social and economic change. What really occurred was a restoration of the pre-Marcos elite that had run the Philippines almost as a fiefdom or series of fiefdoms. If one enormously rich Cojuanco left for Honolulu with Marcos, his cousin—President Aquino's brother—was there to fill the void, taking a seat in Congress and keeping the family prosperous. Secretary of Trade José Concepcion could openly propose legislation to preserve his protected market in household appliances. Landlords could meet in public convocation to plan how to defend their holdings; one even publicly proposed "bribing" journalists to see things their way.[10] It was back to business as usual.

True, EDSA opened the way for a return to economic growth, a prerequisite of political stability in any guise, and compared with the alternative of open civil war or NPA takeover, one should not minimize that benefit. Moreover, with 6–7 percent growth and prospects of a continuation of that trend, the government's room for maneuver will undoubtedly grow.

The debate over economic development goals was accentuated by the stakes in the so-called "mini-Marshall Plan," bandied about by the press and given reality at a July 1989 summit of aid donors in Tokyo. The Multilateral Aid Initiative/Philippines Aid Program (PAP) resulted from the efforts of four members of the U.S. Congress (Senators Alan Cranston and Richard Lugar and Congressmen Stephen Solarz and Jack Kemp), who in late 1987 pressed the case for the program with President Reagan. The administration canvassed support around the world, as well as with the World Bank and the International Monetary Fund, and found agreement in three areas: supporting continued economic reforms, improving Philippine absorptive capacity of external capital investments, and organizing donor assistance around sectoral programs. For the ensuing five years, sponsors wanted to raise at least the foreign assistance equivalent of Philippine negative foreign exchange commitments. At the Tokyo pledging session donors appeared to promise the $10 billion over five years that Manila had come to expect.

The debate on the best economic development strategy for the

Philippines in the late 1980s did not differ essentially from that during the preceding decades. The argument was whether aid flows, in exchange for pledges to free up markets and clean up corruption, would in fact, as the *Manila Chronicle* put it, "just get us mired deeper in the economic rut to which we have been consigned for too long a time."[11] Or in other words, did not the newspaper owner-oligarchs wish to keep the protected Philippine market for their own inefficiently produced goods?

Consider land reform, a psychological and economic cornerstone of comprehensive socioeconomic reform. Although from the start Aquino's government committed itself to land reform—indeed, President Aquino offered the nation's largest hacienda, her family's, as a starting point—the president waited two critical years for action.[12] She believed that, to be effective, land reform had to be done carefully, by the established interests, and only after these had identified themselves. She thus lost the momentum that the EDSA-induced revolutionary enthusiasm afforded her and with which she could have made the needed large-scale, dramatic changes in the program.

The legislation that eventually passed the Congress in some ways was a step backward from the Marcos program. That at least had compensated land owners on the basis of productive value (two and a half times the annual harvest). But now the old oligarchs lobbied for two years to achieve "fair market value" as "just compensation" and got it.[13] Meantime, holdover Marcos administrators and bureaucratic inefficiencies bogged the program down.

The ultimate evolution of the bases question must also be part of the economic equation. Filipinos repeat over and over that American aid is not rent, but saying it does not make it so. It was an open joke in Manila, based on an absolute reality, that during the last difficult phases of the interim bases renegotiations in 1988, progress on the PAP came virtually to a standstill, at American insistence. This made the connection black and white between base concessions and aid. Only after the breakthrough did Washington allow discussions of the PAP to go forward. The multibillion dollar cost to the United States of moving the bases eastward, the value of the land and facilities, the payroll to Filipinos, the nearly $100 million annually in military aid that is in American minds directly linked to base use, and finally the new pledges of economic aid of almost $200 million per year for a half-decade are all tied up in the bases question. It ensures that the bases will be the underlying, if not always the explicit, bargaining point between the two powers, with the issues of aid and security cutting both ways for both powers.

## Democracy and Development

The Philippines was affected by, and in turn affected elsewhere, a global movement toward democratization. Having launched an American program for the spread of democracy within Communist and allied but autocratic states, President Reagan in the end could not spare Ferdinand Marcos from the fires to which he had added so much kindling. The EDSA revolution was surely the most satisfying and exciting of the third world transitions in the 1980s. Ultimately it will succeed or fail not only on its intrinsic political merits but also on the economic buoyancy of the region (an only partly sufficient cause) and the internal economic reforms. And the slowness of the reforms will necessitate all the more effort from the region.

We should also consider the nature of democracy in the Philippines. The apparent similarity of institutions there and in the West, particularly the United States, has led observers to assume an explicit model: a presidency, a senate, and a house of representatives. But these superficial similarities hide more pervasive underpinnings of Philippine politics. One is the Malay basis of society, a consensus culture only appearing to make its political bargains through the institutions of popular power. It is instructive to compare Filipino culture with its sister Malay state, Malaysia, where, as one authority argues, "the strong curbs placed on political conflict and dissent may be seen as reflective of Malay cultural values, which appreciate strong authority and fear conflict and dissension."[14]

The other underpinning is the Spanish heritage. From 1521 to 1898, representatives of the king of Castile held the islands as personal property and exploited them as such. Notions of individual rights did not develop, but a form of personalism ironically did (as in Indonesia also). Philippine political culture was thus an outgrowth of the mixed ethnic heritage of the ruling elite and the fact that social status among that elite derived almost purely from, in David Steinberg's words, "wealth and consumption."[15] These were not the most appropriate backdrops for the kind of sociopolitical development that would buttress democracy.

"To be democratic in adversity is a stern test," Dennis Austin has written.[16] So it is difficult to see democracy surviving more than a few more years into the 1990s off the momentum of the EDSA revolution. Evidently, the country has not yet found a set of democratic institutions that conform to historical Philippine patterns of society or to the needs of the poor. And on that point, population growth is adding heavily to the social burden, this in a country that cannot find the will to restructure values to bring population growth into line with the availability of resources.

The problem is that the ruling elite has self-servingly seen democracy as a discrete political phenomenon and thus for the most part has failed to see the organic connection between economic reform and political and democratic stability. It is a connection the New People's Army has understood, in proposing rather tougher medicine for the national ills.[17] Further, it is not the habit of military elites anywhere to unlearn the capacity for political intervention, once mastered. Until Marcos's regime of martial law elevated the military role well above its historical low visibility and the empowered military then delivered the *coup de grâce* to his rule, the Armed Forces of the Philippines never contemplated a political role. Now the Philippines lives with "coup jitters."[18] A continuing debate between those advocating a tougher military response to the insurgency and those seeing its solution through economic development has largely been resolved in favor of the military, if only to quiet its restiveness.

The United States remains the Philippines' most important international contact—political, military, economic, and sociocultural. As such, the United States has difficult choices ahead in its policy toward the Philippines. It is not fanciful to envisage that by the mid-1990s military intervention may be contemplated, if the security situation continues to deteriorate at a faster rate than real gains are made in the economy—that is, real gains for the peasants outside Manila. Indeed, the Philippines is one of the few countries where American intervention is both conceptually possible *and* thinkable, because it is achievable through existing logistics. The sense of responsibility (or guilt) in America toward the former colony, the utility of the military bases, and the close connections between Philippine and American elites might lead to an overt American role in fighting the insurgency. Armed intervention would serve principally to signal the populace of American will, something that would count for much more in the archipelago than it could ever have in Vietnam.[19]

If that premise is correct, how does Washington fashion policy to avoid that unhappy situation? The critical question is the relationship of development to security. Hitherto, policy has been premised on the *necessity* of retaining the bases; other ingredients have tended to be subsidiary. But if the NPA wins, the bases are worthless.[20] In any event, long-term American security ties with the Philippines are only as good as that country's democratic stability. On balance, it is arguable that the Philippines needs the bases more than the United States, and thus it behooves Washington to bargain less for military access and more for the real reforms in the country's governance and development that alone will secure Manila's future and Washington's ties with the islands.

241

In negotiating, shrewd parties always can discover the touchstone of the other's position. Were U.S. policy to shift toward emphasis on rapid economic reform—not just through land reform but on breaking bottlenecks in aid flows and in market reform (that is, wherever the old oligarchy or corrupt bureaucrats are stifling progress for self-serving reasons)—Filipino negotiators would soon get the point.

Another signal will have to be sent to a broader audience. Washington backed President Aquino with fervor. Although her historic role was in providing the mechanism for ridding the country of a despot, she has failed to provide the creative leadership that could take the country out of its deep malaise. The NPA's persistence is proof enough of this. The United States must be ready to encourage a new leadership capable of understanding, then responding to, that malaise. Although this cannot be done with the heavy hand with which President Magsaysay was picked and backed almost forty years ago, the message must be sent, for the challenge today is greater. Aquino need not be undercut for the message to be received that her act is finished. Whether a Magsaysay-style reformer can emerge before either a military or an NPA-dictated solution is found can hardly be predicted with confidence. The political will of the military, the growing strength of the NPA, and the residual determination of the middle strata of the Philippine polity to make democracy work all suggest that the outcome will be a combination of all three: military coups backing a chosen reformer to combat an NPA that increasingly dictates the terms of political combat. What seems self-evident is that the particular balance of the three will determine the character of Philippine foreign policy in the longer term. In the meantime, American pressures and Philippine responses are the only game in town.

PART FOUR
# Assessments and Conclusion

# 14
## Comparing the Cases

*Raymond Gastil*

This volume considers two questions: (1) Do recent political developments in East Asia point finally to the definitive emergence of democracy in the third world? (2) Is economic development necessary for the firm implantation of the democratic virus?

As material for answering these questions, the preceding chapters have presented extensive and convincing information on the recent history and prospects of the Republic of Korea, the Republic of China (Taiwan), and the Philippines. In spite of many similarities, what emerges most strongly from these descriptions is the difficulty of generalizing from three such different societies. Their political and economic development, though borrowed and flavored from the same outside sources, cannot be expected to follow the same patterns in the future. Even more difficult is the task of using these societies as a basis for thinking more generally about trends in third world economic and political development.

Situated in the contact zone of the Chinese, Malaysian, and Melanesian/Polynesian cultures, the Philippines has been deeply affected by long periods of occupation by two Western peoples. Its nationalism has been superimposed on a variety of peoples speaking different languages. At the top of the social pyramid the recently crafted or rechristened national language has to compete, not always successfully, with English and even Spanish. Economically, the past generation has seen continuing very high population growth rates and a stagnant economy—especially for the average person. Given the strong, if oligarchical and violent, democratic tradition dating back at least to before World War II, the recent establishment of democracy under Corazon Aquino has been more the reestablishment of an already well-developed tradition than the beginning of a new one.

South Korea and Taiwan are both well within the Sinic or East Asian cultural world. Both have been affected for centuries by massive influence from the Chinese mainland. Both have also had the intensive experience of decades of Japanese occupation. The peoples of both speak and write essentially the same language at all levels of society (although dialectal differences have political importance, particularly on Taiwan). Both have experienced rapid economic growth in recent years, growth that has been remarkably egalitarian for a developing society. Democracy in the sense of political rights and civil liberties, however, is not deeply rooted in the cultures of the peoples of either society. Recent democratic developments have the character of experiments, of innovations in societies joining in the flush of economic success a world society of market economies that have long practiced political and civil democracy under the rule of law.

Yet these two societies also have much to distinguish them. The Republic of Korea has until recently fitted the pattern of many third world states that have tried repeatedly to establish democratic institutions, only to have their attempts thwarted by military interventions in the name of national security. Since World War II South Korea has experienced relatively democratic interludes, and the experience of working in opposition parties is by no means new to the society—although the parties have remained personalistic. Yet no major political parties, whether government or opposition, can be said to be well entrenched. The struggle for democracy has been largely between the military establishment and civilian society. By 1988 South Korea seemed to have achieved, or all but achieved, a working democracy. But this democracy will for some time continue to exist on sufferance. The military commands will watch and wait and may reestablish their by now almost traditional rule.

By contrast, the Republic of China has until recently been under the firm and uninterrupted rule of the Kuomintang (KMT), an elite, top-down party borrowing organizationally from Leninism. While force and violence have played a major part in maintaining this power, in theory the security forces have always served a civilian administration rather than the other way around, as in South Korea. This could change overnight with the passing of the older generation, but for now the distinction remains significant—in neither the Philippines nor China (Taiwan) has there been a tradition of military rule. It should also be noted that the progress of democracy has been slower in Taiwan against the entrenched power of the KMT than in the Republic of Korea. Remarkable gains since 1986 should not obscure the fact that previous opposition party activity in Taiwan has been scattered and minimal. This and the end of the Chiang dynasty may account for the fact that political activity in China (Taiwan) is for the moment much less personalistic than in the Philippines or South Korea.

Like many third world countries, all three states have serious identity problems. Yet the causes and possible results of their identity problems are quite different. The people of South Korea are sure of their identity as Koreans; yet their emotional identification with the people of North Korea, artificially cut off by a cold war that was none of their doing, remains a running sore. North Korea's development into one of the most repressive states in the world, one of the least responsive to recent trends in political and economic development, places a question mark over the future of democracy in the Republic of Korea. We must always wonder whether economic setbacks, growing antiforeign sentiments, and the desire for unity might lead large numbers of South Koreans to trade present freedoms for a united nation.

The well-known identity problems of China (Taiwan) are equally perplexing but, in the absence of an invasion, somewhat more reassuring as far as democracy is concerned. To some extent the preservation of the fiction that the Republic of China represents all of China has served as an excuse for slowing the evolution of democracy on the island. As a result the further development of democracy is likely to build a firmer distinction in the minds of the people of Taiwan between themselves and those on the mainland. Since Taiwan has a much higher standard of living than the mainland and the great majority of its people are generations removed from close identification with the mainland, democracy as and if it develops will be seen as a symbol of a people's separateness and specialness, certainly not a good that would be lightly traded away for the benefits of unity with a massive society in which Taiwan would be a small and powerless province.

The identity problem of the Philippines is similar to that of many new states. Its solution will require continued effort at nation building, at bringing different peoples, different religious groups, and different classes to see themselves as part of one people, a people willing and able to work together for the common good. The third world has many examples of new nations in which democracy has lost out to systems that can more readily overcome the lack of an effective sense of nationhood.

To answer the two original questions more comprehensively, we need to put the experience of these three countries in the context of what we know about the relationship of democracy and development throughout the world over the past two hundred years. Democracy

247

and economic development as we know them today arose in Western Europe and spread through trade, colonization, missionary activity, and the gradual internationalization of education and communication over more than two centuries. In 1750 there were no democracies in the modern sense, and economic development was still in its beginning stages. Early "peasant democracies" at the grass-roots level, such as those in some of the units of Switzerland, the thirteen colonies, or Iceland, were certainly not based on great wealth or a result of the accumulation of wealth. The United Kingdom, however, was in the forefront of the development of both large-scale democratic institutions and the engines of economic development. The diffusion and expansion of this initiative throughout Europe and much of the world eventually produced the democratic life and the levels of wealth that we know today.[1]

It would be fair to say, then, that democracy and economic growth came into the world together, came from similar roots, and somewhat reinforced one another. Unfortunately, because of the interlinkages of history, we cannot hope to find an experiment that isolated these two. Without such a crucial experiment we cannot say that one produced the other or even that they require each other—although a reasonable argument can be made that they do.

Throughout the nineteenth century, development proceeded, nations formed into modern states, and democratic institutions became accepted in state after state. By the late nineteenth century there may have been ten modern democracies, by World War I or the early 1920s perhaps twenty or more. But in the 1920s a reversal of the democratic trend began with the growth of Communist and Fascist regimes and their diffusion and emulation. This countertrend began before the economic collapse of 1929–1933 and affected some of the world's most economically advanced countries. Before the trend was reversed by military defeat, the economically and intellectually most advanced countries of Europe, Latin America, and East Asia—Germany, Argentina, and Japan—had moved away from democracy. Capitalism, market economies, economic development—these did not prevent the destruction of democracy. Yet economic reversals often played a major part in the destruction.

After World War II a new phase began in both the development of democracy and economic development. Democracy was imposed on Italy, Japan, and most of Germany. Decolonization was imposed on the European empires, with the notable exception of Russia. Suddenly there were free, independent, democratic regimes throughout most of the world. America provided technical assistance and aid almost everywhere; the students of the world came to its universities. The massive destruction of World War II was followed by an age of optimism, tempered by the specters of Communist expansion and the danger of nuclear war.

In the event, many hopes were fulfilled and many dashed. The forced experiments in Germany, Italy, and Japan worked better than anyone would have imagined. Democracy became more fully established throughout Western Europe than it had ever been. Important advances in democracy occurred in the United States and in much of the British Commonwealth. These same countries also experienced dramatic economic growth, growth that was broadly based and extended to all classes. Yet democratic experiments in Africa and the Middle East failed almost without exception. Economic development also proceeded slowly if at all in these areas. Even the dramatic infusions of money through the expansion of the market for oil seemed to make little fundamental difference. In Latin America progress on both fronts was spotty and easily reversed. Today democracy seems to be doing well in the region, but progress in both regards remains undependable. In East Asia, outside the Communist orbit, democratic growth has been spectacular throughout the period. Democracy has been preserved in Japan and is now apparently building in the countries reviewed here. In Southeast and South Asia the record has been more mixed. Muslim states such as Pakistan and Bangladesh have largely repeated Middle Eastern patterns in both kinds of development. Non-Muslim Burma has been a failure. India has managed to hang onto democracy while fueling considerable economic development. Further east events have been more promising. But Malaysia and Singapore, two countries with consistently positive economic performance, have never achieved complete democracy. Indeed, today their democracies are in steady retreat. The record for Indonesia remains mixed: it is certainly not a democracy.

One conclusion from consideration of this record is that democracy must be firmly based to be durable and that its basis must be more than capitalistic economic institutions or even growth. Ghana and Nigeria have tried several times to make democracy work. Soon Nigeria will try again. Perhaps the depth of attachment to democracy is simply absent in the generality of their populations. In such older British colonies as India or the small island states of the Caribbean, democracy has generally thrived without great wealth or particularly capitalistic systems. But economic problems have played a large part in the recurrent downfall of democratic regimes in much of the third world, and they are likely to do so again.

In 1989 the institutions of Western democracy and the Western market economy seem to be gaining ground. There are now nearly sixty democracies in the world, and perhaps the number of market

249

economies should be placed somewhat higher.[2] To these should be added, possibly, some of the post-Socialist regimes produced by the great anti-Communist revolution in East Europe and parts of the Soviet Union in 1989 and 1990. But nearly all countries are affected by these institutions in one way or another. The assumptions that underlie them, sometimes in the guise of human rights, seem increasingly accepted throughout the world, including parts of the Communist world. Increasingly this is one world. But one may wonder what happens if the one world economy gets into difficulty or if the trade spats of today become the trade wars of tomorrow. Under such conditions, how firm will be the staying power of these institutions in new democracies? Will there be a repeat of the 1930s? Or will we have gone far enough, generalized our experience enough, to bring most of the world through deep crises without reversion to repressive systems?

In the Philippines, the Republic of Korea, and the Republic of China, past history and recent performance suggest somewhat different outlooks for democracy. Although it is much the poorest of the three, the Philippines seems to have the most firmly based democracy. Nothing, not even the most successful economic development, can substitute for decades of experience with operating democratic institutions. Yet the multiple economic and social problems of the Philippines may overwhelm it. But if democracy is lost, it will be lost, as in Nigeria, only temporarily: elites will continually strive to reestablish democracy, for it alone will remain a legitimate system. Objectively, the much wealthier economies of Taiwan and South Korea should be able to weather the problems of the future while preserving progress toward democracy. Yet experience with this new system is slight in these countries. Competing legitimating principles in their traditions can be invoked to displace a democracy under economic or nationalistic pressure. We can only hope that present trends last long enough for their peoples to make democracy an integral part of their cultural traditions, a part of the past that will be increasingly difficult for any power-hungry individual or group to displace.

# 15

# General Assessment of Democracy and Development in East Asia

*David S. Chou*

In assessing democracy and development in east Asia, I was asked to focus on the Republic of China (ROC) on Taiwan, although I will also consider the general situation. Two questions were posed: first, do economic changes over the past several years preserve, augment, or undermine recent gains for democracy? Second, what theoretical or generalized relationships exist between democratization, on the one hand, and socioeconomic, cultural, and international variables affecting the ROC's future, on the other? I address these questions first and conclude with some brief observations on the general situation.

## Prospects for Democracy in the ROC

While prospects for democracy in the ROC are very bright, dangers on the horizon may change the picture, unless they are handled with care.

**Recent Gains for Democracy.** The optimistic view is based primarily on three developments: the lifting of martial law, the emergence of competitive party politics, and the peaceful transition of power in the government and the Kuomintang (KMT).

Martial law officially ended on July 15, 1987, a sign indicating the coming of more genuine democracy. It had been in existence since 1949, suspending such constitutional rights of the people as organizing political parties, staging strikes and demonstrations, and publishing newspapers. The lifting of martial law meant restoring these rights to the people.

Prior to the termination of martial law, the political atmosphere had already undergone subtle changes. The first opposition party, the Democratic Progressive party (DPP), was founded on September 28, 1986, before the late president Chiang Ching-kuo revealed his

251

intention of ending martial law to *Washington Post* Chairman Katharine Graham in October 1986. In November 1987 another opposition party, the Labor party, was formed. The new parties are technically illegal since the new law governing civil and political organizations is still pending in the Legislative Yuan. Nevertheless, the government has not only tolerated them but also actively sought a dialog with them on pending legislative proposals. While the dialog has not been institutionalized, already it has been considered proper and desirable for the functioning of the legislative body and for maximizing political harmony and conciliation.

The founding of opposition parties has ushered in competitive party politics. Although two minor parties, the Youth party and the Democratic Socialist party, have existed alongside the KMT, they are not "opposition parties" in the strict sense of the term and are too weak to compete with the ruling party. The significant change in the electoral process came in November 1986, when a competitive two-party election was held, the first ever in the history of China.[1] Politicians who opposed the KMT previously ran as a group of nonparty or independent candidates. In 1986 they ran under the banner of the DPP, obtaining about 29 percent of the votes cast.

The lifting of martial law has also increased press freedom. The ban on the establishment of newspapers ended. The number of newspapers has increased from a dozen to more than thirty-seven. The control over mass media has passed from the Taiwan Garrison Command to the Government Information Office, which does not see its primary role as censorship. Press restrictions have been greatly eased. What were considered political taboos are now the subject of public discussion. The press has begun discussing unsavory episodes of the past four decades, such as the incident of February 28, 1947.[2] Those who considered themselves wrongly imprisoned during the years of Chiang family rule are demanding their names be cleared. A freer press is publishing articles questioning the integrity of some Chiang family members. Some in the opposition party are even suggesting taking down the statues of Chiang Kai-shek that dot the city of Taipei.

Opposition parties, competitive party politics, and media freedom have been considered essential for genuine democracy. They are now part of political life in the ROC.

The transition of power in the government was carried out quickly and smoothly. Less than four hours after Chiang Ching-kuo died on January 13, 1988, Vice President Lee Teng-hui assumed the presidency. Contrary to speculation, Chiang's death did not unleash the military.[3] In fact, the military had long been tamed, thanks to the system of periodically rotating military leaders and checks and balances between the commanders and the political commissars. There was at first a little uncertainty whether Lee could step into the shoes of Chiang Ching-kuo as the KMT chairman. Nevertheless, in response to public opinion as well as to the expressed wishes of the younger and more moderate members of the KMT, the Standing Committee of the Central Committee elected Lee as the acting chairman, thereby quashing a move by some old guards to stop Lee.

It is clear that dizzying changes have swept the ROC in the past few years. The prime mover behind the changes was President Chiang Ching-kuo, instituting reform from above. The changes, however, have taken on a momentum of their own. The leadership in the post-Chiang ROC is also committed to maintaining that momentum. In spite of violent clashes between the police and demonstrators, KMT leaders rejected a suggestion that martial law be reimposed. They obviously share the view that modernization is essentially perpetual change constantly generating new social tensions and political problems and that the violence of demonstrators and social tensions are but birth pains of democracy.

The KMT will not beat a retreat on the reform of the parliament. Senior members of the parliament are already retiring and more will do so in the near future (although retirement may not be en masse nor compulsory). Local self-rule will expand. The mayors of Taipei and Kaohsiung will be elected directly by the people. The governor of Taiwan, however, will still be appointed by the central government. Many people believe the direct election of the governor to be a fairly thorny problem because the effective rule of the ROC government covers only Taiwan and a few offshore islands of Fukien Province. An elected governor might be thought to possess a greater popular mandate than the president of the ROC.

There will probably be no strong man or charismatic leader in the post-Chiang era. This is perhaps a byproduct of democratization. Lee Teng-hui has weathered challenges from the old guard and was elected the KMT chairman by the Thirteenth Party Congress in July 1988. As the president of the ROC and the KMT chairman, he will be first among equals in the collective leadership. He may become a popular and strong president, and his prestige is rising. While he has refrained from making major policy announcements, he has already decided that the ROC should return to the Asian Development Bank. He also prevented the government from presenting to the public two hijackers from mainland China as freedom seekers.

The KMT will still dominate a multiparty ROC, partly because it has built strong grass-roots support and partly because opposition parties are plagued with serious factional disputes and power struggles and lack organizational strength and financial power to challenge the KMT's dominance. Thus so far as the party system is concerned, the ROC has a good chance of achieving a stable democracy. Samuel P. Huntington has pointed out that a modernizing country may achieve high levels of actual and presumptive political stability if it possesses at least one strong political party.[4]

**Dangers on the Horizon.** Among the dangers that could alter the ROC's democratization, none is more serious than the call for an independent Taiwan. Some radical members of the DPP have openly advocated Taiwan's independence. Others have argued in favor of the same goal in the guise of national self-determination. The issue of independence is, of course, sensitive. It bears directly on the ROC's security vis-à-vis mainland China. Beijing has said that it would invade Taiwan if it tried to declare itself independent. It is also illegal and considered seditious or treasonous for anyone on Taiwan to pursue the independence line actively. As the government is resolutely against a move to independence, a very serious identity crisis seems to be in the offing.

Radicals in the DPP tried to include an independence clause in the party platform, sparking not only debate within the party itself but also in society in general.[5] After much debate, a vote was taken to drop the controversial "Taiwan independence" proposal from the platform at the conclusion of a two-day party congress in April 1988. It passed instead a resolution to replace the proposal, forming a task force to study the issue. Most of the members of the task force the DPP appointed in May, however, tend to support independence.[6] The DPP leaders also said in April that the DPP supports a person's right to advocate Taiwan's independence, although the party does not support it. They issued a statement spelling out two conditions under which the party would change its stance on the independence issue: first, if the government tries to sell out Taiwan to Peking; second, if the government does not implement genuine constitutional democracy. In November 1988, the task force came out with a report that described and analyzed eight different approaches for dealing with the future of Taiwan. It withheld any recommendation on them but emphasized that the choice should be made jointly by the people of Taiwan, not by one party or faction within a party.[7]

Another potential danger for democracy is the explosion of mass demonstrations. The police counted 729 demonstrations from January to May 1987 alone, 70 percent of them against the government.[8] Many indicated the heightened desire of the people to protect their environment, which is deteriorating daily, largely as a result of rapid industrialization and past neglect on the part of government and society.

Local workers also staged demonstrations to protest management policies. They increased in number and intensity. Significant new developments have occurred on the labor-management scene. Workers, laboring for long under authoritarian management practices and unfair treatment, are no longer passively accepting their lot. They have gained more political power, through demonstrations, union actions, and bargaining. Some of these activities had adverse effects, which spread far beyond corporate borders. For example, on May 1, 1988, train workers struck, stopping trains for the first time in the ROC.

Reasons for Taiwan's proliferating labor protests are many. Chief among them is the newfound awareness of the laborers of the right to seek more reasonable treatment from employers. Their position is now reinforced by two favorable developments. One is that the sustained growth of the ROC's economy continues to boost demand for workers, strengthening their power to negotiate better terms of employment. Another is that as Taiwan's society moves toward greater democracy, it imposes fewer legal restraints on how people express their dissatisfaction. Virtually all protest activities are now legal in Taiwan, as long as they are nonviolent.

Growing labor awareness aside, out-of-date laws and the inability of employers to catch up with the times in leading their workers are other important factors in Taiwan's proliferating labor protests. The Collective Act, for example, was proclaimed a half-century ago and has never been updated. One basic problem with this law is that it lacks a vital provision requiring employers to sign a collective contract with their workers. Because of this omission, most labor unions have difficulty persuading employers to sign these contracts.

Demonstrations have also been staged by veterans, university students, opposition parties, and farmers. In fact, the farmers' demonstration in Taipei on May 20, 1988, turned into Taiwan's worst riot since the 1979 rioting in Kaohsiung. They demanded that the government restrict foreign agricultural imports and carry out a comprehensive farmers' insurance program. Since then demonstrations have shown more self-restraint.

Democratization has increased demands by the people for expansion of political participation and improvement of government services to satisfy their needs. The tempo of change seems to have outpaced the political system's ability to adapt. The increasing frequency of mass demonstrations has sometimes made government bureaucracy impotent in implementing controversial socioeconomic policies. Under these conditions, the system must seek to maintain stability and to augment its capabilities. Stability can be maintained when the people's needs and expectations are fulfilled, at least partially. The government's ability can be augmented only through the process of institutionalization or structure building. The lag in institutionalization behind social and economic change may lead to instability.[9]

### Relationship between Democratization and Other Variables

**Democratization and Socioeconomic Development.** Scholars differ on whether socioeconomic development precedes democratization or vice versa. Britain provides an example that socioeconomic development ushers in democracy, whereas Switzerland shows that democracy can precede socioeconomic development. In spite of these examples, democratization in the ROC tends to confirm the theory of developmentalists like Robert A. Dahl and Seymour M. Lipset that there is a positive relationship between the level of socioeconomic development and democracy.[10] Socioeconomic development tends to change the fundamental way individuals and groups relate to the political process. Advanced economic development produces greater economic security and equity, provides more widespread education, and consequently enlarges the middle class. This in turn generates the pluralist distribution of resources that is in itself an important condition for democracy.

Since the early 1950s, local elections in the ROC have been held regularly. Most people, however, did not care much about politics. As the ROC's economy took off in the 1960s, a politically participatory society gradually took shape. People's political aspirations rose. A better educated and more motivated new generation provided the political system with many activists. Elections have now become fiercely contested events. The ROC has been a leading newly industrialized country and is expected to join the ranks of the industrialized community by the early 1990s. As it continues to grow rapidly, it can promote further development of democracy.

The ROC has not only created economic miracles but has also achieved economic equity. It is one of the most economically equitable societies in the world. Equitable distribution of wealth has mitigated feelings of relative deprivation and injustice among the lower class and consequently reduced the likelihood of extremist politics.

The middle class has long been associated in political theory with moderation, tolerance, and democracy. Now 50 percent of the population in the ROC consider themselves middle class. The decline of the death rate is also held to be an important factor for democracy. Socioeconomic development has reduced the annual death rate of the ROC from 10 per 1,000 in 1952 to 4.9 per 1,000 in 1986. Socioeconomic development has indeed provided the ROC with the necessary conditions for a full-fledged democracy.

**Democracy and Culture.** The political culture of the ROC is heavily influenced by Confucianism and the Three Principles of the People laid down by Sun Yat-sen.

Confucianism is a multifaceted framework of ethical thought. It has undemocratic as well as democratic elements. So far as it stresses reverence for authority, elders, and hierarchical order, it may foster authoritarian rule. But it also calls for harmony, moderation, consensus, and mutual obligations between ruler and ruled. These are elements that facilitate a democratic life. As the ROC becomes an industrialized and pluralistic society, people will tend to discard the undemocratic elements in Confucianism.

The Three Principles of the People are nationalism, democracy, and people's well-being. They have been the governing ideology of the ROC. Since 1949, they have become the most significant elements in the political socialization of the Taiwan area. They also serve as a basic guide for national policy. Their explicit goal is to establish an equitable, affluent national community based on freedom and democracy. Sun visualized that the people would exercise political power and directly participate in political affairs. In his view, government must conform to the people's will. The Japanese aggression and later the civil war, however, prevented the Nationalist government from fully implementing Sun's Three Principles of the People. Because of the emergency situation, the 1936 Constitution of the ROC, which is based on Sun's doctrine, has been partially suspended. But the KMT remains committed to democracy, which is one of the three principles laid down by Sun.

No country can expect to develop genuine democracy if it has no compatible political culture. Since the political culture of the ROC values political participation, fosters awareness on the part of the citizenry, and stresses willingness to compromise, prospects for democratization are very bright.

**Democracy and the International Environment.** In the contemporary world, the political development of states is often affected by the system of international incentives and restraints. The democratization of the ROC has been influenced by international factors.

U.S. aid was obviously crucial to bringing about rapid economic development in the ROC, hence indirectly paving the way for democratization. As a legal basis for unofficial relations between Washington and Taipei, the Taiwan Relations Act reaffirms that preservation and enhancement of the human rights of all the people on Taiwan are objectives of the United States. The U.S. Congress accordingly held hearings on Taiwan's human rights and passed resolutions urging democratic progress in the ROC and an end to martial law. The views of the United States have been given a great deal of attention because of the security, political, and economic ties that have been established over the decades.

Democratization in the neighboring countries has also affected Taipei's political development. The examples of the Philippines and South Korea have encouraged opposition politicians to increase their pressure against the government and strengthened the position of reformers for further democratization.

Mainland China has indirectly contributed to the ROC's democratization. Taipei has perceived a constant, serious military threat from Beijing. It has already been isolated internationally by the mainland. The ROC leaders therefore could not suppress the representative system for fear of losing their legitimacy and support from the democratic world. Both the elite and the masses perceive that democracy makes the ROC more deserving of support from the international community to resist Beijing's pressure to negotiate reunification. The ROC has also engaged in a peaceful competition with mainland China, trying to show the people on the mainland that the ROC's system is much better than the Communist system and more suitable for the Chinese. For that purpose, the ROC has to be not only economically prosperous but also politically free and democratic.

While international factors have affected the ROC's democratization, their role is less significant than domestic factors, an important conclusion.

### Differences and Similarities

If we compare the ROC, South Korea, and the Philippines in their political development, we notice some differences and similarities.

First, all three countries are undergoing a transition from authoritarianism to democracy. They are thus living examples that, while no totalitarian or Communist society can become democratic, authoritarian societies may evolve into democracies.[11]

Second, the United States has continually pressured the three countries in the direction of democracy over the past decades. But

Washington has played a more direct and crucial role in redemocratization of the Philippines.

Third, popular support for the government in the three countries varies. The ROC government has consistently obtained about 70 percent of the votes cast. The Korean government got less than 40 percent of the votes cast in the 1987 parliamentary election. Although the Philippine government enjoyed 77 percent of the votes cast for the new constitution, it consists of a coalition of parties with no common political and economic ideology. Moreover, its large popular support may disappear if it cannot achieve economic recovery.

Fourth, the influence of the military also differs. In the postwar era, the ROC has not experienced any military coup, unlike the Philippines and South Korea. The possibility of a military coup in the ROC is very remote. Military intervention, however, poses a constant threat to the democratization of the Philippines and South Korea.

# 16
# Some Comments on Democracy and Development in East Asia

*Nicholas Eberstadt*

Democracy and development in East Asia are surely timely topics. The political and economic prospects for the countries of East Asia are a matter of keen interest today—an interest by no means delimited to the region itself. The words *democracy* and *development*, moreover, are being increasingly used in discourse about the region. Journalistic reports, local political debates, diplomatic correspondence, and scholarly papers fairly abound with allusions to the trends toward development and democracy that are said to be afoot in the Far East. Even in such ordinarily staid and circumspect confines as the U.S. Department of State, talk about democracy and development in East Asia is now often reservedly enthusiastic; at times, it sounds positively euphoric. A review of the events and circumstances that have attracted so much attention, and prompted such expectant emotions, would certainly seem to be in order.

Nonetheless, I wish to sound a note of caution in these comments. Although specific instances of political liberalization in different spots in East Asia in recent years may be adduced, these various indications fall far short of establishing a trend for the region as a whole, and may themselves individually have been ascribed a greater significance than is warranted. Economic change is undoubtedly transforming the region; yet the direction of change is by no means uniformly positive, and the material advance that has taken place has not consistently served to extend human choice. If development and democracy are today favored terms, they also suffer by their popularity. Degrading or confusing the meaning of these two words is neither a stimulus to clear thinking about political and economic problems nor a kindness to those who are striving for the better life that is held to be fashioned by these ideas.

The chapters composing this volume are both informative and

261

provocative. They have also been wide ranging. My comments, correspondingly, will address specific countries and touch upon more general questions.

## Republic of China (Taiwan)

The four authors on Taiwan have pointed to many interesting and distinctive aspects of the Taiwan experience. One of the most intriguing of these features, however, has been somewhat neglected.

The Republic of China is ruled by a party that was, in its formative years, strongly influenced by the Soviet Union. The founders of the Kuomintang (KMT) looked explicitly to Soviet Russia as they contemplated the development of their own revolutionary party. Sun Yat-sen expressed the sentiment succinctly at the First KMT National Congress in 1924:

> We live in a dangerous time . . . the results of the Russian revolution are visible to all, and we must take it as an example, if we desire to construct a strong, organized, and disciplined party.[1]

The KMT's embrace of the Soviet example was not merely a matter of intellectual receptiveness. The relationship between the KMT and the USSR was, during those years, also intimately logistical. Mikhail Borodin, the agent of the Communist International (Comintern), who had been instrumental in founding the Communist party of Mexico, may have been the most prominent of the political advisers sent by Moscow to help with the establishment of the fledging KMT in China, but he was by no means the only one. General Vasili Bliukher, previously minister of war for the Soviet Far Eastern Republic, was assigned to China to help build a National Revolutionary Army under KMT command. These and other contacts with Soviet authority had a lasting impact upon the nature of the ruling party, and party rule, in the Republic of China. In many ways, the KMT has been affected by the precepts of Leninism. Indeed, it might not be too much to include the KMT in the list of governing parties informed or guided by the Leninist political tradition.

As the chapters emphasize, Taiwan's economic progress over the past four decades has been exceptional. A central factor in the economic performance has been a rapid and relatively steady increase in total factor productivity. Leninist regimes are not ordinarily associated with economic efficiency, much less economic dynamism, these days. In this regard, Taiwan may offer a dramatic and fascinating exception.

Perhaps even more noteworthy, in the context of the party's Leninist heritage, are recent political developments within, and around, the KMT. Between 1986 and 1989 the Republic of China amended its laws and its procedures in significant respects, as several of the chapters on Taiwan have detailed. These emendations redefine the party's authority over state and society. They move the country closer than it has ever been to an open and liberal civil order.

In the past, Leninist parties have been known to embark upon temporary tactical relaxations of policy when circumstance dictated. The Republic of China's recent moves toward political liberalization, however, cannot readily be ascribed to some pressing exigency. They appear, instead, to reflect a deliberate decision on the part of the KMT leadership to fashion for the party a less prominent and less decisive role in the country's daily affairs.

One can only speculate on the directions in which events will lead Taiwan in coming years. The country is still far from being a liberal democracy in the pattern of the modern West. Even if political liberalization in Taiwan were to proceed no further, the post-1986 changes would be signal in themselves. Such a voluntary diminution of party power is unprecedented in the Leninist tradition of government. Is it, as the Soviets might say, simply a coincidence that the only Leninist party that has to date embarked upon such a voluntary transition is also the only such party not committed to the service of Marxist doctrine?

## The Philippines

In discussing the economic situation in the Philippines, many seem to assume that living standards for the country as a whole have undergone a secular and substantial decline in recent years, begetting "growing impoverishment" and "worsening poverty."

Serious deterioration in living standards has beset a number of populations in East Asia during the past twenty years. Man-made famine, for example, has stricken the people of East Timor and those of Cambodia. In 1987, the government of the Socialist Republic of Vietnam announced that a substantial portion of the population under its guidance was on the brink of starvation.

To include the Philippines in such a list, however, seems utterly unwarranted. Available economic and social data indicate that the Philippines has progressed materially over the past generation—albeit at a comparatively slow pace. While a slow pace of advance may not be exactly what the people, or the rulers, of a low-income country would wish for themselves, slow advance is one thing and retrogression is another.

For developed countries, economic data pertaining to popular well-being are often difficult to interpret. Their interpretation is more difficult still for low-income countries, where questions commonly arise about the reliability and comparability of figures. For what it is worth, however, the World Bank annually provides a set of estimates bearing directly on living standards in poor countries. These are its statistics on mortality.

Between 1965 and 1985, according to the World Bank, the infant mortality rate in the Philippines dropped from seventy-two per thousand to forty-eight per thousand—that is, by a third. Death rates of children of ages one through four—a measure sometimes taken to reflect the nutritional condition of the population as a whole—are said to have fallen from eleven per thousand to four per thousand, or by over three-fifths. Life expectancy at birth, by the bank's estimate, rose during this period by seven years for men and eight years for women.[2] One may, of course, quibble with the specifics of such World Bank estimates, but the tendency these figures illustrate is not a matter of dispute. Over the past generation, the Philippine population has enjoyed an unambiguous and substantial improvement in general health. Such improvements would seem rather strongly to suggest that the prevalence of extreme material hardship has declined, not increased, over the past generation.

One further point about the Philippines should be mentioned. The Philippine chapters have enumerated many factors that may affect that country's prospects. To this already lengthy list I would add one more consideration: the Philippine situation could be strongly affected in the future by a particular aspect of its American legacy—the English language. Although Filipino is officially designated as the national language, English is widely and fluently spoken in the Philippines. Indeed, by the World Bank's estimates, something like two-thirds of the population of appropriate age is today enrolled in secondary schooling[3]—and English is the medium of instruction for secondary education throughout the Philippines.

Economically and politically, the country's facility with English may stand it in good stead in the years to come. Should the Philippines embark upon a more outward-looking commercial policy, it will find the general command of today's principal language of international business an advantage—possibly a significant one. An easy familiarity with English, moreover, makes accessible to an entire population the literature of the Anglo-American political tradition in a way that selective translation can only imperfectly duplicate.

## Republic of Korea

The chapters on Korea are particularly welcome, for knowledge about—and even more important—understanding of the Korean scene are distinctly limited quantities. This deficiency exists at a time when the economic, political, and strategic importance of the Korean peninsula has increased markedly. The same cannot be said of foreign insight into the area. The disparity between the region's international importance on the one hand, and, for example, American understanding of the region on the other is striking. I would suggest that this disparity is, in some sense, as great for Korea today as it was for Iran a decade ago. One need not envision cataclysm and catastrophe to recognize that such disparities are unhealthy and even potentially costly.

Over the past generation, the Republic of Korea (ROK) has established an exceptional record of economic performance. Between 1962 (the first year of the First Five Year Plan) and 1986 (the last year of the Fifth Five Year Plan), aggregate output increased over sevenfold and per capita output rose by a factor of almost five.[4] One may fairly speak of an economic transformation in South Korea during those years.

Korea's burst of economic growth is typically ascribed, at least in part, to an auspicious environment created by favorable government policies. It should be remembered, however, that many of the policies promoted by Seoul during these years would customarily be expected to impede rather than accelerate economic growth. The hand of the government has been heavy in most areas of Korean economic life. For most of the 1960s and all of the 1970s, the state controlled the allocation of bank credit; not infrequently, loan decisions were subject to political as well as financial criteria. Credit continues to be allocated preferentially to large corporate concerns, such as the *chaebol*, with predictable consequences for the performance of domestic capital markets and for unit costs and labor absorption within small businesses. Agricultural policy has veered from a seeming intention to drain the countryside of capital in the hope of promoting industrialization in the cities to an embrace of expensive subsidies, price supports, and barriers against international food trade in the name of supporting rural livelihood. Aside from its population control campaign, the government has taken a few initiatives to improve public health; at this point, Korea's mortality level is strangely high by comparison with its income level, especially for those cohorts that constitute the labor force. South Korea has discouraged direct private investment from abroad and has arranged its trade regimen in such a way that the general population may at times subsidize consumption of more affluent populations overseas.

Despite these and other transgressions against ordinary economic reasoning, South Korea's economic performance over the past generation has hardly been lackluster. Indeed, much of Korea's success derives from a single decision—the change from an inward-looking economic policy to an outward-looking, export-oriented policy. The determination to profit from the world economy—to earn foreign exchange by marketing products internationally—has a host of implications for such things as exchange rate management, budgetary discipline, institutional flexibility, technological innovation, labor absorption, and, in a broad sense, learning to deal with disequilibriums. Attempts to learn from and cope with the world economy are consistent with an increase in attentiveness to cost and opportunity phenomena—at the heart of the economic process.

Korea's economy might have progressed even further during the past generation if the country had adopted a more liberal trade regimen. Korea's actual practices of export subsidization and import restriction may have been "second best" from the standpoint of economic strategy, but they have been conducive to eminently respectable aggregate results nevertheless. In economic affairs, as in politics, getting one big thing right can usually more than make up for getting smaller things wrong.

Although Korea's economic contacts with the outside world have multiplied dramatically over the past in general, the Korean political situation has remained a sort of *terra incognita* to foreigners. For a variety of reasons, knowledge about the workings of the South Korean political situation has, until quite recently, tended to be transmitted by the oral tradition rather than committed to the written word. One may begin to appreciate the difficulties facing overseas students of Korean affairs when one learns that the Korean Academy of Sciences in Seoul has maintained for some time a unit whose title translates roughly as the Committee to Edit National History.

Obscure though many aspects of Korean politics may still be, the frailty of the South Korean political structure is a fact that has been apparent to all. The Korean economic edifice was erected on a foundation much like sand: capable of bearing weight, but lacking in cohesion and prone to sudden changes of state with swings in the weather. In the four decades between 1949 and 1987, the Republic of Korea experienced not a single peaceful and orderly transfer of political power. One president was turned out of office by riots;

another came to power in a *Putsch* and ruled until he was assassinated by a trusted aide; a third consolidated his position after leading what came to be called a "constitutional coup." The fragility of the South Korean political system, even in the face of growing military and administrative power and dramatic, continuing economic success, was a curious but distinctive characteristic of ROK rule. If South Korea's allies were aware of this paradox, her enemies were no less so. Indeed, there is considerable evidence that Communist North Korea's strategy for forcible reunification with the more populous and powerful South has been informed for perhaps two decades by the perception that the government in Seoul might be made to collapse in chaos—or might even do so on its own.

As the chapters on the Republic of Korea have noted, some new and highly significant acts have played on Seoul's political stage during 1987 and 1988. An open and genuinely competitive presidential election campaign took place—the first in the history of the republic and indeed in the entire history of the Korean people. A peaceful, orderly, and voluntary transfer of presidential authority was effected. And for the first time in memory, a political party in Korea (the ruling Democratic Justice Party) outlasted the career of its founding figure and lent its loyalty and organizational support to someone other than its original constituting personality. Insofar as these events reflect or contribute to the stability, resilience, and security of the South Korean polity, they are heartening.

To interpret these events as proof that South Korea has attained, or is about to attain, the status of a liberal democracy, however, would be a serious error. There is more to democracy, if we mean by this word the style of rule that people in the West enjoy, than mass plebiscites and bloodless transfers of supreme power.

The concept of democracy that has prevailed in the West over the past generations is one that recognizes the importance of the individual and strives to guarantee and protect his or her rights through rule of law. Even though a new president has been freely elected in South Korea, one cannot honestly say that he has come to power in a country where the rule of law prevails—much less a rule of law in the service of liberty.

Administrative practices in Korea are very often arbitrary and personalistic. Accountability is, in many quarters, a novel and alien proposition. Such notions as impartial authority, equality before the law, respect for private property and the integrity of person, rights of the minority, and due process have yet to make their way into the everday routine of Korean political life.

To proponents of the open society, the rule of liberal law is always deemed desirable. In Korea today, however, the case for establishing such a rule of law is especially compelling. Because of the political events of 1988, the costs of failing to establish a uniform and civil rule of law have risen enormously.

In 1989, South Korea possessed a government with considerable power to reward and punish, a president selected by a minority of the electorate, and a National Assembly divided into political factions (of which four were most prominent). In an environment where the exercise of authority has long been personalized, where such phrases as "loyal opposition" are held to be oxymoronic, where the quest for mastery by and advantage to one's own group is accepted by many as the legitimate objective of politics, the new system of arrangements, as it stands, has the makings of an unstable equilibrium. Unless South Korea can forge from its current circumstances the idea of an all-encompassing political community, it will be tugged in two opposite but similarly perilous directions: toward disintegration of government on the one hand and toward mass tyranny (what J.L. Talmon called "democratic totalitarianism"[5]) on the other. The idea of an encompassing political community is integral to the notion of a rule of liberal law. It would seem very difficult, under current circumstances, for Korea to accept the idea of an overall political community without a serious and sincere effort to promote the rule of law.

Many obstacles stand between Korea and such a rule of law. A variety of them could be listed, but one in particular deserves mention: the spirit of racialism. Often described as "nationalism," it pervades Korean thinking and impresses itself forcefully upon almost every aspect of contemporary Korean affairs.[6] There are many Western proponents of democracy who see nothing untoward in the stirrings of nationalism manifest today in so many low-income countries. Students of politics, especially in the United States, will even suggest nationalism may actually be a handmaiden of democracy in low-income areas. If democracy is meant to connote the system of liberal and enlightened rule that populations in the Western world enjoy, then nationalism is not conducive to democracy. Korean nationalism—the sentiment and theory of racial rule—is subversive of democracy, and is inimical even unto democracy's basic principles.

A gathering of people justified by and organized upon a notion of race cannot provide firm ground for a government guided by abstract and impartial moral precepts. It can only be less hospitable still to a philosophy of government that holds the individual to be important by virtue of his humanity, not his race or ethnicity.

Lord Acton, the great exponent of classical liberalism, succinctly described the differences between nationalism and other philosophies of political authority:

Our connection with the race is merely natural or physical, whilst our duties to the political nation are ethical. One is a community of affections and instincts infinitely important and powerful in savage life, but pertaining more to the animal than the civilized man; the other is an authority governing by laws, imposing obligations and giving a moral sanction and character to the natural relations of society.[7]

Though these words were written in the nineteenth century, they are very pertinent to the situation in Korea today.

The political reforms of the Sixth Republic have unleashed the forces of race against the ideals of liberality. Thus it is in South Korea that we witness, coincident with the heralded political reforms, a simultaneous rise in expressions of anti-Americanism and an outpouring of longing sentiment about the North. Unofficial but increasingly vocal groups talk of the possibility of reunifying with the people in North Korea, willfully deferring or ignoring all the while such issues as the nature of the regime under which that captive population is forced to live, or the terms under which the two Koreas might realistically expect today to reunite. These same voices, which describe themselves as voices of democracy, have grown increasingly critical of, and hostile to, the United States—a country with which they profess to share a common bond of ideals and values. In South Korea's universities, many of the people who have been crying out for academic freedom and agitating for the integrity of scholarship fall suddenly silent when gross and even inflammatory misrepresentations of the American role in Korea arise—even when these misrepresentations are printed in the country's textbooks.[8] And what are we to make of the growing fascination in so-called democratic circles with the long-departed figure of Kim Ku—assassin, xenophobe, would-be minister of "internal security" for postwar Korea—who preached the racial destiny of the Korean people even as he ridiculed the notion of limited constitutional government?

The people of Korea have proved themselves receptive to ideas and values from abroad over the course of their long history. For many centuries, the philosophy, literature, and even the administrative practices of China reverberated in Korean life. Many millions of Koreans have come to accept as their own the Christian faith, despite its initial unfamiliarity and the punishments that the state meted out to believers. The idea of liberal democracy is, in the Korean context, no less alien than the professions of the Christian faith. Like Christianity, the appeal of liberal democracy stems in part from its universalistic perspective and its respect for the individual. Such notions will not easily coexist with a narrowly defined, racially based nationalism. In the long run, Koreans must choose: they can have one or the other, but not both.

## Concluding Remarks

I have attempted to sound specific notes of caution about what has sometimes been described as the trend toward democracy and development in Taiwan, the Philippines, and Korea. Two additional, but necessarily more general, observations seem appropriate for the East Asian region as a whole.

First, while tendencies toward political relaxation or liberalization in Taiwan, the Philippines, and Korea are noteworthy and interesting, they should not be taken as representative or even indicative of the region as a whole. Over the past two decades, East Asia has seen the slaughter of the Cambodians, the immolation of the Timorese, and the tragedy of the Vietnamese boat people. South Vietnam's limited political freedoms were extinguished in 1975, as were those in Laos. To the extent that government may be said to exist in Burma, it is that of a closed, Socialist state. Racialist rule continues to be the order of the day in Malaysia. Openness and political tolerance appear to have been on the wane in recent years in Singapore. In Sri Lanka (if this may be considered part of East Asia), one of Asia's genuine democracies has been reduced to a state of martial law and partially occupied by a foreign army whose invitation to intervene was a formality extended under duress. Although on the Chinese mainland, economic policy was relaxed over the decade ending in mid-1989, the ongoing policy of forcible and even involuntary population control indicates that the Communist government is as committed as ever to the principles of totalitarian rule.[9] The Tiananmen repression confirmed that orientation. In Hong Kong, as is well known, local administration is scheduled to revert from Britain to China in 1997. And all this is to say nothing of the Soviet Union's growing naval and military might in the South China Sea, the Pacific, and the Soviet Far East. One may read in these diverse soundings many things, but an overall trend toward liberal democracy would not seem to be one of them.

A final comment concerns the decline of American power in Asia. The opinion has been expressed that the decline of American power may be salutory for the development of democracy in the Far East and that the diminution of the American capability or presence in East Asia might contribute to the emergence of and strengthening of independent, mature, self-determining governments in the region. It may be impossible to speak with certainty about the future. But the likelihood, under present circumstances, that a purposeful diminution of American influence in East Asia would stimulate the spread of liberal democracy throughout the region seems utterly remote. Even a casual reading of recent history would seem to suggest precisely the opposite of what these advocates—some of them hopeful, others simply weary—evidently wish to believe.

The fact of the matter is that liberal democracy, in those few places in East Asia where it may honestly be said to exist, is wholly and exusively an Anglo-American legacy. In Sri Lanka, democratic rule followed in the tradition to which the island had been exposed through British colonial rule. In Japan, the present form of democracy was imposed upon a defeated and prostrate country by American bayonets. In the 1950s, American power preserved the possibility of liberal democracy for such places as Korea, Taiwan, and the Philippines; Britain did the same in Malaysia and Singapore. In the 1970s, the withdrawal of American power did not do wonders for democratic movements in Vietnam, Laos, or Cambodia.

Like British power before it, American power does not travel in a vacuum. Indeed, it cannot. The actions of the American state overseas are judged domestically by the purposes they are seen to serve; recent events will indicate that domestic support for American programs overseas is jeopardized whenever the moral purposes of these programs seem to be in doubt. In coming years and decades, it is not at all inconceivable that the American presence in East Asia will diminish. Power abhors a vacuum, and one may imagine that a new balance or order might speedily establish itself. It is conceivable that such a new balance would be replete with new democracies. Perhaps they would be "guided democracies," of the variety that President Sukarno of Indonesia imagined himself to lead. They might be "people's democracies," of the type that exists in Mongolia, Vietnam, China, and North Korea. Such a new order might even include other sorts of "democracies." But unless the new order were bolstered by powers that share the beliefs and values that animate the Anglo-American political tradition, this new order is unlikely to include any new *liberal* democracies.

# 17
# The Philippines

*Segundo Romero*

The four chapters on the political, economic, social, and international factors affecting democracy and development in the Philippines constitute a remarkably comprehensive assessment of the state and prospects of democracy and development in the Philippines. In essence they point out that the post-1986 record shows a sustained, deliberate, and so far successful effort by the government of Corazon Aquino to restore democratic institutions. This includes drafting and ratifying a Constitution, reorganization of the bureaucracy and the judiciary, election and organization of the bicameral Congress, and election of local officials. Among the notable highlights of the democratization process, the consensus is that, by any standard, the effort of the Aquino administration to establish democratic political structures and processes is impressive.

Nevertheless, the challenges to democracy and development in the Philippines are formidable. Prolonged and profound poverty, unemployment, and income inequality remain intractable, especially in view of the reemergence of the traditional political elite as the dominant force in Congress and in the local governments. The protracted formulation of implementing legislation on reform and the sluggish implementation of trade liberalization cast doubt on the sufficiency of the political will of the ruling elite to carry out the radical political, social, and economic reforms needed to reverse such poverty, unemployment, and income inequality.

It is clear that government leadership, through innovative and responsive policy as well as committed implementation, is the key to solving these problems. But while there may be short-run economic success even with the government and the bureaucracy as they are, the persistence of democratic government over the long run will depend on the introduction of meaningful and perhaps painful reforms that significantly reduce the existing poverty and inequality in Filipino society. Several sources of the continuing socioeconomic difficulties have been identified, but assessments of their importance have varied.

Richard Hooley and David Rosenberg suggest that the inability of the economy to absorb the 750,000 new entrants into the labor force annually is one of the main problems of economic development. Philippine agriculture can no longer absorb them because there is no new land to develop and cultivation has emphasized nonlabor inputs. Hooley suggests that, through trade liberalization, export-led industrial development could be induced to absorb the surplus labor. A commentator, Edward Lachica, notes that the appropriateness of an export-led economic growth strategy as a major solution to Philippine economic problems remains debatable; the import-substitution strategy continues to have significant advocates, especially among Filipino nationalists and intellectuals.

Carolina Hernandez and Rosenberg mention land reform and social equity reform, already the focus of national policy debates, as the key to economic development and the endurance of democratic government in the Philippines. Another commentator, Frank Denton, however, suggests that industrialization, not land reform, is the key to reducing poverty and unemployment in the Philippines.

The main contribution of Hooley is to provide empirical evidence that popular discontent in the Philippines over the past nine decades has been preceded by significant decline in living standards as measured by real wages. Philippine living standards have been on the decline since 1968, even as per capita income has steadily risen. Hooley believes "the evidence is sufficient by any reasonable historical standards to conclude that democratic institutions are in serious jeopardy if the present situation [a persistent decline in the income of rural and urban workers while income of the middle and upper classes steadily increases] is allowed to continue indefinitely."

This insight could point to a more general formulation of the relationship between political and economic development. Economic decay that is registered in popular discontent leads to the demise not only of democratic regimes but of any regime. If, as the Hooley data suggest, the declining standards of living that challenge the Aquino government today date back to 1968, they are the same ones that induced the people to acquiesce in Ferdinand Marcos's termination of democratic institutions in 1972 and short-cut to economic development through a "revolution from the center," that is, government.

Despite the agreement that the prospects for democracy in the Philippines depend on the socioeconomic program of the Aquino government, two views persist on the prospects for democratic government. One, voiced by Rosenberg, is the pessimistic view. Presenting figures that describe the gravity of problems that predated the Aquino government, he warns that unless reforms are soon forthcoming, there will be either a Communist revolution or a rightist reaction that will see the refeudalization of Philippine society.

The guarded optimists, among them Victoria Denton and Hernandez, express appreciation of the urgency of reform but do not think that a Communist revolution or a rightist reaction is likely in the short term even in the absence of reform. Hernandez points to new faces—nonpoliticians—in Congress as a hopeful sign, even as the traditional elite predominates. The optimists also factor in the intangibles—Filipino traits of flexibility and resourcefulness that crises in the past have induced. Hooley also refers to these intangibles as Philippine society's "special strengths of patience and improvisation and sources of internal resilience, which set it off as a unique, functioning socioeconomic system."

One such intangible is the commitment of the Filipinos to democratic institutions and processes. After Marcos it would be extremely difficult to sell the Filipinos any alternative political system that does not guarantee personal liberties. People of various ideological persuasions are committed to defending the democratic space that was won in February 1986.

One other intangible factor is the charisma of Aquino. No other postwar Filipino leader has approached the stature that she enjoys among her people. Contending leaders from both civilian and military sectors have tried to unseat her; yet she is more securely entrenched. It would be difficult to dislodge the formal democratic institutions that she has established as long as she champions them.

To be sure, these intangible factors in support of democracy have progressively weakened. The euphoria of February 1986 has given way to a sense of realism and even of low-level disappointment. The accession of Aquino to power triggered excessive and incongruous expectations among Filipinos of various walks of life, expectations that could not be realistically maintained. Now people increasingly talk of how things have not changed.

Apart from the implementation of urgent socioeconomic reforms, how could the prospects for development and democracy be improved? Rosenberg suggests an exogenous contribution in the form of a no-strings-attached multilateral assistance program provided by the United States and other democratic countries. The Aquino government, for its part, must increase the participation of the people in their governance and development.

Other contributors mention endogenous factors, such as the style of the leader and the commitment and ability of the bureaucracy to implement socioeconomic development programs directed at uplifting the conditions of the poor and underprivileged. One commentator, Larry Niksch, suggests that a "permissive authoritarian style" might help focus the bureaucracy's efforts on development objectives. He emphasizes the importance of executive control over the bureaucratic process through oversight and supervision. He also suggests that the civilian government, not just the military, should fight the political battle against the insurgency. Indeed, the Aquino government may have prematurely and unnecessarily closed itself to some useful tactics and strategies employed by Marcos. The Aquino government early embarked on an effort to distance itself from the Marcos regime. The abolition of the Marcos-dominated Batasang Pambansa and the attempt to recover the hidden wealth of Marcos through the Presidential Commission on Good Government were on the whole wise political decisions. Others remain debatable, among them the reluctance of the Aquino leadership (1) to create a political party, or at least a movement to consolidate and harness the "people power" support of the Aquino government against graft and corruption and for national discipline; (2) to revive or replace grass-roots organizations at the village level; or (3) to undertake an aggressive and comprehensive political education and public information program to explain and advocate the government's position on issues.

These and other tactics and strategies were exploited by the Marcos regime, which set up the Kilusang Bagong Lipunan (Movement for a New Society), Samahang Nayons (Farmers' Cooperatives), Kabataang Barangay (Village Youth Corps), and a Ministry of Public Information. Marcos also formulated and advocated the "ideology of the New Society." The lingering support for the Marcos regime may be traceable to its effort to organize and structure support over several years, and it might take the Aquino government a similar effort, not so much to redirect political loyalties as to create new orientations supportive of the ideals of the people power revolution.

In assessing the prospects for democracy in the Philippines, we should keep in mind that the initial acquiescence of the Filipinos in Marcos's authoritarian rule indicated a willingness to consider the Asian model of a government-controlled approach to economic development. If Marcos's "constitutional authoritarianism" had been successful in making a newly industrialized country of the Philippines, the Philippine pattern might have been more like that of Taiwan and Korea. Eventually, economic prosperity under authoritarian rule would have fueled democratic aspirations, provided it spawned the appropriate socioeconomic circumstances—universal education, a bigger middle class, reduced income inequality, and reduced differences in regional economic development. Such a level of economic development would have made participatory democracy more feasible, in contrast to the present effort to stimulate economic development through democratic institutions and processes but under continuing oligarchic conditions in society.

The greatest threat to democracy in the Philippines, apart from the failure of government to induce economic development and an improved standard of living, may very well be the continuing poverty of democratic practice. Just as the rhetoric of Marcos did not substitute for democratic practice, neither do the democratic institutions under the Aquino government reflect a healthy state of democratic practice. Outside of electoral politics, democratic practice has always been severely limited in the Philippines, whether under the presidential democracy of 1946–1972, the authoritarian regime of 1972–1986, or the democratic restoration of 1986. Political participation at the local level is limited. Governmental efforts to bring development down to the *barangays* have focused on the delivery of prepackaged services rather than on stimulating the active involvement of the people in helping plan and implement projects intended for their benefit.

Every administration has recognized that there is too much centralization, partly because the Philippines form an archipelago and because of the inertia of colonial policy. Yet efforts to decentralize decision making must be undertaken at the village, city, province, and regional levels; government remains hopelessly centralized in the capital. Despite the change from authoritarianism to democracy, Philippine society remains a spectator society, with the common *tao* largely uninvolved, except as an object of the government's development efforts. It also remains a bottlenecked society.

The planting of the seeds of democratic transformation has been quicker in the Philippines than in Korea and Taiwan. What would have happened if Aquino and Salvador Laurel had failed to form one opposition ticket against Marcos in the elections of February 1986, in the same manner that Kim Dae Jung and Kim Young Sam split the opposition vote to let Roh Tae Woo win the presidential elections in Korea in December 1977? Equally important, the speed with which the new Constitution was drafted by an appointed convention locked into the Constitution the democratic ideals of the revolution.

Some change has also occurred in the structure of pressure politics. The open progressive movement (left-oriented but legal) is an achievement of the Aquino government. It has weaned from the armed Communist struggle many actual and potential adherents.

These cause-oriented groups and individuals now participate in electoral politics, help defend the "democratic space" created by the Aquino government, and have given life to the "parliament of the streets" as a parallel avenue for popular participation in addressing national issues and problems. The open progressive movement has helped marshal popular energies against the ills of Filipino government and society.

After having surmounted the crisis of legitimacy, the government must be able to respond to the crisis in political participation without being overwhelmed. If genuine political development is to attend democratization, demands for popular participation must be responded to as opportunities for converting local energies into policy inputs rather than stifled as law-and-order problems. To stifle them would be to exacerbate rather than to mitigate the frailty and emptiness of the formal democratic processes in the Philippines and invite the revolution or reaction of which Rosenberg warns. The prospects for the survival of formal democratic government in the Philippines are good. But the prospects for demonstrating that such a government can bring about economic development and distribute its fruits to the Filipino masses, not just to the elite, are dim.

It is difficult to generalize about development and democracy in East Asia, looking only at the recent experience of Taiwan, Korea, and the Philippines. One similarity is that the three countries have manifested strong aspirations for democratic political institutions. But so have countries in the rest of the world. One difference is that while Taiwan and Korea aspire to the formal democratic institutions already in place in the Philippines, the Philippines aspires to the economic growth and development of Taiwan and Korea. Which sequential approach to democracy and development will prove more successful by the end of the century?

# 18
# Democracy and Development in East Asia—Toward the Year 2000

*Thomas W. Robinson*

The chapters in this volume have concentrated on the relationship between economic modernization and political democratization in three East Asian countries. At least in Taiwan and South Korea an increasingly close and mutual dependency has emerged between successful economic development and the growth of political pluralism. The Philippines apparently provide a negative example of the same proposition: a declining economy provided an important condition in the downfall of a right-wing authoritarian regime, while further economic debilitation could play a central role in the overthrow of Philippine democracy by left- or right-wing totalitarianism. But while there is a rough correspondence, indeed reciprocity, between changes in the two spheres in these three entities, enough is still unexplained for one to suspect the influence of other major determining elements.

## Development without Democracy?

Perhaps most important, for significant periods economic development can take place without democratization. Indeed much of the economic success after 1960 in South Korea and Taiwan took place under political systems that were deliberately undemocratic. Authoritarianism—and perhaps even totalitarianism if one extends the analysis to China and other Asian Leninist, centrally planned countries— might even be a necessary condition for economic development, at least at a relatively early stage. And the reasons are clear. First, repressive, top-down governments are better able to regiment a population for the massive sacrifices necessary for early industrialization. These include keeping industrial wages very low, extracting large surpluses of labor from the countryside to feed a growing urban industrial work force, and conducting large-scale literacy and public health campaigns among people who still lack the requisite habits and attitudes for successful economic development. Second, the initial stages of industrialization need development of a thorough infrastructure, large amounts of capital, great volumes of imported technology, and expansion of the industrial base producing relatively simple manufactures at low prices. A nondemocratic polity can accomplish these goals just as well, and perhaps with greater efficiency, than a government answerable to a popular will that neither understands nor necessarily agrees with the goal and the means of industrialization.

Third, most countries, including every Asian country, have for almost all their long histories been agricultural societies under authoritarian political rule and lack most of the requisites of democracy. Democracy seems to require a lengthy gestation, a complex social structure, an adequate degree of educational attainment among the general populace, and a general attitude of tolerance. These are often lacking in most countries. There is also the need for experience with a genuine rule of law and with respect for individual rights. These too are generally in short supply. Attention must also be paid to a nation's political culture. Political culture tends to emerge relatively early in a country's history and to persist with relatively little change over long periods: like culture in general, it reflects the general nature of society, which in a preindustrial setting is stable for hundreds or thousands of years. Upon industrialization it can act only as a drag upon political change and catch up with changed conditions only slowly.

The Philippine political experience, as well as that of some other Asian nations (including South Korea before 1960), tells us that the process of constructing a democratic order can sometimes be initiated without concomitant rapid industrialization. The important cause appears to be foreign influence. The Philippines was an American colony until 1945. Some propensity toward democratization was induced by the American experience, just as some tendency to resist native absolutism resulted from the introduction of Catholicism by the Spanish. Spain and the United States in turn transmitted portions of their own—though quite different—political cultures to the Philippines. A similar process, albeit with widely varying outcomes, occurred in many other Asian colonies of the European powers, including India, the principal Asian example of a postcolonial Asian democracy lacking until recently a modern industrial economy. There is also the important instance of Japan, which escaped colonialism but was well down the road to democracy early in its modern economic transformation. But for an unfortunate international environment (an Asian balance of power, for example, that tempted Japan to expand into a power vacuum after World War I and a major global economic depression that drove Tokyo into economic imperialism) and aspects of its own political culture, Japan could have remained on the democratic path instead of deviating so severely from it in the 1930s and 1940s and having to be forced back in that direction by military defeat and occupation.

What kind of international influence, for and against democracy, is important in Asia? The British colonialists left a tradition of democracy (even though severely truncated) that obviously did have a positive impact on India, Sri Lanka, Pakistan, Malaysia, and Singapore. The French and Dutch colonialists conversely left a similar desire for democracy in Indochina and Indonesia but governed with such an iron hand and with no thought to compromise with nativist political aspirations that the quest for freedom had to take a violent, ultranationalist form. Moreover, there is the interesting case of Soviet influence in Asia. Moscow under Leninist rule made major efforts to export its form of political organization, as undemocratic as the globe has ever seen. These efforts were enormously successful: Marxism-Leninism found such high favor among so many Asians that several principal Asian nations like China, Vietnam, and Cambodia elected— albeit through war and revolution—to adopt that manner of economic-political organization. Soviet conquest permanently transformed the traditional order in two others, Mongolia and North Korea, and Soviet influence greatly altered the political landscape in many others. And the American influence in South Korea and Taiwan after World War II was so central that no account of the transformation, economic or political, of these two societies (indeed of many others as well) is possible without major attention to the American role. Land reform, foreign aid, security guarantorship, transmission of cultural and political values, and American toleration of unequal terms of economic competition were all important elements informing both the economic modernization and the emergence of political pluralism in each of these societies. Conversely the lack of American influence in the Asian Communist states—and to a lesser extent in the former European colonies—goes a considerable distance toward explaining the nonemergence of democracy in those states.

At least during the initial stages of the modernization drive, then, democracy and development are only roughly related. Important intervening variables impinge sufficiently in both the political and economic spheres as to call conclusively into question any straightforward one-to-one correspondence between the two and raise the issue of whether, in more recent stages in both spheres, the relationship might remain complex. Indeed historical Asian examples (to say nothing of other geographic areas) demonstrate that democratization, given economic development, is not inexorable or for that matter that economic development need not continue unabated—or be enhanced—once a certain (presumably comparatively advanced) stage of democratization has been reached. Political and economic slippage is clearly possible and should probably be expected. Japan experienced just that before World War II, South Korea did also between 1960 and 1988, the Philippines moved downward politically and economically during the later Marcos years, and democracy was either overthrown or has yet to get a healthy start in Pakistan, Sri Lanka, Burma, Bangladesh, and most of the Southeast Asian states, to say nothing of the six Asian Marxist-Leninist nations.

## Increasing Links

Nonetheless evidence is mounting in favor of increasing linkages between democracy and development once a certain point, or era, has been reached in one or both spheres. For one, changes in the social structure upon industrialization apparently favor emerging political pluralism. Urbanization, rising educational levels, the creation of a large working class, the emergence of a strong middle class, the demographic transition, bureaucratization of the workplace, and the need for modern work habits all are consequences of industrialization that provide strong underpinnings for a democratic movement. For another, higher stages of economic development apparently demand more complex forms of political activity. The most obvious example is the shift from quantitative growth stressing extensive use of the means of production, especially labor, to qualitatively based growth emphasizing intensive use of the existing capital stock and substituting technology for labor. Not only can that kind of economy afford to distribute political power from the state or the small number of private owners of the means of production to the rest of the population, especially middle management, but such a change becomes a necessity to further growth.

In fact the appearance of higher orders of technology as a fourth factor of production (joining the classical Smithean trilogy of land, labor, and capital) at higher stages of economic development becomes a principal element in eventually pulling together economic modernization and political democratization. Technology begets the information revolution, which greatly enhances cross-cultural communication and hence knowledge of the outside world; favors product uniformity across national boundaries; makes access to foreign cultures more efficient; requires higher levels of education, making acquisition of a foreign language and foreign training nearly imperative for a rising portion of college students; introduces native technologists to international norms of behavior and to the language and standards of international science; and becomes a driving force for broadly improving material standards of living. While none of these alone is essential for democracy, in combination they are a powerful impetus.

Moreover they are critical elements in economic development. Indeed without technological innovation, either domestically or internationally derived, economic progress is not possible. And because technological change is both increasingly rapid and increasingly costly, it is nearly impossible for developmental latecomers to acquire world-class, competitive technology through, or even largely by means of, nativist efforts. Because that technology must be imported, the country is pulled economically and politically into the international arena and subjected to all the strong forces of new ideas and ways of doing things that compose the modern global system. Thus technology forces economic modernization and political development to proceed along increasingly close paths.

That would not necessarily spell democratization were it not for two other factors. One, technology must operate in as free an atmosphere as possible to influence economic development most efficiently. Authoritarian and totalitarian countries, with informational compartmentalization, are the enemy of technology, and democracy by its nature is its friend. Second, most of the advanced and economically successful nations are democracies. Developing nations must obtain top-of-the-line technology largely from the democracies, and the latter are most often interested in transferring it to other democracies rather than different types of polities. Or those democracies tend to make technology transfer conditional on economic changes— the promise of instituting market-opening measures, protection of intellectual property, and the like—that favor a free market economy and hence, in the long run, political liberalization.

Moreover the successful establishment of an integrated, interdependent global economy by the democracies of Europe, East Asia, and North America has an enormous effect on nondemocratic polities. However complex or poorly understood is the mechanism linking democracy and development, the economic success of the democracies in the post–World War II world strongly favors those in authoritarian or totalitarian regimes who favor both conversion to a free market and internationalization of the economy and also political liberalization. Conversely socialism has abjectly failed, both economically and politically, in the eyes and actions of the very peoples whom socialism was supposed to benefit. That had been clear to the

283

cognoscenti for decades, but the events in China, East Europe, and the Soviet Union in the late 1980s demonstrated that fact for all. While the combination of democracy with a market economy seemed historically to be a winning one, until socialism failed so utterly in such obvious manners it was still possible to argue that two models of economic and political development were worth considering. After 1989 there was only one (with many internal variations, to be sure).

The prodemocratic revolution of the late 1980s was hardly confined to the Socialist world. In several authoritarian nations, in Asia and elsewhere, the trend toward democracy also appeared and gathered momentum. In Burma the people revolted in mid-1989 against the military government, were brutally suppressed, but showed by voting the next year overwhelmingly to oust the military from power, that they could not be turned back. In Pakistan the military government was succeeded by a civilian administration under Benazir Bhutto. Under her rule, however, the country was torn apart by religious and communal strife, military opposition, and corruption, and Pakistan's second experiment with democracy was in crisis in less than two years. In Nepal an antimonarchical, prodemocratic rebellion forced the Chogal to agree to contested, free elections and most other expressions of democracy that transformed the political landscape in that country. And in Latin America the trend toward democracy, apparent for more than a decade, culminated with the electoral removal from power of the Sandinista government in Nicaragua. Even in authoritarian Asian nations, the trend toward a more pluralistic system was apparent, as in Thailand, Malaysia, Indonesia, and Singapore. In all these cases a rough correspondence existed between the opening toward democracy and economic development via the free market version of reasonably rapid economic progress.

Although at the turn of the 1980–1990 decade democracy appeared to be linked increasingly with development in Asia and elsewhere, two major facts stood on the other side. For one, in many polities the relationship between economics and politics did not clearly favor linking democracy and development. Communist Asian states—China, Vietnam and its Indochina dependencies, and North Korea—though hardly impervious, nonetheless attempted, each in its own ways and with varying degrees of success, to contain the democratic virus and to stress economic growth on country-specific variations of the Socialist development model. While the viability of these attempts was increasingly doubtful, the survival of these regimes for yet a while longer indicated the complexity of the democracy-development tie. In other Asian nations military or authoritarian regimes continued to exercise a firm grip over their peoples and their

THOMAS W. ROBINSON

economies. This was the case in Sri Lanka and (to a lesser extent) in Bangladesh, where downward momentum toward further political and economic disaster accelerated. And in many other nations no trend toward democracy was apparent nor was any obvious linkage evident between economic development and political openness. That was quite clear in many of the Islamic polities of the Middle East, most of which persisted in authoritarian or even totalitarian governments despite oil riches, and most of the African nations, where extremist ideologies, civil war, and economic stagnation or actual shrinkage were unfortunately the norm.

## Success of Democratization?

So if there was in Asia a trend toward democracy and linking growth with openness, surely there was no similar global tendency. Are the Asian instances, especially in Taiwan and South Korea, essentially an aberration, or is Asia at the forefront of trends that will sooner or later become worldwide? The above analysis, as well as much in the previous chapters, indicates that there are too many impediments, unknowns, and intervening variables to conclude that, in Asia at least and with increasing probability elsewhere, democracy and development are the probable future and that their mutual dependency is assured.

This unfortunate and perhaps too-agnostic conclusion is buttressed by the second unassailable fact. The history of the transition to democracy is hardly rectilinear, nor is it ever smooth. That is surely the case for the Western European and North American democracies, where the emergence of democratic forms of political organization took a long time and suffered many setbacks. Indeed democracy in many cases was overthrown by totalitarian regimes, or progress toward democracy was rendered stillborn by seizure of power by a small group of militarists or ideologues, who then fastened their rule for many decades. The well-known experiences of Germany and Russia continue to be instructive, to say nothing of the imperfect nature of democracy over long periods in France, Britain, the United States, Canada, and other Western nations. In Asia itself the overthrow of democracy in Japan—until the post–World War II era the only one in Asia—by a fascist-militarist clique just when it appeared that democracy had been successfully established must always be kept in mind.

Confidence about the success of democracy amid development in Taiwan, South Korea, and the Philippines therefore seems premature. A few years' experience is not long enough. And already signs are appearing that the future could see major challenges to both democracy and development in all three countries. In South Korea the political situation at the turn of the 1989–1990 decade was none too stable. Although three of the four political parties had combined, leaving Kim Dae Jung's Party for Peace and Reunification the sole opposition, President Rho Tae Woo's own position was itself hardly secure, and it was doubtful that he could win another popular election. Moreover student unrest continued to take a violent form that at times gathered support from an increasingly diverse spectrum of society. Many of the often massive strikes were extremely violent, especially when the government suppressed them by force. These actions tended to polarize Korean society and to negate part of the work of the previous years, which had favored democratization through avoiding showdowns and confrontations. In addition South Korean political culture did not dovetail with the requisites of democracy. Koreans tended to think in terms of polar opposites and more often than not attempted to solve problems through confrontation and violence rather than through compromise. Democracy in South Korea was thus hardly a surety.

In Taiwan the situation was somewhat different, but the outcome was also threatening. The comparatively sudden extension of various political freedoms to the whole population left many relatively unprepared for the responsible exercise of freedom. Some took the term to mean license, resulting in a precipitous rise in crime and a general outbreak of public disorder. A law-and-order backlash emerged, symbolized by the appointment of General Hao Pou-tsun, the Taiwan Army garrison commander, as deputy premier. Of equal importance was the question of Taiwanese nationalism. With the emergence of the Democratic Progressive party into full-fledged legality as the standard-bearer of anti-mainlander, anti-Kuomintang sentiments, and with the approximate 80 percent of the residents—and hence, under democracy, voters—on the island being Taiwanese, the probability was rising rapidly that the DPP might soon come to power. Although the party was factionalized and the majority pledged not to seek independence from the mainland, the party could adopt a new program. And since Beijing never varied from its threat of military action against a declaration of Taiwanese independence— imminent or actual—there remained a lively prospect that military conquest could snuff out democracy in Taiwan. Or the Kuomintang could decide to reverse course in the face of such an internal and external threat and to reestablish its own unilateral rule over the island.

In the Philippines the situation was different still but even more precarious. By the turn of the decade the Aquino government, brought to power by a popular democratic revolution against Marcos authoritarianism, had squandered its mandate through a congenital inability to carry through an economic revolution. Land reform, the single most important and obvious element in such a revolution, was frittered away by Corazon Aquino's lack of leadership and the reluctance of the legislative representatives, many of whom were major landowners. Industrial rates of growth and investment did not rise sufficiently even to cover the population-driven rise in the work force, much less move to the double-digit increases necessary to make up for past declines and to set the country firmly on the road to full-scale modernization. Politics returned to its previous form, based on rivalry between large landowning families who dominated the Congress and who plotted and intrigued against each other for the presidency. Increasing numbers of the military, desperate from seeing economic and political transformation as the only means of keeping the Communist New Peoples Army from coming to power in a violent revolution from below, concluded that the Aquino government could not lead that transformation and that the only path to national salvation lay through military coup and direct rule. By late-1990, therefore, the Aquino administration had been the target of no less than nine attempted military coups; the most serious, in December 1989, nearly toppled the government and laid bare Mrs. Aquino's dependency on American military support. Meanwhile the NPA, which had suffered a clear setback as a result of the Aquino revolution, recovered strength (which could only, as before, depend on popular grass-roots—mostly peasantry but increasingly urban worker—support of an increasingly demoralized and poverty-stricken population) and once again threatened to take power by force. The prospect for democracy in the Philippines was thus guarded at best as both economic and political determinants combined against it.

### Security Factors

International factors also made democracy and development in the three entities somewhat more dubious. In Korea the situation in the North could no longer be kept separate from that in the South. Pyongyang appeared near the end of its economic rope, as it could no longer devote between a quarter and a third of its annually produced wealth to the military or keep 8 percent of its population in uniform, all in the name of keeping ahead of a South Korea with more than four times its gross national product and a population more than twice its size. The Kim Il Sung succession was to occur reasonably soon, and given the probability that his son, Kim Jong Il, would not be able to make fast his own rule, a struggle for power was bound to take place. Two separate clocks were simultaneously ticking, therefore, and the danger was mounting that the North would in desperation—either before or as part of the succession process—take military action against the South. The surrounding powers were all trying to safeguard the situation by mutual consultation, by moving to cross-recognition, and by warnings to Kim of the folly of an invasion. But few were able to get through to the North Korean dictator, who also felt even more pressure stemming from the anti-Communist revolutions in East Europe and the trends and events of the late 1980s in China and the Soviet Union. At some point Kim might seize upon a periodic upsurge in political disorders in the South and command his forces to cross the DMZ. It would be ironic indeed were the movement toward democracy in South Korea to be one of the causes of a new Korean war.

As for Taiwan, the security issue was as always fourfold. First, would the mainland remain quiescent militarily in the Taiwan Straits any longer? Second, would the domestic situation in China resume movement, after the Tiananmen Incident, toward political transformation and eventually allow a negotiated and peaceful reunification? Third, could Taiwan entice the mainland to lower its threat of a military and economic blockade through the inducement of economic investment and trade? And fourth, could the United States be convinced of the need to continue its military and diplomatic security guarantorship of the island?

The military question was becoming more serious. With the near-disappearance of the Soviet threat to China, Beijing could for the first time in a quarter-century consider its options regarding Taiwan without worry over a Russian attack from the rear. A strong Fukien frontal force could therefore be reestablished. China could thus restore its capability to attack Taiwan should either or both of the traditional *casus belli*, about which it had always warned Taipei, appear: evidence of Taiwan's acquisition of nuclear weapons and imminent declaration of independence by a government elected by, and fully responsive to, the Taiwanese majority. The probability that either or both conditions could be present was rising at the turn of the decade. And while Taiwan was doing its best to build a modern military, especially to deter air attack, the mainland was moving with equal rapidity in the same sphere and, given the size disparity between the two, will eventually stand qualitatively equal to Taiwan as well as quantitatively far more powerful.

The domestic political situation in China was cloudy after Tiananmen and could remain so indefinitely. The Chungnanhai ruling group was fearful of any but marginal movement back toward the relative political openness before June 4, 1989. It was complicated by the presumably short time remaining before the Deng Xiaoping succession, the near surety of a disorderly struggle for power, and the relatively poor prospect of a "liberal" ruler coming to power in the short to medium term. The politics of the Deng succession will affect Taiwan in two manners. First, if the succession struggle is relatively lengthy and therefore inconclusive for a considerable period, more political issues, including policy toward Taiwan, will probably be drawn into the fray. And second, once China again possesses a strong, unitary leadership at the top, it will be in a better position to deal with Taiwan from a position of strength. Its resolve might be modulated by the effects of Taiwan's policy of economic investment in China and by its cautious policy of seeking political conversations with Beijing. But these, or similar, developments are unlikely to deter significantly any successor Beijing regime from eventually bringing Taiwan under its rule.

There was less concern, at the beginning of the 1990s, about the strength of the American security commitment, buttressed now by the perception in Washington of a democratizing Taiwan. Nonetheless the important changes in the Asian security environment—the end of the U.S.-Soviet standoff in the region, the rise of many major and middle powers, and the unclear willingness of the American people to continue to fund a military force commensurate with their Asian security responsibilities—all pointed to a dilution of Washington's willingness to continue its anomalous role as Taipei's security guarantor against Beijing. Moreover by the end of the century the effects of the 1983 American-Chinese agreement concerning arms supply to Taiwan will be increasingly important, as the yearly decline of American sales will by then have cut severely into the amounts of equipment and technology transferred. When matched by the year 2000 with the probable large increase in Chinese military capability, the product of gradual but continual force modernization, the balance in the Taiwan Straits could tilt severely in Beijing's favor. Taipei's fate will thus be even less in its own hands and even more susceptible to the course of American-Chinese relations and hence to events and policies over which Taipei will have increasingly less control. All the more reason, therefore, why Taiwan might conclude it had nothing to lose by declaring full independence or attempting to acquire nuclear weapons and thus precipitate confrontation or actual invasion.

Regarding the Philippines, the most important security development was the changing American motivation to deploy—and capability of so doing—a significant military force for general peace-keeping purposes in the Western Pacific. As the Philippines insisted on reclaiming Clark Field and Subic Bay, the United States also took a declining interest in these military installations, which for nearly a century have been one of the cornerstones of American security policy in Asia and the practical basis for defense of the Philippines. In an era when a serious foreign threat to the Philippines had all but disappeared and when the United States was clearly less desirous of using the Philippine facilities to assure regional stability and peace, Washington's motivation to protect the Aquino regime from its domestic enemies, Left and Right, was also declining. The upshot could be that when Manila needs the Americans most, they will be unavailable.

## The Future

The future of economic development in Asia, particularly in Taiwan, Korea, and the Philippines, is also checkered. First, South Korea and Taiwan, having reached the point of economic maturity, increasingly had to pay the price of success: rising wage rates and therefore product prices, consequent decline in international competitiveness, retaliation by other countries for restricted markets, and competitiveness of lower-wage countries. Their rates of growth, for these structural reasons, must inevitably decline. Second, Asian economic life as a whole was even more tied to the global economic situation. As the decade began, a global recession was looming, protectionism was gaining ground in the United States, capital flows were being redirected to Europe or remaining within domestic economies, and interest rates were remaining stubbornly high on both sides of the Pacific Ocean. Third, a major economic contest was shaping up between the United States and Japan. American anger against alleged Japanese unfair practices rose precipitously, while Japan continued to take market shares away from the United States along a broad front of products. If the United States did move to cut off the American market, the consequences not only would be severe for Japan but could spill over to other Asian countries with trade practices judged similar to Japan's. That would surely include South Korea and Taiwan, if not the Philippines.

Conversely, if these challenges could be met successfully, the longer-term economic future appears bright. For one, China and the Soviet Union are emerging as great trading nations and as loci of major investment interest not only of Japan and the United States but also of Korea and Taiwan. The scale of Asian international economic life could thereby measurably enlarge, and the political and economic transformation of the two presently Socialist societies could proceed. For another, and perhaps more important, the task could proceed of constructing a great Asian interdependent economic system encompassing not only the Asian nations bordering the Eastern Pacific but also those on the eastern side of that great ocean: North, Central, and perhaps some countries of South America. That task will take leadership and persistence, especially by the United States and Japan. But if successful, the new economic system could become a powerful engine to bring development and democracy to many Asian nations and to perfect the political and economic development in others, including the three discussed in this volume. A great economic-political tide would thus swell, in which democracy and development would so blend that questions of their relation would be put aside once and for all.

A similar tide might appear in the political sphere. Existing democracies on both sides of the Pacific, led by Japan and the United States, might find it necessary as well as desirable to invest their energies in perfecting their own democratic orders. Indeed at the onset of the 1990s directions in those two leading democracies appeared to point to that end, to say nothing of South Korea, Taiwan, and the Philippines. If democracy were made even more attractive through a series of domestic reforms, prospects for its success would improve immeasurably in many Asian states that now are unsure of which political direction to take or that remain authoritarian or totalitarian.

Taken together, the international influence of development and democracy over the 1990s and beyond could become commanding. Democracy and development would then cease to be largely a domestic question (if ever it was) as the relationship between them would be internationalized. In sum, it is becoming reasonably clear that the conditions for a close tie between democracy and development stem not only from all of the complex factors within societies noted in this volume but as well from the changing nature and scope of the Asian and global economic and political systems themselves. Democracy and development in South Korea, Taiwan, and the Philippines stand to succeed or fail because of regional or global changes, not just because of how these three societies deal with economic and political problems at home.

# Notes

CHAPTER 2: POLITICS IN THE REPUBLIC OF CHINA, *Lu Ya-li*

1. By saying that democratic reform in Taiwan was initiated by the leaders themselves, I do not mean that social pressure did not have a role to play. But in comparison with such countries as Korea, the reform was initiated by the leadership when social pressure was still relatively weak.

2. The term "soft authoritarianism" was used by Edwin Winckler in his "Institutionalization and Participation on Taiwan: From Hard to Soft Authoritarianism," *China Quarterly*, no. 99 (Sept. 1984). The term "authoritarianism with developmental features" was used by Jürgen Domes in his "Political Differentiation in Taiwan: Group Formation within the Ruling Party and the Opposition Circles, 1979–1980," *Asian Survey*, no. 10 (Oct. 1981), pp. 1011–28.

3. In 1969, the first "supplementary" election was held. Other "supplementary" elections were held in 1972, 1980, and 1986. As of April 18, 1988, the total number of members in the National Assembly was 924, of which 84 were not senior members. The number for the Legislative Yuan was 306, of which 96 were not senior members. The number for the Control Yuan was 66, of which 31 were not senior members.

4. For a perceptive analysis of Taiwan's economic development from 1952 to 1972, see Walter Galenson, ed., *Economic Growth and Structural Change in Taiwan* (Ithaca: Cornell University Press, 1979).

5. According to Taiwanese sociologists, the upper class accounts for one to 1.5 percent of the population, and the middle class accounts for 30 to 35 percent of the population. The middle class can be further divided into the new middle class consisting of professionals and white-collar workers and the traditional middle class consisting of small shop owners and owners of small factories. The working class consists of manufacturing workers, service workers, and the like and accounts for 40 to 45 percent of the population, while small farmers account for 19 percent of the population. The remaining are "marginals." These figures are given in H.H. Hsiao, "The Social Structure and Political Dynamics in the Changing Taiwan," cited by Yao Chia-wen in his *Min-chu, Tsu-cho, Chui Tai-wan* (Democracy, Self-Determination, How to Save Taiwan) (Taipei, n.d.), p. 50.

6. See Robert Ross, "China's Strategic Role in Asia," in James Morley, ed., *The Pacific Basin: New Challenges for the United States* (New York: The Academy of Political Science in conjunction with East Asian Institute and the

tion and the Other Four," in Cynthia L. Chennault, ed., *Modernizing Asia: Economic and Cultural Dimensions of Political Change* (New York: Asian Studies Center, St. John's University, 1990); and "The Economies of Island and Mainland China: Taiwan as a Systemic Model," *Issues & Studies*, vol. 24, no. 12 (December 1988), pp. 12–28.

## CHAPTER 4: SOCIOCULTURAL DEVELOPMENTS IN THE ROC, *Ting Tin-yu*

1. Both Legislative Yuan and National Assembly elections were held in 1986. These elections reelected only about one-third and one-tenth of the legislators and members of the National Assembly, respectively. The rest of the parliamentary members were originally elected in 1947. Because the KMT has suspended reelections since then, these representatives have remained in their posts for more than forty years.

2. Martin M. C. Yang, *Socio-Economic Results of Land Reform in Taiwan* (Honolulu: East-West Center Press, 1970), pp. 38–85.

3. Budget Department, *Taiwan Statistical Data Book* (Taipei: Republic of China, 1981), p. 221.

4. W. Y. Shirley Kuo, Gustav Ranis, and John C. H. Fei, *The Taiwan Success Story: Rapid Growth with Improved Distribution in the Republic of China, 1952–1979* (Boulder, Colo.: Westview Press, 1981), pp. 30–34.

5. See also Shail Jain, *Size Distribution of Income* (Washington, D.C.: World Bank, 1975); and Richard E. Barrett and Martin King Whyte, "Dependency Theory and Taiwan: Analysis of a Deviant Case," *American Journal of Sociology*, vol. 87, no. 5 (1982), pp. 1064–89.

6. The overall Tangwai movement in local elections, the *Meilitao Magazine*, and the Kaohsiung Incident in 1979 are examples of these political movements during the late 1970s.

7. Jurgen Domes, "Political Differentiation in Taiwan: Group Formation within the Ruling Party and the Opposition Circles, 1979–1980," *Asian Survey*, vol. 21, no. 10 (1981), pp. 1011–28; Thomas B. Gold, *State and Society in the Taiwan Miracle* (New York: M. E. Sharpe, 1986); and Ting Tin-yu, "Who Votes for the Opposition in Taiwan: The Case of Chia-yi City" (Paper presented at International Conference on Taiwan, A Newly Industrialized Society, sponsored by the Department of Sociology, National Taiwan University, Taipei, 1987).

8. David Robertson, *A Theory of Party Competition* (England: John Wiley and Sons, 1976), p. 3.

9. A. Downs, *An Economic Theory of Democracy* (New York: Harper, 1957).

10. James M. Enelow and Melvin J. Hinich, "Nonspatial Candidate Characteristics and Electoral Competition," *Journal of Politics*, vol. 44 (1982), pp. 115–30.

11. S. Martin Lipset, "Democracy and Working-Class Authoritarianism," *American Sociological Review* (1959), pp. 482–501.

12. Gerhard Lenski, *Power and Privilege: A Theory of Social Stratification* (New York: McGraw-Hill, 1966).

13. Peter L. Berger, *The Capitalist Revolution* (New York: Basic Books, 1986).

14. Heinz Eulau, "The Ecological Basis of Party Systems: The Case of Ohio," *Midwest Journal of Political Science*, vol. 1 (1957), pp. 125–35; Phillips Cutright, "Urbanization and Competitive Party Politics," *Journal of Politics*, vol. 25 (1963), pp. 552–64; Douglas S. Gatlin, "Toward a Functionalist Theory of Political Parties," in William J. Crotty, ed., *Approaches to the Study of Party Organization* (Boston: Allyn and Bacon, 1968), pp. 217–64; and Frank J. Sorauf, *Party and Representation* (New York: Atherton, 1963).

15. Charles M. Bonjean and Robert L. Lineberry, "The Urbanization–Party Competition Hypothesis: A Comparison of All United States Counties," *Journal of Politics*, vol. 32 (1970), pp. 305–21; David Gold and John R. Schmidhauser, "Urbanization and Party Competition: The Case of Iowa," *Midwest Journal of Political Science*, vol. 4 (1960), pp. 62–75; Kenneth Janda, *Data Processing* (Evanston, Ill.: Northwestern University Press, 1965), pp. 175–81; and A. Nicholas Masters and Deil S. Wright, "Trends and Variations in the Two-Party Vote: The Case of Michigan," *American Political Science Review*, vol. 52 (1958), pp. 1078–90.

16. C. I. Eugene Kim, "Significance of Korea's 10th National Assembly Election," *Asian Survey*, vol. 19, no. 5 (1979), pp. 523–32.

17. Richard J. Samuels, "Local Politics in Japan: The Changing of the Guard," *Asian Survey*, vol. 22, no. 7 (1982), pp. 630–37.

18. Jimmy C. M. Chao, "From Limited to Extended Participatory Rights: The Current Political Process in the R.O.C." (Paper presented at the annual meeting of the International Sociological Association, New Delhi, 1986); John F. Copper, "Taiwan's Recent Election: Progress toward a Democratic System," *Asian Survey*, vol. 21, no. 10 (1981), pp. 1029–39; and Richard L. Engstrom and Chu Chi-hung, "The Impact of the 1980 Supplementary Election on Nationalist China's Legislative Yuan," *Asian Survey*, vol. 24, no. 4 (1984), pp. 447–58.

19. Sheng Shing-yuan, *A Study of the Electoral Competition between the Kuomintang and Tangwai Central Supporting Association in 1983 Supplementary Legislative Yuan Election* (Taipei: Laureate, 1986).

20. Mau-kuei Michael Chang, "Partisan Preferences in Taiwan" (Paper presented at the International Conference on Taiwan, A Newly Industrialized Society, sponsored by the Department of Sociology, National Taiwan University, Taipei, 1987); Fo Hu and Yu Ying-lung, "The Voter's Choice: An Analysis of Structure and Typology" (Paper presented at the annual meeting of the Chinese Association of Political Science, Taipei, 1983); Mei Tsai-hsing, "Voting Behavior in Military Dependents' Villages of Tso-ying, Kaohsiung City: A Comparison between the 1981 City Council Election and the 1983 Supplementary Legislator Election" (M.A. thesis, Sun Yat-sen Institute, Sun Yat-sen University, Kaohsiung, 1984); Ting, "Who Votes for the Opposition"; and Yu Ying-lung, "Systematic Orientation and Voting Behavior—A Study of the 1980 Taipei City Central Supplementary Legislator Election" (M.A. thesis, Department of Political Science, National Taiwan University, 1982).

21. Lei Fei-lung, Chen Yih-yan, Ting Tin-yu, Lee Pei-ti, and Sheng Shing-

CHAPTER 7: ECONOMICS IN KOREA, *John T. Bennett*

1. *Economic Statistics Yearbook 1988* (Seoul, Korea: Bank of Korea), p. 11.

2. Whang Seokyung, "Korea's Education System," *Korea's Economy*, May 1988, pp. 20–24; Noel F. McGinn et al., *Education and Development in Korea*, (Cambridge, Mass.: Harvard Univ. Press, 1980).

3. International Labor Organization, *Yearbook of Labor Statistics 1986*; Economic Planning Board, *Social Indicators in Korea 1987*, Seoul Korea.

4. At this time, Samsung, Hyundai, and Goldstar have offices in Silicon Vally as does the Korea Institute for Electronic Technology. In addition, Daewoo has bought an American chip maker, Zymos, and an American computer maker, Corona, now called Cordata.

5. According to company officials, Hyundai required its new dealers to put up $1–2 million in facilities detached from show rooms for other car brands, and to include service bays and to carry spares. Because many had missed out when the Japanese dealerships were first established, far more applied to become dealers than could be accepted, even though the qualifications were considered stringent for a new brand from an unknown company.

6. Economic Planning Board as quoted in the *Korea Herald* (Seoul, Korea), Dec. 16, 1988.

7. Yung Whee Rhee, "The Catalyst Model of Development: Lessons from Bangladesh's Success with Garment Exports," The World Bank, unpublished paper, 1987.

8. At the end of 1988, Korea had outstanding foreign liabilities of $32 billion and foreign assets of $25.3 billion, making its net foreign liabilities $6.7 billion, according to the Economic Planning Board as quoted in *Korea Herald*, December 16, 1988. In 1989 and 1990, Korea was a net foreign creditor.

9. Successive international meetings of the major trading nations, starting with the Plaza Agreement of September 1985, have used coordinated intervention in the currency markets to stabilize adjustments and to prevent a collapse, while encouraging exchange rate adjustment in the direction indicated by market forces. In addition, peer pressure in the Group of 5 nations (the United States, Germany, Japan, the United Kingdom, and France) has begun to move national economic policies, such as the reduction in the U.S. federal deficit, in the direction leading to a long-run stable equilibrium.

10. Whang, "Korea's Education System."

11. See for example, Oles Gadacz, "Labor Pains of a New Deal," *Business Korea* (Seoul, Korea), September 1987, pp. 25–27, and Lee Keum Hyun, "No Longer a 'Silent Partner,' " *Business Korea*, December 1988, pp. 66–75.

12. See John T. Bennett, "Labor and Wages in Korea," *Korea's Economy* (Washington, D.C.: Korea Institute of America, February 1984), and Kwon Okyu, "Recent Labor Disputes and Wage Increases in Korea," *Korea's Economy*, pp. 16–17, August 1988.

13. In addition to sources cited in note 11, the author had discussions with Korean labor economists, like Park Fun Goo at the Korea Development Institute, who expressed this concern.

14. For example, Kim Kihwan, when he was vice minister of trade and industry, Deputy Prime Ministers Rha Woong Bae and Kim Mahn Je, and senior secretary to the president for Economic Affairs Park Seung. See "Park Seung: A Believer in Decontrol," *Business Korea* (Seoul, Korea), July 1988, pp. 19–21.

15. Industrial policy is the use of tax advantages, subsidies, and approvals to enter business activities and loans, both domestic and foreign, as instruments to foster industries or activities. For a history of the use of some of these instruments, see Yung Whee Rhee et al., *Korea's Competitive Edge: Managing the Entry into World Markets* (Baltimore: Johns Hopkins University Press, 1984).

16. Gunnar Myrdal, *Asian Drama* (New York: Twentieth Century Fund, 1968). A "hard state" is one that acts against its own people, especially interest groups.

17. Such a pessimistic view is expressed in chapter 2 of Edward S. Mason, *Modernization of the Republic of Korea* (Cambridge: Harvard University Press, 1980).

18. Ibid.

19. Mark Clifford, "Filing for Divorce," *Far Eastern Economic Review* (Hong Kong), April 21, 1988, pp. 58–60; Kim Jin Moon, "Fighting to Regain an Empire," *Business Korea* (Seoul, Korea), May 1988, pp. 19–22.

CHAPTER 8: SOCIOCULTURAL DEVELOPMENTS IN KOREA, *Kim Kyong-dong*

1. For discussion of earlier modernization theories, see Kim Kyong Dong, *Rethinking Development: Theories and Experiences* (Seoul: Seoul National University Press, 1985).

2. Various issues related to dependency-World System theories are discussed in Kim Kyong Dong, ed., *Dependency Issues in Korean Development: Comparative Perspectives* (Seoul: Seoul National University Press, 1987).

3. The Chinese word *yang* literally refers to sunshine or light, and *yin* to the absence of light, or shadow. Chinese philosophy has accorded them the meaning of two cosmic principles, forces, agents, or elements. They are a pair of opposites, contradicting each other. Yet without their interaction there is no production of things and events. They are at once contradictory and complementary. See Wing-tsit Chan, *A Source Book in Chinese Philosophy* (Princeton: Princeton University Press, 1973); and Kim Kyong Dong, "The Issue of Modernization Revisited: East Asian View" (Revised paper originally entitled "Explaining Change: An East Asian View," presented at the Theory Section—Transpacific Conference of the American Sociological Association Annual Convention, New York, August 1986).

4. More condensed discussion of the emerging social forces is to be found in Kim Kyong Dong, "Social Change in Korea: The Dynamics of Tension Management and Conflict Resolution," in *Managing US-Korea Trade Conflict* (Washington: Committee on Ways and Means, U.S. Congress, 1987), pp. 50–59.

Doronilla, "The Media," in R. J. May and Francisco Nemenzo, eds., *The Philippines after Marcos* (London: Croom Helms, 1985).

13. A study of presidential and legislative output by Abraham Sarmiento in 1983 indicated that the preeminence of the executive in legislation rested not only on the quantity but also on the substance of presidential decrees and other enactments.

14. See Alex B. Brillantes, Jr., *Dictatorship and Martial Law: Philippine Authoritarianism in 1972* (Quezon City: Great Books Publishers, 1987), especially chap. 3 and 6 on the role of the Supreme Court during martial law.

15. See Carolina G. Hernandez, "The Philippine Military: Under Marcos and Beyond," *Third World Quarterly* (October 1985), pp. 907–23, on RAM's organization and objectives.

16. See "U.S. Policy toward Marcos," National Security Council Study Directive, November 1984; reprinted in Schirmer and Shalom, eds., *The Philippines Reader*, pp. 321–26.

17. See Romeo L. Manlapaz, "The Mathematics of Deception: A Study of the 1986 Presidential Election Tallies" (Diliman, Quezon City: Third World Studies Center, University of the Philippines, 1986), for a scientific assessment of the election results indicating Mrs. Aquino's probable victory in the elections.

18. Social Weather Stations, Inc. (henceforth SWSI), *Public Opinion Reports: 1986–1987*, Political Indicators table 16, "On the New Constitution," p. 28.

19. This definition of politics was made by the grand old man of the old Nacionalista party, Eulogio "Amang" Rodriquez, Sr.

20. See Article VII, Section 18 on Emergency Powers, *The 1986 Constitution of the Republic of the Philippines*.

21. Ibid., Article XVI, General Provisions, Section 5, subsection 3.

22. Ibid., subsection 4.

23. Ibid., Section 6.

24. For an analysis of the military's future in consonance with constitutional prescriptions, see Carolina G. Hernandez, "The Philippine Military in the 21st Century," in F. Sionil Jose, ed., *Solidarity Conference: A Filipino Agenda for the 21st Century* (Manila: Solidaridad Publishing House, 1987), pp. 235–48.

25. The statistical data on popular perceptions about the Communist insurgency before July 1985 and March 1987 are from SWSI, Political Indicators table 14, "The NPA/NDF," pp. 21–24.

26. The statistical data on popular perceptions about the insurgency in October 1987 are from SWSI, *Public Opinion Report: October 1987*, Political Indicators table 13, "On the Insurgency," pp. 2–4.

27. Ibid., Political Indicators table 18, "On Human Rights Abuses," pp. 12–13.

28. Seth Mydans, "2 More Top Philippine Communists Arrested," *New York Times*, March 30, 1988.

29. From a survey by the Institute of Popular Democracy as cited in "Between Deadlines," *Philippine Daily Inquirer*, January 24, 1988.

30. John Bresnan, ed., *Crisis in the Philippines: Under Marcos and Beyond* (Princeton, New Jersey: Princeton University Press, 1986).

31. SWSI, *Public Opinion Reports: October 1987*, Political Indicators table 2, "Performance Ratings of Officials/Agencies," p. 3.

CHAPTER 11: ECONOMICS IN THE PHILIPPINES, *Richard Hooley*

1. R. A. Dahl, *Polyarchy: Participation and Opposition* (New Haven, Conn.: Yale University Press).

2. D. A. Rostow, "Transition to Democracy," *Comparative Politics*, vol. 2 (1970).

3. Carole Pateman, *Participation and Democratic Theory* (Cambridge: Cambridge University Press, 1970).

4. D. Lerner, "Communication Systems and Social Systems: A Statistical Exploration in History and Policy," *Behavioral Science*, vol. 2, no. 4 (October 1957), pp. 266–75.

5. Carl H. Lande, *Leaders, Factions, and Parties: The Structure of Philippine Politics* (New Haven, Conn.: Yale University Press, 1965).

6. R. A. Higgot, "From Modernization Theory to Public Policy: Continuity and Change in the Political Science of Political Development," *Studies in Comparative International Development*, vol. 15, no. 4 (Winter 1980), pp. 26–58.

7. D. Rothchild and R. C. Curry, *Scarcity, Choice, and Public Policy in Middle Africa* (Beverly Hills, Calif.: University of Calif. Press, 1978); N. T. Uphoff, and W. Ilchmann, *The Political Development of Development* (University of Calif. Press, Berkeley and Los Angeles: 1972).

8. Seymour Martin Lipset, *Political Man: The Social Bases of Politics* (Garden City, N.Y.: Doubleday, 1960).

9. Gabriel Almond and James S. Coleman, eds., *The Politics of Developing Areas* (Princeton, N.J.: Princeton University Press, 1980).

10. Ibid.

11. Irma Adelmann and Cynthia Morris, "A Factor Analysis of Social and Political Variables and GNP," *Quarterly Journal of Economics*, vol. 79, no. 4 (1965), pp. 555–78.

12. G. Bingham Powell, Jr., *Contemporary Democracies: Participation, Stability, and Violence* (Boston: Harvard University Press, 1982).

13. Simon Kuznets, *Modern Economic Growth: Rate Structure and Spread* (New Haven, Conn.: Yale University Press, 1986); Hollis Chenery et al., *Redistribution with Growth* (New York: Oxford University Press, 1974).

14. Lipset, *Political Man*.

15. Michel Crozier, Samuel H. Huntington, and Joji Watanuki, *The Crisis of Democracy* (New York: New York University Press, 1975).

16. Abram Bergson, "Development under Two Systems: Comparative Productivity Growth since 1950," *World Politics*, vol. 23, no. 4 (July 1971), pp. 579–617; and Chenery et al., *Redistribution with Growth*.

17. Mancur Olson, Jr., "Rapid Growth as a Destabilizing Force," *Journal of Economic History*, vol. 23, no. 4 (December 1963), 529–52.

18. Benedict J. Kerkvliet, *The Huk Rebellion: A Study of Peasant Revolt in the Philippines* (Berkeley: University of California Press, 1977).

5. I conclude, from an acquaintance dating from 1969, that President Aquino's friendship for the United States is not tactical or conditional; it is principled and basic to her foreign policy—unlike what might have been expected from her late husband had he assumed the presidency.

6. Thus a regional comparison of trends showing fatalities per day in the five Luzon regions (not including the national capital region) had an average in 1985 of .558; in 1988 the average was 1.138, almost precisely double. Raids and other attacks on stationary targets (AFP detachments, municipal halls, etc.) in 1985 reached 89, in 1987, 145, and by March 1988 had an annualized rate of 138. Reference Folder on the AFP, March 1, 1988, given to the author by Defense Secretary Fidel Ramos.

7. A historical peculiarity of elite politics in the Philippines is the tendency for the richest to support radical elements, usually for purposes of developing a "fire sale" mentality among foreign investors (read Americans). Most of these (for example, the once powerful Lopez family) were burned in Marcos's martial law regime, making it likely they would not forswear the potential protection of America in the future. They certainly have held onto their green cards.

8. Cited by Ambassador Leonard Unger, in an essay on Philippine foreign policy, unpublished.

9. Significantly, one of the few genuine diplomatic strategists of the republic, Alejandro Melchor, who served President Aquino as ambassador to Moscow, was dismissed in 1989, just as he was by President Marcos from his post as executive secretary.

10. At a well-reported convocation in Davao, author's files, March 1988.

11. Editorial, "We Must Not Pin Much Hope on PAP," *Manila Chronicle*, July 3, 1989.

12. The plan for the distribution of Hacienda Luisita, the immense Cojuanco sugar plantation in central Luzon, was deeply flawed, in offering to the peasants thereon nonfungible certificates of ownership that only changed their status de jure, not de facto.

13. See Rigoberto Tiglao, "Caught in the Act," *Far Eastern Economic Review*, July 13, 1989, p. 15.

14. Larry Diamond, "Introduction: Persistence, Erosion, Breakdown, and Renewal," in Larry Diamond et al., eds., *Democracy in Developing Countries: Volume Three, Asia* (Boulder, Colo.: Lynne Reinner Publishers, 1989), p. 16.

15. Cited in "The Philippines: The Search for a Suitable Democratic Solution, 1946–1986," Karl Jackson, in Diamond, Linz, and Lipset, *Democracy in Developing Countries*, p. 235.

16. Dennis Austin, "Liberal Democracies in the Non-Western World," (Prepared for the conference "Liberal Democratic Societies: Their Present State and their Future Prospects," London, August 1989).

17. See Victor N. Corpus, *Silent War* (WC Enterprises, 1989), written by a one-time senior NPA leader. This gives a comprehensive overview of NPA strategy and goals.

18. See W. Scott Thompson, "The Prospects for Democracy in Southeast

Asia" (Prepared for the conference "Liberal Democratic Societies: Their Present State and Their Future Prospects," London, August 1989).

19. Of course it is the precise objective of the NPA to draw the Americans in as deeply as possible to the counter-insurgency campaign, thus permitting the NPA to make the tag of lackey stick to the AFP—whence the killing of Colonel Nicholas Rowe outside JUSMAG in April 1989. As *The Manila Chronicle* put it,

> The war footing the NPA has taken against American advisers in the country should therefore be seen for what it is: an attempt to raise the stakes and escalate the conflict by luring the Americans into active and overt involvement in the insurgency war.
>
> Should this happen, the insurgents will finally succeed in selling the line . . . that Americans run the country. . . .
>
> The Aquino and the US Governments should not allow themselves to be drawn into the insurgents' grim agenda. ("Rowe Killing Could Shut off Foreign Aid," April 25, 1989)

20. The Guantanamo parallel is presumably less pertinent for bases 6,000 miles—rather than 90 miles—from home shore. Nevertheless, the late Senator Benigno Aquino, during exile, amused Americans anxious about his intent vis-à-vis the bases if he assumed the presidency with the statement that "if Fidel Castro can't even push you out of bases on his territory, I hardly think a 'radical' like me would contemplate being able to get rid of the bases."

## CHAPTER 14: COMPARING THE CASES, *Raymond Gastil*

1. Surprisingly little has been written on the progress of democracy over the past hundred years. For a recent consideration and reference to the literature on democratic development, see G. Bingham Powell, Jr., "Social Progress and Liberal Democracy," in Gabriel Almond, Marvin Chodorow, and Roy Harvey Pearce, *Progress and Its Discontents* (Berkeley: University of California Press, 1982), pp. 375–402, esp. note 8, p. 378. See also Raymond D. Gastil, *Freedom in the World: Political Rights and Civil Liberties, 1984–1985* (Westport, Conn.: Greenwood Press, 1985), pp. 257–69. On economic development the literature is much broader. Some older references are Colin Clark, *Conditions of Economic Growth*, 3d ed. (London: Macmillan, 1957); Colin Clark, *Population Growth and Land Use* (London: Macmillan, 1977); and Simon Kuznets, *Modern Economic Growth* (New Haven, Conn.: Yale University Press, 1966).

2. For the current number of democracies and market economies, see Raymond D. Gastil, *Freedom in the World: 1987–88* (New York: Freedom House, 1988), esp. pp. 30–34, 73–83. On the number of market economies, see also Jean J. Boddewyn and Joseph J. Falco, "The Size of the Market Sector around the World," *Journal of Macromarketing*, vol. 8, no. 1 (Spring 1988), pp. 32–42.

# Index

People's Republic of China (PRC). *See also* Communist party of China
Asian-Pacific region and, 39
economic growth, 131
Philippines and, 237
political situation, 289
public satisfaction, 51
South Korea and, 166
Taiwan and, 8–9, 91–93, 254, 258, 288
*Perestroika*, 120, 131
Philippine Civic Action Group, 174
Philippine Democratic party-*Lakas ng Bayan* (PDP-LABAN), 179, 230
Philippine Military Academy, 174, 191–92
Philippine Revolution (1896–1902), 223
Philippines. *See also* East Asia
Philippines, economic developments
agriculture, 206, 216, 218–19, 220, 274
aid, economic, 238–39, 275
background, 17–24, 27–30, 172, 190, 194–96, 200–204, 215, 273
budget deficit, 194, 208–9
bureaucracy and, 208
democratization and, 187–88, 211, 212, 216, 279
foreign debt, 219, 237
foreign exchange rate, 210
government priorities, 219–20
industrial sector, 207, 210, 211
labor, 188, 205–7, 210, 211, 217, 219, 274
land reform, 216, 220–22, 239
Presidential Commission on Government Reorganization, 195
restructuring/reforms, 194–95, 207–9, 211, 273–74
trade, 200, 209, 211, 216, 234, 274
United States and, 23, 24, 234, 290
wage rate/income, 200–203, 205, 207, 208, 210–11, 217, 220, 232, 274
Philippines, international environment. *See also* Association of Southeast Asian Nations
background, 22–24, 191, 235–36
democratization, 240–42
foreign policy, 233–34, 237–38
Japan, 223
United States, 23, 232–34, 235–36, 238–39, 241–42
Philippines, political developments. *See also* Aquino, Corazon; New People's Army
background, 16–18, 20–22, 24, 29–30, 160, 171–72, 186, 232

communism and, 172–73, 176, 180–90, 274–75, 277
constitution, 175, 181–82, 189, 277
democratization, 186–92, 193–94, 204, 211–16, 226–30, 234, 277, 280, 286–87
elections, 225–27, 228–29, 278
judiciary, 176, 179–80
Marcos regime, 172–77, 179–80, 183, 203–4, 214–15, 224–28, 276. *See also* Marcos, Ferdinand
martial law, 172–77, 190, 203, 224–25, 226, 241
military and, 176–77, 180–82, 188, 189, 191–92, 225, 230, 241
Muslims, 173, 176, 183–85
political parties/fronts, 175, 177–79, 182–86, 188, 224–25, 227, 229
press and, 179
protests, 199–200, 202, 210–11
reforms, 176–83, 185, 187–88, 190–91, 193, 195, 207, 209, 216, 230–31, 238, 273, 274–76
social classes, 176, 218–19
United States and, 22, 24, 183, 290
Philippines, sociocultural developments
background, 20–22, 213–16, 240–41, 263–64, 275, 277
education, 189, 222, 264
families, 223–26, 227, 228, 230–31, 238
infant mortality, 217–18, 264
population, 207, 217–18, 220, 240
poverty, 217–18, 222, 231
protests, 199–200, 202
religion, 215, 223, 228
social classes, 176, 218–19
symbols, power of, 227–29
Pimentel, Aquilino, 179
Plunk, Daryl M., ii, 10, 105–18
PnB of People's party. *See Partido ng Bayan*
Political development. *See also* Democracy; individual countries by name
course of, 27, 280
Political parties. *See also* Political theories
Communist. *See* Communist party
Democratic Justice party (DJP; South Korea). *See* Democratic Justice party
Democratic Progressive party (DPP; Taiwan). *See* Democratic Progressive party
Hsinchaoliu, "New Wave" (Taiwan), 43
Kilusang Bagong Lipunan (New Society Movement; Philippines), 175–76

317

A NOTE ON THE BOOK

*This book was edited by*
*Dana Lane and Ann Petty of the publications staff*
*of the American Enterprise Institute.*
*The figure was drawn by Hördur Karlsson,*
*and the index was prepared by Julia Stam Petrakis.*
*The text was set in Palatino, a typeface designed by*
*the twentieth-century Swiss designer Hermann Zapf.*
*Coghill Composition Company, of Richmond, Virginia,*
*set the type, and Edwards Brothers Incorporated,*
*of Ann Arbor, Michigan, printed and bound the book,*
*using permanent, acid-free paper.*

The AEI PRESS is the publisher for the American Enterprise Institute for Public Policy Research, 1150 17th Street, N.W., Washington, D.C. 20036: *Christopher C. DeMuth,* publisher; *Edward Styles,* director; *Dana Lane,* editor; *Ann Petty,* editor; *Cheryl Weissman,* editor; *Susan Moran,* editorial assistant (rights and permissions). Books published by the AEI PRESS are distributed by arrangement with the University Press of America, 4720 Boston Way, Lanham, Md. 20706.